974.72

MIDDLE ISLAND PUBLIC LIBRARY
Coram, New York

DISCOVERING
LONG ISLAND

1076

REFERENCE · · NOT TO BE
TAKEN FROM THIS ROOM

By the Same Author:

NANTUCKET
THE FAR-AWAY ISLAND

ANNAPOLIS
ANNE ARUNDEL'S TOWN

OLD WILLIAMSBURG
AND HER NEIGHBORS

Each with frontispiece in full color and many pen and ink drawings by the author.

DISCOVERING LONG ISLAND

by

WILLIAM OLIVER STEVENS

Illustrated by
THE AUTHOR

DODD, MEAD & COMPANY
NEW YORK　　　　　1939

COPYRIGHT, 1939
BY DODD, MEAD AND COMPANY, INC.

ALL RIGHTS RESERVED
NO PART OF THIS BOOK MAY BE REPRODUCED IN ANY FORM
WITHOUT PERMISSION IN WRITING FROM THE PUBLISHER

PRINTED IN THE UNITED STATES OF AMERICA
BY THE VAIL-BALLOU PRESS, INC., BINGHAMTON, N. Y.

TO

ED and SALLY,

Who know and love Long Island

ACKNOWLEDGMENTS

The Author pauses at the threshold of this volume with the wish to express his thanks to all those who have helped him in its preparation. Of the authorities in print which were consulted, their name is legion. They range from newspaper clippings to heavy tomes, from monographs like Mrs. Jeannette E. Rattray's pamphlets on Montauk and East Hampton to complete volumes like Miss Jacqueline Overton's *Long Island's Story*. Much interesting material was discovered in the columns of the *Long Island Forum*. A special word of acknowledgment is due to Commander A. H. Miles, U.S.N., for his article in the Naval Institute *Proceedings* on the *Princeton* disaster. His is the one definitive account of an obscure but striking tragedy in our history.

To the staff of the library of the Long Island Historical Society in Brooklyn thanks are due for many helpful courtesies. Mr. Chester R. Blakelock, Executive Secretary of the Long Island State Park Commission, was tireless in supplying material on the State parks, both printed and pictorial. Also he personally conducted the writer on a visit to some of these great public playgrounds. Mr. Robert F. Kelly, of the United States Polo Association, and Mr. Stephen Wallis Merrihew, editor and founder of *American Lawn Tennis,* were good enough to supply information regarding their respective sports. Officials of the World's Fair very kindly checked on the data here given on that Exposition. Mr. Meade C. Dobson, Managing Director of the Long Island Association, contributed many helpful suggestions.

Above all, the Author is under a heavy debt of gratitude to the historian, Mr. Morton Pennypacker, who made accessible

ACKNOWLEDGMENTS

all the resources of his famous Long Island historical collection in the East Hampton library. In addition, he scanned the first draft of the manuscript for corrections, a service for which the Author is most warmly appreciative. But for any inaccuracies that may have crept in, despite all precautions, the responsibility must rest on the undersigned alone.

WILLIAM OLIVER STEVENS

INTRODUCTION

Something over sixty years ago a dozen young New York artists, calling themselves the "Tile Club," hit on the idea of a sketching trip together.

"Where shall we go?" was the first question. Various places were suggested, such as the Adirondacks and the Maine coast, without reaching a decision. Finally someone ventured, "Why not go to Long Island?"

"That sand place?" said one fellow member.

"There's nothing there," said another with scorn and contumely.

"How do you know?" retorted the man who had made the proposal.

"Why," replied another, "nobody was ever known to go there!"

"What," shouted his neighbor, "nobody ever went there? Then that's the place of all others to go to!"

That view of Long Island settled the question. "All right!" cried the club in unison, and to Long Island they went. During our own excursion through these pages we shall come occasionally upon their footprints. They were a remarkable group of artists, men who a decade later were the headliners in American painting, sculpture, and architecture, such as F. Hopkinson Smith, Saint-Gaudens, William M. Chase, Thomas Moran and Stanford White; as "honorary members," they had with them some musicians, who became equally famous.

The argument that moved the Tilers to choose Long Island will not serve to justify this travelogue sixty years afterwards.

INTRODUCTION

There are plenty of people who do go to Long Island nowadays. But often, to the uninformed, it is too near the metropolitan area to be taken seriously as interesting. Like a jewel of a wife and mother, or a patient, longsuffering husband and father, Long Island has been too near home to be appreciated. We take it for granted, thinking of it chiefly in terms of bedroom and office, merely as a suburb of New York, which is the nation's front door.

But that isn't the real Long Island at all. It is full of varied beauty and romantic history. If, for example, East Hampton, Hither Hills and Montauk Point were in England, instead of right at the door of a great American city, people would cross the Atlantic to see them and send home postcards breathing rapture over the scene. And the same people would go to Holland for the sake of seeing "those cunning windmills" who would never think of finding similar windmills on Long Island. In the Old Country, too, where there is some little beauty spot, the tripper is obliged to part with a sixpence or a shilling to enter what is called a "Fairy Glen." Here the lakes and woods and seashore at their finest are set aside in what is the world's greatest public park system, free to all. No, it is high time that we appreciated our home body. She still has her beauty, as well as her usefulness; and as for her past—well, she has had her moments, as we shall see.

Dropping the figure of speech and becoming geographical, let us look at Long Island. There it lies, a strip of sand dumped by a glacier in the Atlantic. It stretches eastward from New York City, parallel with the shore line of Connecticut and separated from it by Long Island Sound. The Island is shaped like a fish, with its head nosed up against Manhattan Island, and, unhappily, that greedy metropolis has bitten

INTRODUCTION

off the head so that the western end has become just an extension of the great city. Steadily, the city continues to gnaw eastward, too, as motorcars of today, roaring over broad parkways, and probably airplanes of tomorrow, roaring even more loudly through the broader skyways, may destroy all that is left of present beauty and historic past. It is a melancholy thought that for our grandchildren the whole Island may become a sort of colossal Suburbia, one huge dormitory for the men and women who do their work in Manhattan. But against that dire prospect stands the figure of Robert Moses, the Park Commissioner, who has already done miracles in creating parks on the Island and who, if his hands are uplifted, will keep the bungalows and tenements and apartments within their proper metes and bounds.

For there is too much that deserves to be saved for the future to be imperiled by the "realtors," and perhaps the reason why so much still remains is due to the fact that most Americans, even those of the eastern seaboard, are not aware that Long Island is worth visiting. The line of vacation travel on the Atlantic coast follows the mainland routes. The trippers, who journey by motorcar, run from Maine to Florida and back again without leaving convenient thoroughfares like Route Number One, and all that most of us know of Long Island is a trip by a subway express to Coney Island, during a visit to New York. The millions who will flock to the World's Fair in 1939 will probably rush across the bridges and back again, never suspecting what a delightful and varied bit of their country lies within easy reach of their cars.

The western end, as just remarked, is swallowed up by the metropolis. Gone is the rustic charm of the old "Breuckelin" and "New Utrecht" of the Dutch settlers, and of their outlying

INTRODUCTION

villages and farms with their trim gardens, their orchards and their cottage architecture. All that area is now completely citified. The Brooklyn of today is "the city of homes and churches," also of parks, libraries and museums, but it is emphatically a great modern city, not a countryside to explore.

Back in early Colonial days a line was drawn south from Oyster Bay to separate the Dutch part of Long Island from the English part to the east. It is chiefly this eastern two-thirds of the Island that is the interesting area for discovery, because it is rural Long Island. Here also is a part of New York state that isn't in the least like the rest. Lying just south of the shore line of Connecticut, peopled by fellow colonists from Connecticut, together with some from Rhode Island and Massachusetts, this part of the Island suggests old New England. Here the ancient houses are of the New England "salt-box" type; the white churches of the Wren tradition might have been lifted bodily from any Connecticut village. In ways of life, standards of religion also, the Long Islander of this section belonged to the English colonies of the east and north rather than to the Dutch settlements lying to the west and along the Hudson. Unfortunately very little of old Dutch Long Island has survived the march of Progress. The contrast is even more striking today between the western third of Long Island, with its suburban or metropolitan character, and the truly rural and seagoing aspects of the eastern part.

In fact, one of the first characteristics to strike the visitor is that this *insula longa* is a land of contrasts. Along the North Shore, facing the Sound, rise high wooded bluffs with a stretch of gravelly beach at their feet. On the western side of this shore there are harbors that tend to be narrow and set deep in the high

INTRODUCTION

coast line. On the eastern half of it there are no harbors at all, only an unbroken line of bluffs. On the other hand, the South Shore, facing the Atlantic, is low-lying, with an infinite number of wide, land-locked estuaries and bays; in fact, its Great South Bay alone extends over half the length of the South Shore. Between, in the middle of the Island, runs a stretch of dull, flat, almost treeless country, the worst of which is a wilderness known as the Pine Barrens. In this middle area lie endless acres of farm land, covered with potatoes and cauliflower. For miles in this region one might well imagine himself in a prairie state like Indiana. On the North Shore, South Shore and in mid-Island are the famous state parks, superbly landscaped, connected with four-lane highways—the "parkways"—which are the motorist's delight. In contrast with these beautifully kept areas and highways there are wide salt marshes and little dirt roads running through unspoiled woods and countryside.

The greatest contrast is that between the suburban and city tracts lying near New York and the village character of the towns to the east. As against the countless miles of bungalows, cottages and apartment houses, with all their modern conveniences (and sometimes nuisances) are villages with broad, elm-shaded streets and greens, lined by the small houses of a hundred or two hundred years ago. Many of these are content with such antiquated plumbing as may still be found in the castle of an English lord, but they are pleasant to the eye.

So one could extend contrasting details indefinitely. Suffice it to say that Long Island has everything except mountains, cataracts and the Grand Canyon, and all within the space of one hundred and twenty miles.

INTRODUCTION

A similar variety extends to the inhabitants of this island. A colored preacher once summed up the important races of the world by saying, "They's Hottentots and Europeans; they's Abyssinians and Virginians." These major races may be found here, although the proportion of Virginians is regrettably small. In addition, all the minor tribes of mankind are represented, for the western end of Long Island is at the port of entry for immigrants from every corner of the world. As for occupations, there are farmers, fishermen, boatbuilders, idle Indians, pink-coated huntsmen, polo players, tennis champions, aviators, writers, artists, actors, poets and politicians. In contrast to the "economic royalists" living in huge white elephants of country estates there are ex-fishermen sitting contentedly in little shacks drawing federal relief, the latter, no doubt much more at peace with the world. All these divergent types and many more are inhabitants of Long Island.

If the present-day Long Islanders make an odd kaleidoscope of races, habitations and manners, the characters of the Island's past are even more oddly assorted and picturesque. It is an interesting procession that walks through the three centuries of its history: Dutch Patroons, English Puritans, Quakers, Rebels, Tories, British officers of the army and navy, pirates, eminent divines, free-love colonists, free-verse poets, pugilists, novelists, whaling captains, painters, actors and cranks—it might be difficult to produce a similar strip of American territory which could show such a variegated portrait gallery of its past. The whole gamut of character is there, from virtue to villainy, from George Washington to Captain Kidd.

With all that spangled background of the past, as well as the present, there should be a better reason for exploring Long Island than that which drew the Tile Club thither; and the thesis

INTRODUCTION

of this book is that the Island is a fascinating place to explore, which is what the Tile Club members found out for themselves. In the following pages, therefore, let us make a voyage of discovery to this *insula longa,* which is also, to a great degree, *insula incognita,* lying at the very front door of America.

CONTENTS

CHAPTER		PAGE
I	TO THE NORTH SHORE	1
II	MORE OF THE NORTH SHORE	27
III	TO THE NORTH FORK	53
IV	GARDINER'S ISLAND	75
V	SHELTER ISLAND TO SAG HARBOR	99
VI	EAST HAMPTON	119
VII	OLD TIMES AND OLD-TIMERS OF EAST HAMPTON	145
VIII	MONTAUK	163
IX	THE OTHER HAMPTONS	182
X	THE SOUTH SHORE	204
XI	THE PARKS	225
XII	ISLAND PRODUCTS	247
XIII	SPORTS	263
XIV	OLD BROOKLYN	297
XV	"THE WORLD OF TOMORROW"	326
	INDEX	347

CHAPTER I

TO THE NORTH SHORE

WE have a distinguished precedent for this voyage of discovery. George Washington had been the duly elected first Chief Executive of the United States for exactly a year when it was suggested to him that he pay a visit to Long Island. On a fine day in April he took the ferry to Brooklyn, then a small country town, and from there started forth in state, as befitted the Father of His Country. His coach was capacious and elegant, drawn by four perfectly matched grays in jingling silver-mounted harness. Outriders galloped ahead to clear the road, a suite of staff officers, resplendent in buff and blue, accompanied their Commander-in-Chief on the seats of the coach or rode their horses alongside. In the rear, well powdered with dust, followed a cavalcade of negro slaves who, the records say, tried to make the other servants at every place of lodging on this journey do all the work. For they had their pride of place, too; did they not belong to General Washington?

That Presidential visit must have been very impressive. People ran across the fields to catch a glimpse of Washington as the coach rumbled past. In recent years, trees have been planted wherever he stopped to eat, drink or sleep, and at least one bedroom is preserved today as Washington used it.

For these prosaic days, however, and for us plain citizens, we must rely on less picturesque means of getting about. One way that can be recommended is to be gently wafted to our Island from the Connecticut shore by means of certain ferries. After sitting a long time behind the wheel of a car it feels good to stretch our legs on the deck of a boat, get a whiff of salt water and enjoy the wide expanse of Long Island Sound, lying before our eyes like a sheet of pale blue silk sprinkled with powdered diamonds. Here and there against the blue, flashes the white patch of a sail, almost always of some pleasure craft in these days. It is possible also to see on these waters some lumber schooner, or a seagoing tug dragging a string of coal barges, yet when Washington made his trip there was anywhere from ten to twenty times as much activity on the Sound, for it was in those days a busy highway for fisheries, commerce and travel.

A glance at the road map shows a ferry running from New London to the prongs of the two forks of the eastern end of the Island, Orient Point and Montauk. Another runs from Bridgeport to Port Jefferson, in the middle of the North Shore. If the traveler takes this route and happens to board the *Park City,* he will be thrilled to know that this was the vessel which was caught out in the great hurricane of September 21, 1938. Unable to make headway, she dropped her anchors six miles off Middleground shoal and there, with fires out, she lurched and rolled at the mercy of wind and waves all that afternoon and night, with six passengers huddled on the floor of the "reception room," expecting every minute that the vessel would fall to pieces. As it was, her wooden bulwarks were bashed in. Next morning her distress signal was sighted by a Coast Guard cutter which succeeded in towing her back to Port Jefferson. Probably few boats of her size ever took such a beating and stayed afloat.

Other ferry routes are indicated on the road maps, and it may be said without contradiction that for a traveler coming from points in New England this ferry method is the pleasantest way of reaching Long Island.

TO THE NORTH SHORE

But probably nine-tenths of those who plan a motor trip hither will make their point of departure New York City. That fact makes the most logical route to follow in these pages a path that leads eastward from one of those gigantic bridges that span the East River from the mainland to the Island. These are the Queensborough, the Triborough and, newest of all, the Bronx Whitestone. Since all these make connections with wide boulevards and parkways, the problem of driving through miles of city blocks is not nearly so formidable as might be expected.

However, the man who comes from "God's Country" (the New Yorkers call it the "Sticks") will have to learn to watch the lights. In this Greater New York area nearly all the traffic lights change at once and you must stop sharply at the next corner, even though the light itself is far ahead. This is not always easy, for these lights seem to be perched in all sorts of places, left, right or overhead. Just as you roll over a crossing, you are suddenly aware that away down the boulevard there's a tiny red eye leering at you, and you wonder if an Arm of the Law is coming up from behind to hand you a ticket.

Some of these bridge routes out of New York converge on Flushing Meadow, the site of the World's Fair, and from this focus the motorist can strike out in any direction. Also one may follow Queens Boulevard to the Grand Central Parkway. For the purpose of this voyage of discovery, however, we shall take the shorter route of Northern Boulevard (25 A) and go as fast as the law permits. For it must be admitted that our roadway takes us through a grim, ugly expanse of a great city's outskirts, and pretty dirty skirts they are, too.

This unfortunately is true of every large city from New York to Los Angeles; our back yards are never attractively laid out. A comparatively recent zoning law has tried to amend the situa-

DISCOVERING LONG ISLAND

tion in New York by restricting warehouses, gas tanks and similar necessary disfigurements to the landscape to certain areas. Had this law been in operation from the beginning a great deal of the unhappy aspect of the approaches to New York might have been avoided.

As it is, there are still left, in spite of the rapid spread of the metropolis into Queens, numerous residential areas which the traveler along the arterial highways is likely to miss. There is a road, for instance, just to the east of Flushing, leading from the heart of Bayside, north to the Sound and the military reservation at Fort Totten, which, with its arching trees and glimpses of blue water in the distance, is as lovely as anything in New England or old Virginia. In Flushing itself there are broad avenues, lined with fine old homes, which the man speeding along Northern Boulevard will never see. The same is true of that other much-traveled route, called, but not greatly resembling, Queens Boulevard, from which the motorist gets no impression whatever of the charms of Forest Hills, Kew Gardens or the residential section of Jamaica, with its groves of maples and oaks. The truth is that the whole western end of Long Island, and particularly this part of Queens County, lies in the realm of Suburbia—the Land-of-the-Five-Cent-Fare. As a result of the inexpensive transportation to the heart of the metropolis, a fantastic mushroom growth of small homes has sprung up.

One of the most unbelievable of these is best seen from a high point on Grand Central Parkway, about ten minutes after one enters that roadway. Here one may look off to the right across what was once unbroken farm land but which now seems to be an endless series of tiny roofs, line after line of them reaching almost to the horizon, each one scarcely distinguishable from the next. What actually happened was that tractors were put into

TO THE NORTH SHORE

the farm country here and houses set up in half-mile rows, each house on its own similar plot and each gable and doorway and window patterned after that of its neighbor. So rapidly did this section develop that roadways could not be built fast enough to keep up with the construction and the lumber trucks had to be hauled by tractors through seas of mud.

All that is past, however, and today each little house has its own trim lawn and cluster of evergreens, as carefully kept as a landed estate. For actually these are not merely houses; to tens of thousands of people they are home, though it may be wondered at times how an owner tells them apart and what comedies or tragedies may ensue if he fails to do so. One of Long Island's favorite commuters and poets of the present day, Christopher Morley, once wrote, perhaps while riding through this same area:

> Heaven is not built of country seats
> But little, queer suburban streets.

But the province of this book does not really lie in this region and we must hurry farther out on the Island without delay.

All of Long Island lying west of an imaginary line drawn south from Manhasset Bay is that old Dutch section which, as noted already, has been bitten off by New York City. East of this imaginary longitude begins the real Long Island, the one we are out to discover.

But while we are rolling along through this city area with nothing to occupy our attention but the elusive traffic light ahead, we might improve our minds with some facts about the history of the Island. And since this is the age of Progressive Education we shall make the process of instruction as brief and as painless as possible. A few dates are here laid down, which the reader may take to heart or skip entirely. In 1609, under the employ of the Dutch East India Company, the Englishman Henry Hudson discovered Long Island, though some historians will probably insist that Leif the Red, the Viking, got here six hundred years earlier. At any rate, Hudson went ashore from the *Half Moon*, landing on a beach near the present Coney Island. He records that at this place he made "a great haule of fish." In 1614 Adrian Block, the Dutchman, made the passage of the Sound. He first reported the fact that this long strip of land was an island and drew a map of it. In 1636 some Dutchmen from New Amsterdam—the little settlement then beginning to flourish on the end of Manhattan—crossed over to the head of what is now Gowanus Bay, Brooklyn, and began the first white settlement. This lies around the corner from Governor's Island and Buttermilk Channel, and is now a mess of long piers and wharves and warehouses. In 1936, by the way, Long Islanders celebrated the tercentenary of their history with pomp and circumstance and a specially minted fifty-cent piece.

At the other end of this island came the English. In 1639 the Earl of Sterling made a sale of another island, lying in the eastern fork of Long Island, to one Lion Gardiner, described as "an officer and a gentleman." He had recently come from England, had fought the Pequots and had built a fort at Saybrook at the mouth of the Connecticut River. Other English settlers followed on the eastern Long Island coast, coming from Connecticut and Massachusetts, founding the villages of Southampton and Maidstone (later East Hampton). Still others on the North Fork founded the settlement of Southold. Here also, in later years, came a few French Huguenots to escape persecution. From then on the population grew, English at the east end, Dutch at the west, with the Indians scattered between.

ONDERDONK PAPER MILL, ROSLYN

TO THE NORTH SHORE

Of these aborigines there were originally thirteen tribes, Delawares of the Algonquin nation. But the Iroquois claimed that these tribes owed tribute and allegiance to them. Once, in 1655, on the advice of the Dutch, the Long Island Indians held back on their tribute and the Iroquois fell upon the island and slaughtered the rebels without mercy. The Canarsie tribe, for example, was practically wiped out. After that the Long Island red men sent their wampum promptly.

The white men treated them fairly enough. There was good feeling between the races, and there are no stories of massacres and reprisals. But, as everywhere else, rum, measles and smallpox, consumption and syphilis, the gifts of the white man, slew their tens of thousands. By the seventeen-sixties the tribes were practically all gone, though a few wretched handfuls existed here and there. Today, in the Shinnecock region, there is a small reservation for the remnants of the Long Island red men.

The rest of Long Island history is a part of that of our country at large. The Revolutionary War found the area defenseless against the British forces. The Battle of Long Island in 1776 was a ghastly defeat for Washington and the makeshift American army. In fact, the whole rebel force might have been captured and the rebellion ended then and there but for one of those Long Island fogs, which enabled the Americans to row with muffled oars across the East River to the New York side. Benson Lossing, in his *Pictorial Field Book of the Revolution,* says of the escape: "Surely if the stars in their courses fought against Sisera, in the time of Deborah, the wings of the Cherubim of Mercy and Hope were over the Americans on this occasion." To translate this passage for the present-day reader who never heard of Sisera or Deborah, and does not know the allusion to the stars or the Cherubim, it may be explained that Lossing is only saying elegantly that the fog saved the day. Thereafter the wretched inhabitants of Long Island had to take the oath of allegiance or flee to Connecticut. In any case, the old, the sick and the infirm had to take what the British army and the Tories brought upon them in the way of raids and plunder and burning.

The War of 1812 was almost as bad in this respect, but it did not last half so long. The rest is a matter of local chronicles, each of which can wait until its turn comes, for probably this history lesson is overlong already.

Let's turn to geography. Of course the red highways on the road map are the important ones, broad and smooth, and much traveled, especially on a Saturday or Sunday afternoon; but before starting on this tour of discovery, the traveler should bear in mind that these red lines are useful only for getting to places in a hurry. It is the little blue lines wandering in and out crisscross over the red routes that deserve attention if one desires to see the real, unspoiled Long Island. Some of these are hard-surfaced and just as navigable, if not so broad, as the big highways. Others are of oiled dirt. The stuff flies up and adheres to the back of the car, it is true, but it will come off, and these out-of-the-way places are by all odds the most interesting to explore. They wind in and around bays and inlets and fishermen's shacks; they run headlong to a beach and end right there; they dive into deep woods and come out unexpectedly upon some tiny settlement that hasn't changed its appearance since the year 1800. So the really adventurous soul will spurn the red lines, the broad common routes of travel, and wander off on one narrow blue line after another for the fun of seeing where it goes. That is the way to make discoveries.

As we scan the map, leaving for the moment the lines of red and blue for the places they lead to, the wayfarer is immediately

TO THE NORTH SHORE

struck by the amazing names of Long Island towns. Of course there are, anywhere in America, the Indian names. Cities all over the country labor under such titles Kankakee, Keokuk and Kalamazoo. Those on the Long Island area are not so bad as they might be, but they are not all of honeyed sweetness to the ear. Take the quartette, Quogue, Aquebogue, Patchogue and Cutchogue, all rhyming with "fog" rather than with "rogue." This suffix "ogue" is said to be the Indian name for fish. And how could a stranger guess the right way to pronounce Happauge, Ronkonkoma or Wyandanch?

Others, which may be hybrid English and Indian, are worse. Consider Speonk, Yaphank or Sweezy, for instance. Then in plain, unmistakable English behold Scuttlehole, Hardscrabble and Barnes' Hole. It must be very embarrassing for dwellers in those parts. For example, when an Englishman writes a letter from his country place the address at the top of his note paper reads something impressive like this:

>The Lindens,
>   Upper-Chipping-Wobbley by Woking,
>   Hants.

Imagine answering your English friend by heading a letter with "Quogue," "Speonk," "Yaphank" or "Barnes' Hole"! It's just another one of those cases where the poor American would be drowned in a wave of inferiority, and the letter would never be written.

Of course there are plenty of other names that suggest the homeland, such as the Hamptons, Devon, Southold and Suffolk. Then there is a rather unusual assortment of Biblical names, the most inspiring of which is Babylon. Considering the shocking remarks made in Holy Writ on the manners and morals of the

DISCOVERING LONG ISLAND

original Babylon, especially the phrases used by the author of "Revelation," it is hard to understand how any group of pious English settlers should have chosen such a name. Or maybe they weren't as pious as we think.

But these Puritans who came over from New England lacked imagination, or at any rate a feeling for beauty in nomenclature. Some of the worst of the names have been changed by a more aesthetic later generation. For example, "Cow Bay" is now "Manhasset"; "Skunk's Misery"—fancy that one—is now "Malvern"; "Punk's Hole" has become "Manorville"; and "Mosquito Cove" is "Glen Cove." But we still have Great Hog Neck, which isn't pretty; and Great Neck, also, which has inspired its obvious pathological quip.

Speaking of names, the real, legal title of this island is not Long Island at all, but "Nassau." That is the way it reads on early eighteenth-century maps. It has not been changed, though it never was popular: "Long Island" it was by common consent and Long Island it still is.

As we continue eastward through what begins to look like a countryside, we have on our left the area of Great Neck, famous for its handsome estates, and just across, on Manhasset Bay, is Port Washington.

Out in the Sound, off Sands Point, stands a rocky islet supporting a lighthouse. This is a well-known marker for sailing races in this part of Long Island Sound, and it still bears the grim name of "Execution Rock." The story behind this name is that back in early Colonial times, when punishments were cruel and judges were merciless, prisoners condemned to death used to be taken out to this isle and chained to rings set in the rock at low watermark. There the poor wretches were left until nature had taken its course.

TO THE NORTH SHORE

Around and about Port Washington are drives such as the road to Sands Point, which are good examples of the kind of exploration that can be done if one has the time and the inclination. For the present, however, we shall press on, straight ahead, to the town of Roslyn, as the first port of call. Here is a pleasant place to stop, stretch our legs, look about and perhaps enjoy lunch.

Just at the turn by the clock tower stands the Washington Tavern, or the old Bogart House, one of those places where President Washington stopped on his tour. Right alongside the main highway in the village is an ancient grist mill, now a "tea shoppe," which is an attractive place for refreshment. It has an outlook in the rear toward Hempstead Harbor and there is a small water wheel, rather concealed from view to be sure, but you can hear the mill stream gurgle cheerfully under it. Inside the mill the character of the old building has been carefully preserved, and under the ancient beams is displayed a loan collection of Colonial and Revolutionary relics. This mill was erected as long ago as 1701, and has been recently restored.

Across the street from this spot is the mill pond and a very attractive park, within which we discover another restored mill. This one is more picturesque than the first because its wheel is in plain view outside and tosses the water gaily as it turns. But it is not working—only playing. This mill is now the "dugout" for the local American Legion post. Here is a tablet reading: "Harold Godwin, 1856—1931, whose generosity and love of Roslyn restored this historic building, erected in 1744, scene of the first paper mill in the state of New York and visited by Washington in 1790."

The story is that when the first President stopped here on his tour he visited the mill and, under the guidance of Mr. Onderdonk, the proprietor, made a sheet of paper with his own hands. And a beautiful piece of paper it is, too. There is a sample of it preserved in the library of East Hampton, which we must not forget to see when we go there.

It was a fine and thoughtful act of generosity for Mr. Godwin to create the park, for not so many years ago this region was an unsightly and smelly swamp and the old mill had long since gone to ruin.

The name Roslyn, by the way, is a charming exception to the list of "Quogues," "Speonks" and so on which excites the mirth of the visitor to Long Island. It seems that when, in the year 1844 it was decided to rename the town, then called Hempstead Harbor, somebody remembered that the Scottish troops stationed here on the shore of the harbor during the War of 1812 were always singing a song about "Roslyn Castle."

"The place should be called 'Roslyn,' " someone suggested, and so Roslyn it became. The memory of these enemy troops could not have been very unpleasant if the descendants of the people with whom they were at war, and on whom they were quartered, commemorated their stay by naming their town after the soldiers' favorite song.

William Cullen Bryant had his summer home here in Roslyn, and it would never do to say good-by to the village without reviving the literary memories of the past associated with Bryant. In 1846, just after the town had changed its name, the poet-editor bought an eighteenth-century farmhouse here with forty acres around it. At that time Roslyn was literally a village, for it could boast no more than 250 inhabitants. Bryant immediately transformed his house after the architectural taste of the eighteen-forties, and made it something fearful and wonderful to behold, but he loved it dearly. "Cedarmere," he called it, and there he spent not only the weeks of his summer vacation but also week ends throughout the fall. As he grew older he spent more and more of his time here, and he was buried in the Roslyn cemetery. He bequeathed his library to the village, and this collection became the nucleus of the public library of today.

One corner of his estate Bryant gave to his daughter and her husband, Parke Godwin, who was associated with him on the editorial staff of the New York *Evening Post.* To their cottage, as well as to the Bryant home, came literary friends. Not far away Charles Dana of the *Sun* had a summer home, and for a remote Long Island hamlet, as it was in those early years, there was a coming and going of a remarkable number of interesting people.

A favorite guest and dear friend of the Godwins was Margaret Fuller, that brilliant, vibrant personality whose reflection shines in the heroine of Hawthorne's *Blithedale Romance,* and who, with Charles Dana and Nathaniel Hawthorne, was a member of the famous Brook Farm Utopians. She loved to come to Roslyn, to go on long walks and picnics, to swim in the Sound and to talk long and late with the Godwins on high intellectual themes. But by and by she went to Europe for an indefinite stay. In Italy she married the handsome (and penniless) Count Ossoli, gave birth to a child, wrote the history of the abortive revolution of 1849 in Rome and took ship back to America to find a publisher for her book.

Of course the Godwins looked forward eagerly to welcoming her back to Roslyn after an absence of more than three years. On the night of July 19, 1850, Mrs. Godwin was so overwhelmed by a sense of impending danger to someone dear to her that she was unable to sleep and walked the floor all night. The next day in New York her husband met Bayard Taylor, who broke the news to him that during the night the ship bringing Margaret,

DISCOVERING LONG ISLAND

her husband and child had been wrecked off Fire Island and that all three were lost.

The Roslyn neighborhood has a modern literary fame also, for not far from this village is the imaginary region of Salamis, "imprisoned in foliage, locked up in a leafy embrace." Road maps do not mention the place, but there are readers who have traveled to and from Salamis many times in the pages of Christopher Morley's books. Somewhere in the "tumultuous privacy" of that place is hidden the "Knothole," the retreat from which have come, these many years, those delightful books which have captivated all of us. Here, too, lived the adventurous Gissing who set out with his steam roller to discover where the blue begins. If one wants to catch the true spirit of the commuting Long Islander, there is scarcely a better way of doing it than reading those essays about a Suburban Sentimentalist, "Magic in Salamis" and "Long Island Revisited," in Christopher Morley's *Plum Pudding* and *Pipefuls*.

From Roslyn we may continue on the highway, for the sake of getting on across country until we reach a corner indicated on the road map as "Muttontown." This is another romantic name to add to our Long Island collection. Statistics inform us, if we are interested, that Muttontown boasts 282 inhabitants and "is a community of large estates." Anyway, the crossroads serves our purpose as a good point at which to quit the highway and steer north toward Locust Valley, en route to Oyster Bay. In this area one should not hurry, for it is a singularly pleasant land. To the left is the town of Glen Cove, another one of those attractive suburban communities, having a wide water front on both Hempstead Harbor and the Sound. Around Glen Cove are famous estates, such as those of the Pratt family at Dosoris,

TO THE NORTH SHORE

and the private island retreat of Mr. J. P. Morgan. All this region is typical North Shore country, where broad estates and small farms may be found lying side by side; where tall trees shade the roads, and here and there shines the gleam of water.

On one of these roads we pass the entrance to the Piping Rock Club. The rock was once a gathering place for Indian councils, but now the name is famous for its associations with polo and golf. The estate called "Planting Fields" recalls another Indian tradition, that of a tract of ground which was used by the tribe of this region for the cultivation of corn. The present estate is famous for its flowers, particularly its fields of daffodils. At Mill Neck we see an ancient mill pond on which swans are floating. This is on the place of Mr. Irving Brokaw, and in winter it serves as a skating pond. Mr. Brokaw, it need hardly be said, is the father of figure skating in America.

If one is specially interested in relics of Long Island's historic past, the most important one in this section is a small gray building which stands across the road from the Friends' Academy, a famous old Quaker school in Locust Valley. This building is the Matinecock Quaker Meeting House, dating from 1725, and little altered since that date. It is still used by the Academy for its chapel services, and the visitor who is curious to see what an early eighteenth-century Quaker meeting house was like should apply at the office of the Academy for permission to enter. Pains have been taken to preserve the severe simplicity of the original. It is very primitive still, but certain comforts have been added since 1725. A plain wood stove at each end keeps the place habitable during winter meetings, and there are cushions on the pews for the comfort of the boys and girls of the present Academy.

A curious device to be seen here is the sliding partition which was designed to be drawn down between the males and the females so that there should be no unseemly distraction while the congregation sat waiting for someone to be moved by the Spirit. Of course, if the girls had looked straight ahead during

MATINECOCK QUAKER MEETING HOUSE

meeting their faces would have been completely and properly hidden by their Quaker bonnets, but it seems that the young ladies would turn to take a look at their boy Friends, and that partition had to be built.

All in all, with its gray-painted broad planks and rough-hewn timbers, this building is probably as good an example of the oldest type of Quaker meeting house as may be seen anywhere.

But if horses are more to the traveler's fancy than meeting houses, he will be interested to notice that diagonally across the road there stands a monument with a remarkable inscription:

TO THE NORTH SHORE

APPROXIMATELY TWENTY PACES
TO THE SOUTH OF THIS SPOT
MESSENGER
FOALED IN ENGLAND IN 1780
BROUGHT TO AMERICA IN 1788
BURIED WITH MILITARY HONORS ON JANUARY 28, 1808
DESCENDED FROM ENGLAND'S GREATEST THOROUGHBREDS
SON OF MAMBRINO AND OF A DAUGHTER OF TURF
BRED BY THE FIRST EARL OF GROSVENOR

*

NO STALLION EVER IMPORTED INTO THIS COUNTRY
DID MORE TO IMPROVE OUR HORSE STOCK
NONE ENRICHED MORE THE STOCK OF THE WHOLE WORLD
TODAY HIS BLOOD IS CARRIED BY MOST AMERICAN THOROUGHBREDS

*

AS THE GREAT FOUNDER
OF THE BREED OF STANDARD LIGHT HARNESS HORSES
HIS BLOOD IS NOW DOMINANT
IN AMERICA, THROUGHOUT EUROPE AND IN AUSTRALIA
AMONG HIS DIRECT DESCENDANTS EVERY TWO MINUTE TROTTER
"NONE BUT HIMSELF CAN BE HIS PARALLEL"

*

IN TRIBUTE TO
HIS ENDURING GREATNESS
THIS MEMORIAL HAS BEEN ERECTED BY AMERICAN HORSE LOVERS.
A.D. 1935

This monument erected to the glory of a horse more than a century and a quarter after his death is something of a record among animal memorials.

There is another towering monument here in Locust Valley

DISCOVERING LONG ISLAND

erected to the memory of a Captain Underhill who commanded the English forces in the only battle fought with the Indians on Long Island. But this is in a family burial plot lying at the end of a private road, and not readily accessible to the traveler.

North and east of the village run more attractive country lanes. The very names are rural and inviting, such as "Horse Hollow Road," "Feek's Lane," "Factory Pond Road." And if a glimpse of the Sound is desired it is only a short run to Bayville and along a narrow neck of beach to Center Island, which makes the eastern barrier to Oyster Bay and which is the home of the Seawanhaka Corinthian Yacht Club. Whether we approach this way or go directly by the shortest route, we arrive finally at the town of Oyster Bay as our next destination. This community, now so closely associated with the memory of Theodore Roosevelt, was an Ancient of Days long before he ever came to live here.

As we drive in on West Main Street, just before reaching South Street we see at our left a little house of curious shape. There is a sign over the entrance indicating that this is "Raynham Hall," and that visitors are welcome on Tuesday and Thursday afternoons at the rate of twenty-five cents each. This was once the home of a prosperous merchant, Samuel Townsend, who built it in 1740, but it has suffered monstrous changes since. Sharp gables, projections and French windows have been added to the front. Inside, where a central chimney once stood, the visitor looks up through a sort of gallery on the floor above into a skylight of garish-colored glass. Also, there is not much left of the house of 1740 to recognize, but one can imagine something of what it was like, especially in its cramped dimensions. Even wealthy men were building little houses for themselves in the seventeen-forties. The fine, wide manor houses we shall see later

TO THE NORTH SHORE

on our travels belong to the generation thirty and forty years afterwards. The house was named originally for Raynham Hall in Norfolk, England, and Townsend used to call it "Little Raynham." Small as it seems now, Townsend was a man of consequence in his town. He was a member of the first Provincial Congress, and later of the committee which drew up the Constitution for the State of New York.

Sadly as the old dwelling has been disfigured by Victorian "improvements," its historical traditions are still strong. During the Revolutionary War some British officers were quartered here, notably Colonel Simcoe, of the Queen's Rangers. Now the Townsends were good patriots all, although most of their neighbors were Tories. But the pater familias had three pretty daughters, Audrey, Sarah and Phoebe, and, naturally, the English found them enchanting. While the girls were all for the rebel cause they were not entirely averse to the gallant attentions of these gentlemen. All the village boys were off with General Washington, and the girls saw no harm in keeping in practice, so to speak, by flirting with these fascinating specimens of the enemy. It must be admitted that these officers were very distingué and polished. One of them in particular, who often visited Colonel Simcoe here, was not only handsome and charming, but talented. His name was André. Over the transom of the room which he used as his sitting room is scrawled with a diamond: "The adorable Miss Sarah Townsend." Beneath is the softer word "Sally," but that was scratched through, as if he thought it was too familiar. On the next pane he wrote: "Miss A.T. the most accomplished young lady in Oyster Bay." That was Audrey. Poor Phoebe seems to have been ignored by the gallant major. We can see these inscriptions up there still.

To the left is the bedroom of Major André, and in the chamber above is kept the small four-poster in which he slept. As might be suspected from what he inscribed on the glass, he was particularly attentive to the "adorable Miss Sarah." Once, according to tradition, he drew a portrait of her.

One of the objects the visitor is shown today in Raynham Hall is a cupboard which played an important rôle in the story of Major André. Sally's brother Robert was one of Washington's most important secret agents, and she often managed to get news to him from Oyster Bay. Once he sent a message to her saying that there was a spy somewhere about Raynham Hall, and asking her to keep a sharp lookout. Shortly afterwards a man who was supposed to have rebel sympathies came to the house and slipped a letter into the cupboard addressed to "James Anderson." After he left Sarah scanned it sharply. True, it looked like an ordinary business letter, but she determined to watch and see who took it, for there was no James Anderson whom she knew. Later, André entered and began searching the closets in the kitchen. When he found the letter, he hastily concealed it in a pocket without looking at its contents. Then he took a dish of doughnuts, fresh from the fire, and hid them in the cupboard, as an excuse, apparently, for being in the kitchen. Not long after, Sally overheard a whispered conversation between André and Simcoe in which the name West Point was repeated several times. She knew that something was up.

Promptly she summoned an old friend, Daniel Youngs, captain of a Loyalist company. She told him that she needed a certain kind of tea for her party the following evening, and the only place she could get it was at the store kept by her brother Robert in New York. Would he please send a messenger with her order at once? Daniel was very happy to oblige. The result was that the news was in Robert's hands before night, and he

TO THE NORTH SHORE

immediately forwarded it to another of Washington's agents, Benjamin Tallmadge, who operated in Westchester. The latter had just deciphered the dispatch when he received a note from Benedict Arnold ordering him to forward to his headquarters, with an escort, a "Mr. James Anderson." Tallmadge knew then that Arnold must be at the bottom of a plot, involving André.

When the latter was arrested and turned over to Colonel Jameson, the American officer believed his story, and sent him on to Benedict Arnold, as he requested. But Tallmadge, arriving on the scene in the nick of time, proved to Jameson from the evidence that had come from Oyster Bay that André must be a spy and Arnold a traitor. He insisted that the captured man be brought back at once. During André's confinement Tallmadge was his personal guard. Now this young American had been a friend and classmate of Nathan Hale's at Yale, and he needed little warning to see that this British spy had no opportunity to escape the same fate.

Colonel Simcoe, that other officer who was quartered in the Townsend house, was a "higher-up" in this plot to capture West Point and make a prisoner of Washington. Simcoe was a forceful character, and during the Revolutionary War he was the unquestioned boss of Oyster Bay. An Englishman himself, he commanded a regiment composed entirely of American Loyalists. They wore a green uniform with a black hat of curious shape. A block away from Raynham Hall, to the south, is a marker indicating "Simcoe's Hill," a knoll that he fortified. It was he who planned all the details of the plot to take West Point. Meanwhile he, too, was very much taken with Sally Townsend, and wrote a valentine poem to her.

Then when the news came of André's capture, and later the dread tidings of his execution, there were dismay and horror in Raynham Hall. Simcoe ordered his regiment thereafter to wear black and white feathers in their hats as emblems of mourning. As for Sally, feeling that she had had a hand in identifying André with the plot and hence had led him to the scaffold, she was broken-hearted. She never married; the local tradition is that she was really in love with Simcoe all the while and the tragedy in which she was involved ruined her romance with the English officer.

Toward the close of the war Colonel Simcoe left Oyster Bay to join Benedict Arnold in the raids up the James River in Virginia. Since nobody trusted the traitor Arnold, Simcoe carried secret orders to watch him and on the first evidence of more crookedness to arrest him and take command. Later Simcoe was one of those officers who surrendered with Cornwallis at Yorktown. After the war he was appointed the first Governor General of Upper Canada (1791), and visitors to Exeter Cathedral in England may see a fine memorial to him there.

One detail of the Simcoe-Arnold plot for the taking of West Point was for Benedict Arnold to remove two of the links of the great chain that stretched across the Hudson River to keep the British fleet from advancing. This chain had been forged by Sally's uncle, Peter, near the modern Tuxedo, and carted to the Hudson by trains of oxen. These links were forty-five inches long by fourteen inches wide, and when finished the chain extended 500 yards and weighed 180 tons. The two links which Arnold removed, on the pretext that they needed repair, may be seen now lying outdoors at the west end of Raynham Hall, near some large clumps of boxwood, some of which can probably remember when all this happened.

So this little house has some interesting memories. It is now under the wing of the local D. A. R. chapter, and it would be a

TO THE NORTH SHORE

pleasant thing if some philanthropist would come along and help these ladies to restore it to the way it looked when Sally Townsend was sitting in the window, while Major John André sketched a portrait of her.

But Raynham Hall is not the only old house that needs to have its elderly face lifted. If we turn north at the corner of South

THE JOB WRIGHT HOUSE, OYSTER BAY

Street, go one block left to the stop light and continue a few rods farther, we shall see on our left a little alley or back-yard entrance beside a plumbing establishment. Inside this, at our right, sits "the oldest house on Long Island." True, there are a few other claimants for that honor, but the historians seem to award the palm of age to this, the "Job Wright House." Job was the son of that Peter Wright who helped to found the settlement of Oyster Bay in 1653, and in this house, in 1672, he entertained George Fox, the famous Quaker apostle. For all its antiquity and honored associations, it seems to have no friends in its poverty and decrepitude. It sits disconsolate in a dirty alley, with rusty drain pipes and tall weeds around its feet, gaping holes in the roof, its windows gone and chimneys crumbling down. Looking inside, we can see the evidences of the seventeenth-century methods of building, but the interior is piled high with more drain pipes, for this historic house now serves the purpose of a storage shed. In a few years at most there will be nothing left of it, for nobody seems to care.

To the present-day American, however, the immediate association with the name Oyster Bay is Theodore Roosevelt. He is still the tutelary spirit of the village. On the road I asked an elderly man at a filling station about the route to the cemetery where Roosevelt is buried. "Yes, sir," he said, "Teddy sure was a great man. The only time I didn't vote Republican in my life was when he ran on the Progressive ticket. I wish he was alive now. I'd like to vote for him again."

The way to find Young's Memorial Cemetery, where the Roosevelt grave is situated, is to turn right on South Street at the stop light just mentioned. Incidentally the brown brick business structure with a turret which stands on this corner was the "Summer White House" in the years when T. R. was President. A short run of perhaps a mile brings us to the burial ground, which slopes up from the road on our right.

We leave the car and follow a path uphill to our destination. It is only a short distance before we see at our left the Roosevelt burial lot surrounded by a high picket fence of iron, placed there to protect the gravestone from the vandals who would like nothing better than to chip off a bit of it to carry home as a souvenir. It is a plain, unpretentious stone with the simplest possible inscription: "Theodore Roosevelt, born Oct. 27, 1858, died Jan. 6,

1919." For such a man's life and character an epitaph like this is the last word in understatement, but doubtless he would have preferred it that way. Above the inscription is the national insignia of eagle and shield.

As we turn away and look through the trees we catch a glimpse of blue water, and when the leaves are gone one may see also from here the roof of the famous Roosevelt home, Sagamore Hill. Just facing the grave, placed under the shade of tall trees, is a stone bench, inviting the traveler to rest a few moments, and near by is a rock on which is set a bronze tablet with these words: "Theodore Roosevelt said, 'Keep your eyes on the stars and your feet on the ground.'"

Around the corner of the cemetery to the south is the "Roosevelt Bird Sanctuary," which occupies a long narrow vale. This is a living monument to the man who cared so much for nature in general and bird life in particular; who did so much for the conservation of bird and animal life, and found time for these interests from the beginning to the end of his "strenuous life." There are twelve acres here, presented as a gift to the Audubon Society by W. Emler and Christine Roosevelt—cousins of the former President—as a perpetual bird sanctuary. It is especially appropriate that this site was chosen, for Theodore and his cousin Emler, as nature students, used to stroll through these very woods. The reservation has been carefully planted to provide food, nesting and shelter for birds, and around it stands a high wire-meshed fence, topped with barbed wire, to keep out cats, dogs and foxes.

At the entrance to the Sanctuary, where in Theodore Roosevelt's day a road led into the woods, stands a charming memorial fountain of bronze, the work of the sculptor, Bessie Potter Vonnoh. The central figure holds aloft a wide, shallow dish, which is intended to serve as a bird bath, and from which the water drips into the pool with its water lilies below. The practical gardener may wonder how a man climbs up there to clean the bird bath, and the Audubon Society member may question the presence of a bronze squirrel at the base of the statue, for this particular animal has never enjoyed the reputation of being a good neighbor to the birds. The Sanctuary was established in 1924, and this fountain erected three years later.

Nor is this all that exists in Oyster Bay to commemorate the man who made it famous. On the water front, near the railroad station of the village, is the fine Roosevelt Memorial Park. This, too, was a labor of love. Formerly this area was a hideous combination of swamp and dump heaps. The Roosevelt Memorial Association took it in hand, and at the cost of $400,000 transformed it into the beauty spot it is today. It was dedicated on Decoration Day, 1928.

So a Great American, by making his abiding place in life and death in this seaport village, has caused it to be indissolubly associated with his name. And as we leave to continue our journey, we carry away a fresh sense of the worth and power of this man, this colorful personality, one of the knightliest who ever broke a lance in the lists of American history.

CHAPTER II

MORE OF THE NORTH SHORE

FROM Oyster Bay to Port Jefferson stretches the most delightfully picturesque section of the North Shore. Its coast line of high, wooded bluffs fronting the Sound is cut by frequent indentations, reaching deep inland. These become placid, landlocked harbors, fringed with beaches or marsh grass and shadowed by masses of trees and overhanging bluffs. The natural beauty of this region has attracted many to make their homes in the ancient villages that dot the shores, and the fine system of roads makes even remote corners of easy access, especially for summer cottagers.

As we continue on our travels it is assumed that the motorist has his road map and needs no further information as to where to turn or how many miles to check off on his speedometer. Nor will there be any attempt to set forth everything worth noting and remembering on our travel route. Unfortunately, there is many a monument, old homestead, graceful white church, old tavern or charming village which must be skipped simply for lack of space and time. Besides, the explorer must be left the fun of finding out some things for himself; otherwise he isn't exploring. Here the writer begs the pardon of all those Long Islanders whose pride of place may thus be offended by omission in these pages. If this narrative succeeds in suggesting the attractive character of the countryside and its villages and brings back some of the interesting ghosts of its past, that should be enough.

DISCOVERING LONG ISLAND

In entering the region east of Oyster Bay, we notice that the magnificent estates which we admired in the area from Great Neck to Locust Valley have given place to more modest homes, but no less pleasant to the eye in their own unpretentious way. In general, the farther east we go the more we discover ancient dwellings, churches and grist mills, which still survive as relics of Long Island's earlier day.

In our travels along the back country roads of this section we have already noticed an unusual number of locust trees, which seem to resist their enemy, the fungus, rather better here than on the mainland. All of these, they say, go back to the enterprise of a certain Captain John Sands, after whom Sands Point, on Hempstead Harbor, was named. His house, dating from the seventeenth century, is still standing. On one of his voyages to Virginia he obtained a quantity of locust trees and planted them on his place. They grew so well and the timber proved so useful that other settlers planted from his stock, not only on Long Island but in Connecticut, and so they multiplied and spread. There are now miles of them lining these North Shore roads.

The highway we are following has a thoroughly modern surface, but it is not a new route of travel; it is the old "North Country Road," formerly a toll turnpike on which the stagecoaches used to run. It was venerable when President Washington's great coach bounced over it in 1790. In the eighteenth century—in fact, until the railroad came—there were three main arteries of travel for stagecoaches on Long Island, the North, the Middle and the South Country Road, and when the modern highways came to be constructed the old routes were largely followed.

Next to Oyster Bay lies another narrow indentation of coast line, Cold Spring Harbor, once famous as a whaling center. That curious peninsula, Lloyd Neck, which is all but an island,

CAROLINE CHURCH, SETAUKET

MORE OF THE NORTH SHORE

was, in Colonial days, a famous rendezvous for British privateers and supplied much of the cordwood for the redcoats in New York. After skirting the shore line of Cold Spring Harbor, the traveler enters the town of Huntington, another attractive residential town. But it has one unholy practice that the town fathers permit; namely, a parking space in the middle, as well as on both sides, of Main Street. This leaves only a narrow lane on each hand for threading your way to a more spacious avenue. And when some Sweet Young Thing absent-mindedly and suddenly backs out from left or right, you need all your self-control and a powerful brake.

Huntington's most prized possession is that handsome white First Presbyterian Church on the north side of the 25 A highway, on the outskirts of the town. It is a good example of the white pine meeting house of the New England tradition, and if the traveler is interested in architectural details he will want to haul up for a few minutes to take a good look at the wheel windows, the central doorway, the sundial above it and the slender spire. This building was erected at the close of the Revolution, 1784 if you insist on knowing. There was a church here as early as 1665, and its successor, built in 1715, was the one which the British troops took possession of when they arrived here. They made it a barracks, and we trust that the pews were most uncomfortable to sleep on. Finally, the invaders tore the church down for material to build a "Fort Golgotha," so named because it was erected on a burial ground hard by. The order to do this was issued by that interesting early American scientist, Count Rumford, who remained loyal to the King. In this destruction the bell was saved by the soldiers, but as it proved to be an awkward souvenir to carry off to England it was finally returned to the people of Huntington. That same bell still swings in the spire of the present church, and it has rung the summons to worship on this spot for more than two hundred years.

There is a pleasant wartime incident to offset the miseries suffered on Long Island during the two wars with Great Britain, and it happened here in this town of Huntington. During the Revolution a small British midshipman, named Hardy, fell ill of smallpox and a kind-hearted woman, named Elizabeth Williams Potter, cared for him and nursed him back to health. In the War of 1812, a sloop belonging to her son, Judge Nathaniel Potter, was captured by the British fleet, with the Judge's nephew on board. The young man was clapped into irons. Judge Potter paid a ransom to recover his sloop and then went out to the flagship to negotiate for the release of his nephew. When Potter met the Commodore the two recognized each other. The latter was the same Hardy whom Mrs. Potter had taken into her home as a very sick boy more than thirty years before. He was also that same Hardy who had been the flag captain on the *Victory* at Trafalgar and had received Nelson's dying words. When the Commodore realized whom he was dealing with, he released the nephew instantly. Soon afterwards, on board the flagship, Hardy gave a dinner in honor of the Potters. At its close he arose and toasted his American friends in the courtly speech of "an officer and a gentleman."

Another memory of the Revolutionary War is honored by a boulder on the shore of the Sound not far from Huntington. This marks the spot where Nathan Hale landed when he came to visit the Long Island camps of the British in order to find out for Washington what were the plans of the enemy. The road maps show where this monument stands.

If one is in the mood to linger and ramble about a bit, he will find, in the rear of this church, Heckscher Park, which is one of

MORE OF THE NORTH SHORE

many private gifts for public enjoyment which we will come across on Long Island. Besides the usual ponds and playgrounds, there is a museum of art. The doors are kept locked, but there is an obliging curator who will unlock them cheerfully and with no desire for gain. Probably there are not many visitors who take the trouble to come here and ask for admittance.

The walls of the three large rooms in this gallery are crammed with paintings, and to enter and look about is to step into the age of sixty years ago. Here are Schreyer's distingué-looking desert Arabs, together with J. G. Brown's cherubic street arabs. Here are acres of Venetian scenes, landscapes that look as if painted in brown gravy and, most of all, story-pictures, served with four lumps of sugar. But there are also some examples of English school, eighteenth-century portraits and one splendid moonlight scene by the American Blakelock. Besides the paintings, there is a vast assortment of old laces, wax flowers and flowers made of shells, all under glass domes, not to mention Indian arrowheads and other oddities and curios without number. The whole collection looks as if the original owner, finding the big museums cold to his art treasures, and his descendants unable to give them houseroom, built a gallery for them in this park that he gave to the people of Huntington. At any rate, from Schreyers to shell pieces, it is interesting as a picture of what was considered High Art about 1875, not only in America but in Europe.

While we are here in Huntington it is worth remembering that the man who is now regarded as the most famous native son of Long Island, certainly its most original genius, was once a familiar figure on the streets of this town. And he was born only a few miles to the south of it. This, of course, was Walt Whitman, the "good, gray poet." Whether you like his poetry or no, he stands in the front rank of American writers, ahead of all the elegantly groomed figures of our literature from Washington Irving to James Russell Lowell, flaunting his ill-fitting gray suit and wagging his huge beard at all the critics, not caring a rap what anyone says about him. Is his verse merely "barbaric yawp," to quote his own phrase, or is he *the* great American classic to be read in reverence? In his own words, "As some fellow said to some other fellow back in the fifties when a few people got a good deal excited about me: 'If this Walt Whitman ain't a damn humbug—then what is he?' That's so. What is he? Some people are still asking that question." Whatever he was as a poet, Whitman was a product of this farming section of Long Island. He was born and brought up here. He loved it, and wherever he went in later life this was his homeland.

It will mean only a slight detour to pay our respects at Whitman's birthplace, and it is easy to find. Many road maps indicate the spot; at any rate we shall follow Route 110 south out of Huntington. About a mile beyond the junction with Highway 25 we see at our left, right on the edge of the road, the little dwelling which is the shrine of Whitman enthusiasts. It is a shingled farmhouse painted brown, typical of Long Island homes at the beginning of the nineteenth century in having one main two-story part with a small one-story wing snuggled up alongside, something like a hen with a chicken under its wing. Beyond that extend sheds and outbuildings, and a picturesque, ivy-covered barn. It all looks so diminutive that one wonders how the elder Whitmans found room to tuck away their nine children.

The house is now almost smothered in vines and trees, but it is not altered in any essential detail from the way it looked when a twenty-one-year-old artist named Joseph Pennell came here

WALT WHITMAN'S BIRTHPLACE

in 1881 to visit the poet and make some illustrations for Dr. Buck's biography. The place has not yet been made into a Whitman museum, as it will be someday, for it is privately occupied, and certain "no trespassing" signs bid the wayfarer mind his business; but for a small fee it is possible for a Whitman worshiper to step inside and look about with reverent eye, or on departing to pluck a few leaves of grass as a souvenir. On the highway is a rock in which is set a tablet, "To mark the birthplace of Walt Whitman, the good gray poet, Born May 31, 1819. Erected by the Colonial Society of Huntington in 1905."

In the introduction to one of his books Whitman, speaking of his birthplace, says: "West Hills is a romantic and beautiful spot; it is the most hilly and elevated part of Long Island." Whitman's ideas of the romantic and beautiful must have been original, or possibly the countryside looked more picturesque in 1850 when he wrote those words. There are no "Hills" visible. If this is the most exalted part of Long Island the ascent is so gradual that the tourist would never suspect the fact. But clearly it was home, sweet home to the poet. Here he spent his boyhood. With his father and mother he went as a child to hear Elias Hicks preach, and many years afterwards wrote a long essay about him. "An unnamable something," Whitman says, ". . . deeper than art . . . emanated from his very heart to the hearts of his audience."

In a poem called "There Was a Child Went Forth" are these lines which suggest boyhood memories:

The early lilacs became part of this child,
And grass, white and red morning glories, and white and red clover,
    and the song of the phoebe bird.

This particular child, after the family moved to Brooklyn, used to return to West Hills for his summers. He reveled in the sea bathing on the South Shore, racing up the beach and "declaiming Homer or Shakespeare to surf and seagulls by the hour." It would be interesting to know how many youngsters of these enlightened days could declaim Homer and Shakespeare by the hour, especially those whose formal education ended at the age of thirteen. At this point in his life Whitman began as a printer's devil, and from that lowly beginning became a journalist.

The great event in his career was the publication, in 1855, of a volume of twelve poems, without titles, together with a lengthy Preface. The book is called *Leaves of Grass*. It was a dismal failure with the reading public, but Emerson wrote the unknown poet: "I find it the most extraordinary piece of wit and wisdom that America has yet contributed." An astonishing tribute from a Boston Brahmin to this queer, slovenly Long Island farmer's boy! Bryant used to go to see him. Other critics hailed him, notably in England, but there were those also who thought him Perfectly Terrible. Lines like these have always excited unseemly mirth:

> Do I contradict myself?
> Very well then I contradict myself.
> (I am large. I contain multitudes.)

There is still a division of opinion between readers, but the favorable critics have now the upper hand. Whitman's present standing is suggested by the fact that the *Dictionary of American Biography* gives him a spread of eight and a half pages as compared with four and a half for Longfellow. The article calls Whitman "a gigantic and beautiful figure in 19th century letters," and summarizes his poetry as "the most original work yet done by any American poet."

MORE OF THE NORTH SHORE

That note of originality rings with unmistakable clearness in the following familiar passages, not only in their homely language and their lack of regular metrical form and rhyme, but most of all in their point of view:

I believe a leaf of grass is no less than the journey-work of the stars,
And the pismire is equally perfect, and a grain of sand, and the egg of the wren,
And the tree-toad is a chef-d'œuvre for the highest,
And the running blackberry would adorn the parlors of heaven,
And the narrowest hinge in my hand puts to scorn all machinery,
And the cow crunching with depress'd head surpasses any statue,
And a mouse is miracle enough to stagger sextillions of infidels,
And I could come every afternoon of my life to look at the farmer's girl boiling her iron tea-kettle and baking shortcake.

I think I could turn and live with animals, they are so placid and self-contain'd;
I stand and look at them long and long.
They do not sweat and whine about their condition;
They do not lie awake in the dark and weep for their sins;
They do not make me sick discussing their duty to God;
Not one is dissatisfied—not one is demented with the mania of owning things;
Not one kneels to another, nor to his kind that lived thousands of years ago;
Not one is respectable or industrious over the whole earth.

To one sentiment of the poet all of us can say Amen. Late in his life Whitman wrote that "one main genesis-motive of the *Leaves* was my conviction (just as strong today as ever) that the crowning growth of the United States is to be spiritual and heroic." There was something of this prophetic spirit underlying all his writing, a hope for humanity in the democratic ideal, which possibly was an unconscious echo of the eloquence he listened to as a boy from the great Quaker preacher, Elias Hicks, whom we shall meet later in our travels.

To return to our exploration of the North Shore, we can go back to Huntington and again set our faces eastward on Route 25 A. A few miles brings us to Northport, which stands high on the bluff overlooking its own harbor, and may well stand on its boast of having the finest site of all these North Shore towns, with a delightful drive out to the Sound to tempt the wandering motorist.

After leaving Northport our North Country Road seems possessed by the desire to pass the time of day with its old friend, the Middle Country Road, which it hasn't seen since 'way back in the neighborhood of Brooklyn. So it dips toward the south, and where for a short distance the two roads enjoy their reunion is the main street of a village called Smithtown.

This name, like that of another Long Island town to the south, Hicksville, is derived from a local family. And, like Hicksville, to the stranger the name does not suggest glamour or a romantic past. It is only a shade better than Yaphank or Scuttlehole. But that is where the stranger is mistaken. To be one of *the* Smiths of Smithtown is only a little inferior to royalty. It is like belonging to *the* Joneses of Virginia, the ap Catesby Joneses, of course. The English wit, Sidney Smith, once confessed that the Smiths never had any coat of arms, "and have invariably sealed their letters with their thumbs." (That is, instead of with a seal ring.) But Sidney never met the Smiths of Smithtown.

The founder of their blue-blooded branch of the family was a doughty soldier of Cromwell, one Richard Smith ("the Smith a mighty man was he"), who purchased a tract of land in these parts. In dealing with the Indians, for their side of the bargain, he is said to have obtained the promise of all the land he could ride around between sunrise and sunset. Now in these days horses were rare. Smith used a large bull for his favorite means of transportation, and so he set out to encircle as much territory as he could. Where he stopped to eat his lunch, a valley near the present Fort Salonga, is still called "Bread and Cheese Hollow." For this feat Richard Smith was familiarly known hereafter as "Bull-Rider Smith," and his descendants are the "Bull-Smiths" today, to distinguish them from the descendants of Colonel William Smith of Brookhaven, who was once the British Mayor of Tangiers in Morocco. For his services the Governor presented him with a tract of land on Long Island. Members of that rival clan are therefore known as "Tangier Smiths." Which Smiths have the deeper tint of azure in their veins is a moot point.

It must be confessed that Smithtown, as viewed from its Main Street, looks quite "ordinary," if not "tacky," as they say in the South. But nearly all Main Streets look that way. There are nooks and corners that are much more attractive. And, be it said, Smithtown has had its moments in the past. George Washington "baited" his horses at the "Widow Blidenberg's, a decent house," as he noted in his diary, and all the villagers turned out to wave their hats and shout huzzas, doing him as much honor as they could to anyone who was not a Bull-Smith.

In a later day Daniel Webster enjoyed coming here to fish. Near where we entered the town a long woodland lane runs south to a secluded lake, with a deserted mill beside it. Every morning during his vacation here he would start out from his lodgings at a certain "Aunt Sally Vail's," equipped with fishing tackle and lunch box, and adorned with a tall beaver hat—dignified always. (The same Sidney Smith whose testimony about the Smith family has just been quoted saw Webster in England once and said that he impressed him as "a steam engine in trousers," and added that he was a fraud because no man *could* be as great as Webster looked.) From Aunt Sally's a buckboard would drive the famous statesman to the lake, where he would spend the day.

When it came to publishing his orations, Webster used to add elegant flourishes and purple patches to the original as it had been delivered in the Senate. No doubt the Smithtown pond was a good quiet place for working up his thundering sentences while waiting for the fish to bite. " 'When my eyes shall be turned to behold for the last time the sun in heaven,—may I not see him shining on the broken and dishonored fragments of a once glorious Union'—Pshaw, I thought I had a nibble then. Let me see, what shall I say next?—'on states discordant, belligerent; on a land rent with civil feuds, or drenched it may be in fraternal gore!'—No, I'll make that 'fraternal blood'; gore is too strong." And so on till he finished his peroration with, "Liberty and Union, now and forever, one and inseparable." After all, there must be something a fisherman does besides stare at the water. There are probably as many fish in the pond now as there were in his day, but there seem to be no more Daniel Websters, either in Smithtown or in Washington.

The little white church at Smithtown Branch is not much more than one hundred years old, but, like that other church in Huntington, its predecessor on this site had a hard experience during the Revolutionary War. The preacher, Joshua Hart, was so fearless in the way he denounced the behavior of the British troops that one soldier took a shot at him from the pews, but fortunately missed. It is one of those rare cases in history when some member of a congregation has dared to answer back the man in the pulpit, but he might have done it more decorously than with a musket.

OLD GRIST MILL, STONY BROOK

The commanding officer became angry, too, and he ordered the reverend gentleman handcuffed to a negro slave and made to travel on foot all the way to Brooklyn for trial.

"How do you like your company?" sneered the captain, as Joshua Hart started off with his black companion.

"Better than yours!" he retorted, which was not one of those soft answers that turn away wrath.

Near this church a road comes out on the highway—the River Road. Don't pass this by, but turn the car straight up northward and slow down, for this is one of the most beautiful drives on the whole Island. It runs beside a long inlet of the Sound, known as the Nissequogue River, and it passes through an ancient and now almost invisible hamlet of the same name, where the Smithtown Church was originally established in 1675.

The River Road is one of those lanes to be enjoyed at a leisurely pace, for even the man at the wheel must have ample opportunity to look to the right and left, as well as ahead. Shortly after leaving the highway, the road plunges into a tunnel of deep green. The forest branches meet overhead and form a dense shade in the middle of a bright afternoon. Golden green lights, where the sun does manage to filter through, sparkle and flash like flames on leaves and tree trunks. The road goes gently up and down, roller-coaster fashion, but it is hard-surfaced and quite wide enough for passing a semioccasional car coming from the opposite direction. Every now and then one comes upon a fine old house of a bygone age, deep in shrubbery and trees, but so trim and speckless in snowy paint that you know it has become a city dweller's summer home. Elsewhere you see gateposts at the end of a grassy drive, indicating that far up the hill and hidden in the forest is some other summer retreat. And, as we trundle northward, we begin to see through the trees on our left the blue stretch of the Nissequogue River, lined with overhanging woods and sea marshes. This is not so much river as estuary, which widens gradually as it opens toward the Sound.

If time permits, we may drive not only to where one branch of the road ends at the mouth of the "river," but (following our road map) take the other branch which rambles around Stony Brook Harbor. Then we can come back again through "Head of the Harbor," and thence to Stony Brook village. Within this area of a few miles the explorer may enjoy the North Shore of Long Island at its best. Here are dense woods, blue water, lush countryside, fine old houses, all lying fair and peaceful under the summer sky.

Stony Brook harmonizes well with its rural and picturesque setting at the head of a landlocked pocket of a harbor. Where the "stony brook" may be is not clear to the casual traveler as he drives along the road, but there is a water mill here which is worth visiting, and which the brook, no doubt, was responsible for. There used to be many of these water and windmills operating on Long Island, and some of the former had tremendous wheels that dwarfed the rest of the building. One such water mill was still visible, though in poor repair, as late as fifty years ago, at Northport. But this type exists no more. In fact, of all the water mills on Long Island, the last that is doing business is the grist mill here at Stony Brook, and here the water wheel itself is a modest little contraption, boxed in as a protection from winter ice.

It is said that this Stony Brook mill keeps going because, by terms of the deed, the owner is bound to keep the mill in operation in order to hold title to the pond. And it is said also that, despite the Machine Age, this Stony Brook mill is a going concern which shows a neat surplus in black ink at the end of the year.

But the owner today is not the man of such awesome importance to the Stony Brook community as his predecessors used to be. In Colonial Long Island the mill meant so much to a town that its residents offered all possible inducements to get a miller

NORTHPORT WATER MILL, FIFTY YEARS AGO
(*After a woodcut in Scribner's Magazine*)

to settle there and do business. Here in Stony Brook a town meeting in 1698 gave a certain Adam Smith the "Town's right to Stony Brook [exclusive rights to the water power] and two acres of land on condition that he build a good and sufficient grist mill and maintain same." The mill built that year was used until 1750, when it was torn down. The one the visitor sees now is the one that replaced the original in that year.

Because of its age—and the alterations have been very few since it was built—this is a unique example of the eighteenth-century Colonial grist mill run by water. It is quite permissible to enter by the wistaria-hung doorway and look about inside. The framework is of hand-hewn oak timbers, twelve to fourteen inches thick, and the flooring is the same as was laid in 1750. The same machinery is working, too, and it looks surprisingly intricate for a mill of those early days. The grain is dumped into the chutes at the top of the building, falling down into hoppers which lead to the stones.

In addition to the grist business, the mill serves the community by pumping water to houses and stores in Stony Brook village. Besides being so useful, the old mill charms the eye that loves a placid pond, reflecting the trees, a tumble of water over the dam shaded by willow branches and a stream that leads through tall grasses to the head of the Bay. In the earlier half of the nineteenth century a famous painter of farmyard scenes whose work may be seen in the Metropolitan Museum—and there is an example in the East Hampton library—lived in Stony Brook, William Sidney Mount. For his sketching excursions he rigged up a curious traveling cart, with one glassed-in side and a stove in winter. In this he jogged about the country, painting as he traveled. In those happy, far-off days it was still possible for a painter to make a living.

Before abandoning rural lanes to return to the highway, the traveler should ramble out to that dot on the map marked Old Field. Sometimes these back-country routes wriggle like a fever chart, but who expects to "make time" in scenes like these? As we draw near Old Field Point we gain charming views of patches of blue water, shining in the sun, framed in overhanging trees, and finally we bring up at a dead end on the edge of the bluff. Here there stands a courteous police officer who sees to it that thoughtless motorists do not clutter up the road by parking cars just where others need to turn their cars around. For it is

OLD FIELD POINT LIGHT

a tempting place to linger. At your right is the lighthouse, Old Field Light, now a private home, its task being taken over by a government beacon in the rear. Everywhere as far as eye can see stretches the broad blue expanse of the Sound, with a faint suggestion of the Connecticut shore on the horizon.

Then, winding back in a general easterly direction, one road or another takes us to Setauket, lying at the end of Conscience Bay and near one side of Port Jefferson Harbor. These sheltered waters made the Setauket of the eighteenth and early nineteenth century a lively port. From here, even as late as the eighteen-fifties, a famous schooner, *The Flying Eagle,* was sent to Constantinople during the Crimean War with a cargo of rum and pepper, "which," the owner observed, referring to the Turks,

DISCOVERING LONG ISLAND

"I thought ought to warm 'em up." But Setauket has long since slipped into the placid inactivity of most old American seaport towns, though, unlike some of them, it has gained in beauty with the advancing decades.

As we enter the village from our detour to Old Field Point, we come upon a scene of unusual charm. On either side of a bridge lies a wide mill pond, its shores carefully landscaped and planted

FRANK MELVILLE MEMORIAL PARK

with flowering shrubs. On the seaward side is another bridge with a stone mill and a water wheel, where the outlet flows over the dam. A driveway branching off the main road invites the traveler to turn off, pause and look about. Here is the "Frank Melville Memorial Park," presented to the public by Mrs. Melville as a tribute to her husband—certainly as beautiful a memorial by a widow to her husband as can be found anywhere.

Sloping up the hill from this park is the village green, and the center of the historical Setauket. In the open field on the right rises a large boulder with a cluster of small trees growing round it. This bears a tablet commemorating a skirmish that took place in August, 1777, between the British regulars and a united band of Connecticut patriots and local boys. The invaders barricaded themselves in the Presbyterian Church on the hill, where they mounted small cannon in the upper windows and uprooted gravestones for breastworks. These redcoats were certainly no respecters of sacred places. In the fighting the patriots had a tough time of it, for the British were not to be dislodged. When the war was over and the enemy retired from Setauket, they left the church a wreck, and soon afterwards a bolt of lightning gave it the *coup de grâce*. The present building, which took its place, dates from 1811.

There is still plenty of antiquity in the burial ground, however. Some say that the oldest headstone on Long Island lies directly behind this church, but as the poor old relic is smothered in brambles and tall grass and quite illegible when you get down to it, there is no arguing the matter.

The neighboring shrine, of the Episcopal fold, is called the Caroline Church. When the congregation was first organized in 1723 it was called Christ Church; but after Caroline, the wife of George the Second, presented a silver communion service to the church (in 1730) the grateful parishioners renamed their temple "Caroline." Sad to say, when the British troops left the island at the close of the Revolution, the royal silver disappeared with them and has never been returned. The present building dates from 1729—that is something of a date, too, for American churches—and is famous for its odd square-built tower with a spire on top. In the course of two hundred years or more this tower has slipped out of perpendicular, somewhat like the leaning tower of Pisa, though not so drunkenly as that, but it is in no danger of falling. On the tip of the spire is a gilded Union Jack which was put there when the parishioners were still loyal Britishers, and the worship was literally "Church of England."

Visitors may enter and look about inside to see what a church of 1729 looked like, but let them be warned that their eyes will be assaulted by some horrendous specimens of nineteenth-century stained glass. Unfortunately some of the old-time New England Episcopalians felt it necessary to show the difference between their sanctuaries and the "chapels" of the dissenting sects by inserting stained glass in the windows—and just at the time when American stained glass was at its worst. Sometimes even a Calvinist congregation in days of prosperity was not content with the clear glass windows of their meeting houses, but took to raw pinks, and royal purples, and venomous greens, in memory of its dear departed. But such windows are fortunately rare.

However, we should not take leave of the old Caroline Church in a carping spirit. Like the Matinecock Meeting House in Locust Valley, this building has been a place of worship continuously for well over two centuries, and survived two invasions of hostile armies.

In contrast with Setauket, her near neighbor, East Setauket, is very brisk and modern. But here beside the broad cement street there is one forlorn specimen of antiquity which is worth pausing for, an old house in a clump of trees that include some bearded patriarchs of willows. It faces a smart, new filling station and doesn't seem happy about it. This is the old Brewster homestead. No hedge or fence protects it from the roar of traffic and the fumes of gasoline. The grass about it grows long and tangled, but sweet with quantities of mint. The bricks in the chimney are beginning to drop off. The ragged shingles are black with age, and the windows are sagging out of drawing, but if the tourist from the West or South has never seen what the architects call the seventeenth-century New England "salt-box," or "lean-to," house, here is a good one to study. This example has the distinctive features, especially the short roof in front, and the long one sloping down to a single story in the rear.

This house is supposed to have been built by a son of the

PRESBYTERIAN CHURCH, SETAUKET

MORE OF THE NORTH SHORE

famous "Elder Brewster" of early Massachusetts history. Heaven only knows just when and where it was first erected, but it was moved to this site in the year 1665. And people still live therein who are exceedingly proud of their ancient habitation and respond very kindly to the questions of the chance traveler.

The Brewster homestead is another of those venerable dwell-

BREWSTER HOMESTEAD, EAST SETAUKET

ings which are being allowed to die of old age. Among all the federal bureaus and projects—and they are legion—what a pity that there isn't one for the Preservation of Ancient Buildings!

After shedding a tear at the bedside, so to speak, of this expiring old dwelling, left to us from the days of Charles the Second (and Nell Gwyn), let us continue on our way until we slide down a long hill into the cheerful town of Port Jefferson, one of the most important in size on the whole North Shore. The highway leads directly to the harbor. Here in Port Jefferson there are no antiquities visible except these old wharves and boat sheds, but they have a tradition of their own to boast about.

More than a hundred years ago this was a busy shipping center, and the harbor bristled with masts and spars. In the heyday of the American merchant marine the shore was lined with shipyards where stout vessels stood on the ways in all stages of construction. Port Jefferson built not only whaling ships for Sag Harbor, but also larger and more streamline hulls for the long journey round the Horn in the China trade, the "China Clippers." Also, although it isn't good form to mention such things now, there were vessels built and fitted out here which went into the forbidden business of slave-catching on the coast of Africa; in fact, the last slave ship that served in the famous triangular trade of rum, molasses and negroes was dispatched from this harbor. It is all very quiet now, but these forlorn-looking old wharves can remember the early days of bustle and prosperity. Like so many famous New England harbors, Port Jefferson now has to depend chiefly on the "summer people" for its livelihood.

There is not much to see after we drive into town. But there is an ancient "Wilson's Sail Loft," not far from the ferry landing, where a famous sailmaker, R. H. Wilson, made the sails for the yacht *America* in 1851. Though the Yankee cup contender was well designed and well handled, the sails had much to do with the winning of that famous race. The cotton duck of the *America,* the experts claim, held the wind better than the hemp and linen canvas of the English yachts. The visitor who is curious about such matters may go up the stairs of the Wilson's Sail Loft and see on the wall of the little office the original drawing of the *America's* sail and spar plan.

It was a proud day for our grandfathers when the first packet

MORE OF THE NORTH SHORE

from England brought the news of the *America's* triumph over a whole field of crack contenders.

"Which vessel is in the lead?" asked Queen Victoria, as the first sail appeared off the Isle of Wight.

"The *America,* your Majesty."

"And which is second?"

"There is no second," was the melancholy reply. And *Punch,* which was in those days positively venomous as far as the United States was concerned, came out handsomely with the following verse beneath a cartoon:

> Yankee Doodle had a craft
> A rather tidy clipper,
> And he challenged, while they laughed,
>   The Britishers to whip her.
> Their whole squadron she outsped
>   And that in their own water;
> Of all the lot she went ahead
>   And they came nowhere arter.

Which was very sporting, and probably nobody read the news of that race with more satisfaction than Mr. Wilson, the sail-maker of Port Jefferson.

Although stories of Long Island shipwrecks naturally have for their scene the ocean shore rather than the coast that fronts the peaceful Sound, there have been tragedies of the sea on the North Shore too. One of these deserves retelling, for although forgotten now, it created a profound impression in its day. A certain young lithographer named Currier, famous in after years as the senior partner in the firm of Currier and Ives, issued a lithograph of the disaster which was his first popular success and launched him on his career as the pictorial chronicle of the middle of the nineteenth century in America. The scene was the entire coast line between Oyster Bay and Port Jefferson, along which were washed ashore the wreckage and corpses of this disaster.

On the afternoon of January 13, 1840, the Sound Steamer *Lexington* left New York for Stonington, Connecticut. Her decks were piled not only with baggage but with a heavy cargo of cotton in bales. For so small a steamer there was a large passenger list, more than ninety. Among these were a number of ship captains who, after leaving their ships in New York, were on their way home to see their families after long cruises.

About seven that evening a cotton bale just abaft the smokestack caught fire. At that time the vessel was in the middle of the Sound abreast of Eaton's Neck, Huntington Bay. A fresh, bitter wind was blowing, which speedily fanned the blaze into a roaring fire, as other bales caught the sparks. Since the cotton had been stowed amidships the flames soon cut off all communication between the forward and the after parts of the steamer, and the passengers, huddled tightly in the stern, could only watch the conflagration sweep toward them along the deck.

The captain turned the bows of the vessel toward the Long Island shore in an effort to beach her. He ordered the boats away, but with the speed of the steamer, the ineptitude of the crew and the terror of the passengers, each boat was swamped. Soon the tiller ropes burned away, the engine stopped; and then the *Lexington* lay at the mercy of wind and tide, one horrible crackling mass of flame. Many of the passengers, preferring drowning to being burned alive, jumped into the icy water. A few seized on bits of floating baggage or bales of cotton.

It seems strange that there was no vessel within sight of that blaze to come to the rescue. In the earliest account of the dis-

OLD WHARF, PORT JEFFERSON

MORE OF THE NORTH SHORE

aster, as printed in the *Sun,* it was asserted that a sloop, the *Improvement,* had sighted the burning steamer, but her captain, reckoning that if he paused to render aid he would lose the tide necessary to make his port of call that evening, decided to let her alone and went blithely on his way. Whether that was true or not, certainly no help came from any quarter. Out of one hundred and thirty souls on board the *Lexington* only four were saved. One of these, a sea captain named Hilliard, had hauled himself out of the water upon a bale of cotton. Then he dug into it to keep warm, and after floating fifteen hours was finally picked up by a sloop from the Connecticut shore. He was the only passenger to survive. The Second Mate also climbed on to a bale and dug in, but he floated forty-eight hours. Having drifted near the shore just beyond Port Jefferson, he managed, by scrambling over heaped-up ice floes and swimming through open water, to get ashore at Miller's Landing (Miller Place). He was dreadfully frostbitten, but survived. Two other members of the crew were picked up in the water. All the rest, passengers and crew, were lost.

This tale of disaster was told and retold for many years. One circumstance specially appealed to the popular imagination, that of the floating cotton bales to which despairing men and women clung until they died of cold or, as in a few instances, were able to climb upon and then burrow into the cotton. Currier, of course, had to draw his picture entirely from imagination, but he did not miss any detail of horror. If one may be permitted a flippant comment after a hundred years, it is noteworthy that in this lithograph nearly all the male passengers in the water or on the cotton bales are still wearing their silk hats. Perhaps in 1840 a gentleman was supposed to cling to his badge of dignity even in death.

DISCOVERING LONG ISLAND

In the early part of this present century the story of this dreadful winter night on the Sound was surpassed in horror by the burning of the *General Slocum* on a summer day in the East River, but that story belongs to the annals of Manhattan rather than Long Island. And though the burning of the *Lexington* took place a century ago, it is still the most appalling disaster of the sea ever witnessed on this North Shore.

CHAPTER III

TO THE NORTH FORK

OUT at the entrance of Port Jefferson Harbor are huge floating steam shovels, disemboweling the hill that stands as the eastern gateway to the port. They are filling barges with the gravel which goes somewhere to cement mixers. These shovels are ruthless; they brandish their arms, and grab and gobble great mouthfuls, like boys at a boarding-school table. They are demolishing the front of a hill called "Mt. Misery" by the early settlers. Once in a while the pioneers left a name behind to express what they really felt, and despite the fine harbor, the plentiful fish, the friendly Indians, these Port Jefferson Puritans evidently went through some tough winters.

Another grimly named eminence near by is "Mt. Sinai." "Where did that name come from?" we heard a stranger ask a barber in Port Jefferson. "One of them Indian names," replied that fount of knowledge. "They's a lot of 'em on Long Island." Even the pronunciation is so altered that a gold-star Sunday-school pupil would never recognize the name. "Mt. Signer," the inhabitants call it, as if it had to do with someone who complied on the dotted line.

There is a bit of history behind the name of this village. Originally it was called Old Man's. In the seventeenth century a precious scoundrel named John Scott appeared in these parts, forged a deed of sale for a large tract of land, including the site of the village, and then sold it to a trusting friend in England, who was always referred to simply as the Old Man. The purchaser sent his son across the Atlantic to Long Island to look after this property, but Scott sold the young man into bonded servitude to make some extra money on the swindle. Because of this story the settlement came to be known as Old Man's. When, about a hundred years ago, the village applied for a post office, the Department declined to accept such a name, insisting on a more dignified one. Finally, the new postmaster's wife determined to leave it to the Lord. She opened her Bible at random and laid down her knitting needle on the page. When she looked she saw that it pointed to the name "Mt. Sinai." That settled it, and Mt. Sinai this village has been ever since.

There is a small harbor here, the *raison d'être* for the village when it was first settled. A handsome white church stands on the "Mount" within eyeshot of the harbor, and it must have been a landmark for many a homebound fisherman in the old days.

Miller Place is Mt. Sinai's nearest neighbor. This was formerly known as "Miller's Place," with the apostrophe. That name did very well for two centuries, but the postal authorities and the Railway Express Company, suffering from the modern obsession for efficiency, have been going all over this fair land casting possessives and apostrophes into outer darkness. The older inhabitants, to judge by my own experience, grimly hang on to "Miller's Place" regardless, as free men should.

All there is to be seen of this antiquated hamlet lies on either side of the road, and the total population is only a trifle above one hundred, but this is one of the oldest settlements on the eastern side of the North Shore. It goes back to Andrew Miller, who settled here in 1659. Here he created a duck pond—still to be seen at the turn of the road—and a commons, north of that, for the village cattle and horses. The early settlers were said to be well-to-do and educated, and they certainly had a sense of

MOUNT SINAI CHURCH

TO THE NORTH FORK

what was decent and proper. For one thing they would not stand any foolishness from the young people, as the following village ordinance makes clear:

Orders and constatutions maed by the Athoraty of this towne [in 1674] to be duly cept and obsarved: 1.) whereas, It have bene too coman in this towne for young men and maieds to be out of there father's and mother's house at unseasonable times of niete, It is therefore ordered that whosoever of the younger sort, shall be out of there father's and mother's hous past nien of the clock at niet, shall be summoned to the next cort and ther to pay cort charges with what punishment the cort shall se cause to lay upon them, ecksept they can give suffissient Resen of there being out late.

Young people out after nine o'clock! What was the world coming to?

The second clause of this town ordinance was to restrict "tipling," and a fourth checked the ungodly amusement of horse racing. "Whosoever shall run any rases or run otherwise a hors back in the streetes or within the towne platt shall forfeit 10 shillings to the use of the towne." Miller Place was evidently a model of municipal decorum in the seventeenth century, and from all outward appcarances it still is. They do say, however, that certain of the summer young people are known to be "out of there father's and mother's hous past nien of the clock at niet" without being summoned to the next court.

For all their godliness, these Millers and their descendants never had a church of their own, but piled into carriages and wagons of various sorts and made the long journey over sandy roads to Setauket, and then later to the church at Mt. Sinai, when that was built. On the right of the road, which is the main and only street of the village, stands a white building with a belfry which might be mistaken for a church. This is the Miller Place Academy, founded in 1834 by the efforts of a man named Frederick Jones, who became the first teacher therein. His salary for a term of five months was $175. Later the faculty expanded, and

EIGHTEENTH-CENTURY COTTAGE, MILLER PLACE

the salaries became more liberal. Subsequent teachers, all college graduates, received between $316.67 to $400.70 a year, out of which, of course, the professor had to support himself and his family. In those days, April and October were the vacation months—perhaps because of the planting and harvesting—and the rest of the year the pupils were expected to come to school and study.

Even a hundred years ago the activities of the youngsters were not entirely confined to the accumulation of erudition. There was a time, for instance, when a neighbor took his wagon out of the barn and loaded it with bags of wheat to take to the mill early the next morning. When he arose and went forth at daybreak the wagon and his load had disappeared from the face of the earth. Then, chancing to look back at the barn, he saw, perched astride the ridgepole, his missing wagon with every bag of wheat neatly in place. The imps from the Academy had taken the wagon apart, piece by piece, and put it together again on the roof of the barn, and then hoisted up the bags of grain. It must have taken them all night.

Today those young devils have long since gone, with the books, blackboards and birch rods, but within the building are still to be found globes of the world of a date prior to the Mexican War, as the map of the United States shows. The present village has recently taken over the school building for a public library.

Old as it is, Miller Place does not possess now as many of the eighteenth-century homes as one might wish. The oldest of those that have survived is the "Millard House." It stands to the left of the road, a little beyond the post office and general store, as we enter the village. It was built by a grandson of the first settler, Andrew Miller; that is, he erected the first part, and his son and grandson each added a section later. In the two centuries and more of its existence the house has never left the family.

Inside, eloquent of the dangers of the early days, the door is secured by a large wooden lock and two heavy iron bars. Within the tiny vestibule, the door leading to the "parlor" is pierced overhead by three large holes to accommodate the barrels of a musket. These were cut there in the days of the Revolutionary War, when British soldiers and Tory raiders made life in Miller Place wretched and often perilous. One had to be ready to shoot into the vestibule if the enemy broke down the outside door.

The worst menace during the British occupation of those years came from a gang of hoodlums who, under cover of being Loyalists, came from neighboring towns to loot and burn, or crossed over from the Connecticut shore in whaleboats to ravage a defenseless countryside. These were known as the "whaleboat men." By and by they became so ruthless that they robbed friends as well as foe. They would scorch the feet of their victims to make them tell where the hidden silver was located, and did not mind killing if it was convenient. By the time the Revolutionary War came to an end these whaleboatmen had become out-and-out pirates. Miller Place suffered more than its share of raids by these gentry, and watchmen used to be posted on the bluff overlooking the Sound to give warning of their coming.

This is the last of the historic villages on the North Shore until we come to the settlements along the Fork. The reason is that the coast line, instead of opening up into many harbors, as in the area lying to the west of Port Jefferson, from Miller Place eastward presents an unbroken line of bluffs, with a shallow, stony beach at their feet. A shore line of that sort could not offer any attraction to the early settlers. These wooded heights are now thick with summer cottages and villages, such as Shoreham and Wading River, but they are not especially interesting to the explorer.

The landscape itself ceases to be interesting, too. As the motorist comes out of Miller Place upon the highway again, he enters a modern farming area—acres and acres of potatoes and cauliflower stretching across to a dim fringe of scraggly pine forest on the horizon, marking the Great Pine Barrens. If the traveler hails from some prairie state he may burst into nostalgic tears, for the scene might be Illinois, Indiana or southern Michigan, without changing one detail of the landscape.

Along this stretch of the North Country Road one hundred

TO THE NORTH FORK

and fifty years ago there were probably the same number of sparsely scattered farmhouses as now, or fewer. But a steady stream of travel flowed along it, not only the stagecoach from New York, but the small fry of peddlers, cobblers, chairmenders, tailors, barbers, tombstone cutters, portrait painters and evangelists. Some had their own little carts, and others trudged afoot with pack on back, except for friendly lifts. All were heading toward the group of seaports stretching along the Great and Little Peconic Bays on the North Fork shore.

In this North Fork area, from Northville on, the scenery changes again. The limitless fields of potatoes give place to smaller farm patches. Again along the roadside appear eighteenth- and early nineteenth-century homes, with their simple lines, little square windowpanes and the broad chimney atop the middle of the roof. Also along the road stand fine old trees, in contrast with the small, scrubby oaks lining the route we have just followed after leaving Miller Place. In short, after a parenthesis of very modern landscape, back we come to old Long Island. The queer Indian names of this region add to the flavor of antiquity. Here are Mattituck and Cutchogue; and a few miles farther on, the map reveals Hashamomuck Beach. The stranger will think twice before he ventures to pronounce that!

In Cutchogue stands a close rival to the old Job Wright house in Oyster Bay. Like its rival, it isn't easy to locate, but it lies just off the main road, shortly before we come to the small white church which is now the public library. A few paces to the west of this building there is a driveway—hardly more than a path—crossed by chicken wire. The tourist must hop this with as much dignity as possible and wander a few steps through a flock of expostulating chickens to a clump of locust trees, in the midst of which stands the superannuated dwelling. It has a huge clustered chimney over its salt-box roof, and the experts of the Historical American Buildings Survey say that before the house was given its present shape there had been an older structure, going back to a year not far from the time when Charles the First was beheaded, and when the earliest of the English pioneers sought a foothold here.

Under the lean-to roof these experts discovered the original wall with its Elizabethan casements, whereas in the rest of the house the newer-type windows have been built in. Between the outer and the inner walls seaweed has been stuffed for insulation, and the chimney is made of bricks which are identified as having been brought from England. Ancient as this building is, it has been uninhabited for at least fifty years. Like the Job Wright house, it has been used as a shed for housing farm implements, and small boys have delighted in smashing the windowpanes and stealing everything that could be removed. It, too, awaits some fairy godmother to save it and restore it to its former state, though that will have to happen soon or there will be nothing left to restore.

Southold, the next town beyond, is worth a considerable pause, because it certainly is one of the three most ancient English settlements on Long Island, and it claims to be the eldest, though Southamptonians dispute the fact. The charming white church, with clock tower and weather vane, which is the present pride and joy of the village, is the fourth Presbyterian meeting house erected on this site, and this one dates back to 1803. The first one was probably made of logs with loopholes, as a place not only of worship, but of defense. In the library of the Long Island Historical Society in Brooklyn is exhibited the old gun rack, where the men of Southold parked their guns during the services.

TO THE NORTH FORK

This congregation was organized by its pastor, the Reverend John Young, in October, 1640, and this is said to be the oldest church society in New York State. Opposite the present church building is one of the earliest graveyards on Long Island, containing many tombstones which were imported from England. At the foot of Founder's Avenue, on the Bay, is a municipal park, marking the spot where those first settlers set foot in 1640.

These dates will serve to suggest why Southold claims precedence in seniority, even though Southampton was founded in the same year. It is true that in her old age her total population barely squeaks above the 1500 mark, but she still holds her head high. No great events ever shook the tranquillity of this seaport. One of her citizens, Ezra L'Hommedieu, became noted in State affairs, but in general no Southold citizens have become what one would call national figures in any walk of life during its three centuries. "Th' applause of list'ning senates to command," and all the rest of it, "their lot forbade," because they were too busy fishing, whaling or making voyages to the West Indies. One generation after another went down to the sea in ships to make a livelihood. Some of these sailormen were buried in the old graveyard; more of them left their bones on the bottoms of the Seven Seas.

The ghosts that come back to these pages, from the past of Oyster Bay, for example, were impressive and colorful figures: Colonel Simcoe in his green uniform, Major André in scarlet, Commodore Hardy in navy blue and the gay Townsend girls who, it is likely, never forgot their ribbons or their curls. In contrast, let Southold bring back another, very plebeian person named Joshua Penny, who was born here. We happen to know all about Joshua's career because in 1815, with the help of a friend who had more "book larnin'," he wrote out his story and published it in pamphlet form: *The Life and Adventures of Joshua Penny.* No book was ever published on Long Island which aroused more interest. Copies of it are exceedingly rare today, because in its time the pamphlet was literally read to tatters.

Only a few high spots of the story can be touched on here. As a boy Joshua Penny went to sea, and in time drew what he called the "great wages" of $2.50 a month. In Liverpool he signed up on a slave ship; but while the blacks were being delivered to the Jamaica market, a press gang from a British frigate came aboard and Joshua was among those taken. At the time this frigate was riddled with an epidemic, and of the forty sailors taken off the slaver eleven were dead by the next morning. Joshua fell sick, too. "There goes another dead Yankee," he heard an officer say. "He'll be dead by ten o'clock." But Joshua survived somehow and, against his will, became a bluejacket on a British man of war.

The frigate took him to Capetown, and there he managed to escape into the bush, where he lived a year among the Hottentots. Caught and brought back to the fleet, he had his taste of a flogging. "My senses left me," he writes, "when I had three strokes of the cat. . . . The surgeon informed the captain of my condition but he said, 'He shall take his dozen, dead or alive!' "

When the fourth of June came, the sailors were allowed to get drunk because it was the king's birthday, so when the fourth of July arrived Penny approached the First Lieutenant for permission to get drunk. "Go along forward, you Yankee rascal!" roared that officer, who promptly reported him to the captain for impertinence.

"What do you mean," cried the captain, " by asking permission

DOORWAY OF MILLARD HOUSE

to do what you know is contrary to the regulations of the ship?"

"I recollect, sir," answered the irrepressible Penny, "that a month ago you gave the English liberty to get drunk because it was their king's birthday, and now I want the liberty to rejoice on *my* nation's birthday."

The captain broke into a laugh at this and gave orders that two gallons of wine and one of brandy be sent from shore for the members of the Yankee mess in the forecastle.

"We all liked this captain," Penny observes. "The glasses passed merrily round in our Yankee mess of thirty in number, and they began to sing Hail Columbia, Happy Land." Evidently for the thirty impressed Yankee seamen the two gallons of wine and the one gallon of brandy proved adequate for the laudable purpose in hand.

Again Penny escaped, this time hiding in the rocks of Table Mountain, with none but unfriendly baboons for his companions. There he kept himself alive for a whole year, using the woodcraft he had learned from the Hottentots. When he thought himself safe, he ventured out again and shipped aboard a merchantman. After crossing the ocean repeatedly, he was able at last to come back to land on Orient Point. He had been absent from home for fifteen years and was long since given up for dead. In all that time he had had no serious accident, but in landing on his own home shore his boat was upset by a squall and his knee fractured. His captain had to carry him on his back half a mile to the nearest house, and he had to lie in bed for months. But his knee healed itself somehow, and he went back to sea for a living.

When the War of 1812 broke out, Joshua was eager to even up his score with the British who had kidnaped him and kept him, an enforced seaman, in their fleet. He was at this time a lighthouse keeper at Cedar Island in Northwest Harbor, and while his wife tended the lighthouse, Joshua sailed about in a fast sloop to see what he could do to annoy the British. He became interested in the idea of floating mines, and tried once to blow up Commodore Hardy's flagship by one of these devices. The British commander was extremely annoyed by this performance and caused a sharp lookout to be kept for "these damned Yankee barnacles." He also ordered a hunt to be made for the enterprising Joshua, offering a prize of $1000 for information leading to his arrest. "Someone in Sag Harbor," said Joshua, "sold a Penny for a thousand dollars." He gave the information, and Joshua was snatched out of his bed by a British search party, in his hiding place near the now extinct village of Northwest. Thereafter he languished for nine months in a very chilly dungeon in Halifax, expecting every day to hear that he would be hanged for "unlawful warfare." Finally, he was exchanged and sent home. Then the war ended, and he sat down to write his memoirs.

Penny's adventures sound fantastic enough, even in the barest outline, but probably there was many another Long Island boy, even from Southold, who could have matched them, but they did not have anyone to help them write it down. The lives of these seafaring youngsters represent an era in American history as extinct now as the age of feudalism.

In contrast with the antiquity of Southold, her neighbor, Greenport, is comparatively modern. As a town it was not incorporated until 1838, and to be a centenarian is mere infancy on Long Island. However, there were enough people living here and there on the premises to cause a schoolhouse to be set up as early as 1797, and in 1805 it is recorded that the "Preceptor's" salary had been boosted to the extravagant figure of forty dollars a quarter. And there had been for three or four years a post office here with the name "Stirling," after the English lord who

TO THE NORTH FORK

owned most of the territory in these regions during the mid-seventeenth century. (This post office reported for its first quarter the magnificent gross intake of $19.33.)

In 1830 an official document relating to the building of a wharf here calls the settlement "Greenhill," though there is nothing remotely resembling a hill near by. But a year later the name became "Green Port," and that it has held to, though it has long since become one word. In 1831 it is described as having "Fifteen dwellings completed and several in progress, five stores, a warehouse and numerous mechanic shops." In Stirling Creek, which a century ago was deeper and wider than now, there were at that time "two whaling ships fitting out; 350,370 tons . . . and in short Greenport is a very eligible, flourishing and beautiful place." Thus wrote the Secretary at the meeting in which the name of the place was duly chosen.

When the railroad extended its service to Greenport in 1844, the burghers thereof had visions of magnificence. The town was to be a great terminal for New York City, both for rail and water. In that year there was no railroad on the mainland between Boston and New York. Travelers could ferry to and from Greenport and make the rail connections at either end for Boston and New York. Greenport possessed a splendid harbor, too, landlocked and wide, opening on Gardiner's Bay on the one hand and the Peconic Bays on the other. Here packet and freight ships might lie with passengers or merchandise for New York. But these dreams faded when the railroad was built on the mainland. The chief reason that had delayed it so long was the fact that the route between Boston and New York by land had to cross eighteen deep and wide rivers, involving costly bridges.

This same geographical fact is responsible for the presence here of a very distinguished traveler, George Washington, who came this way in 1756, when there wasn't any town of Greenport. But there was a country inn where he could rest for the night, and the site of that caravansary is now marked by a boulder near the Presbyterian church. (The date of 1757 on the tablet is incorrect.) The innkeeper did not realize the fact at

THE HEAD OF THE CREEK

the time, but when a tall young Virginian, with his retinue of servants and horses, rode up to request a night's lodging, this arrival proved to be the one event which would mark his hostelry for future generations to remember.

When Washington made his tour in 1790 he came to Long Island as President, already hailed as the Father of His Country, and recognized in Europe, as well as in America, as one of the great men of his age. But in 1756 George was only twenty-four years old, and although he had won a fine reputation in Virginia for his conduct in the Braddock disaster of the year before, his

TO THE NORTH FORK

name meant nothing in Long Island.

This trip is one of the little-known episodes in Washington's life. After the Braddock campaign the question arose as to whether Washington was or was not the Commander-in-Chief of the Virginia troops. Another officer from Maryland claimed

A CORNER IN GREENPORT

that his royal commission took precedence over the Colonial one of Washington. Dinwiddie, then Governor of Virginia, on being appealed to by Washington, replied that he had no authority to settle the dispute, but recommended that Washington make the journey to Boston and lay the case before Governor Shirley there, because Shirley was in command of all the provincial troops. He added that Washington had better go without saying what his mission was, for fear the other fellow would get wind of it and arrive first. This Washington agreed to do, though he assured Governor Dinwiddie that if he were denied the command of the Virginia troops he would certainly resign.

As soon as possible he started off on his journey by horseback from Alexandria to Boston. And when he left New York he followed the advice of a certain Dr. Alexander Hamilton—not the one history knows—and crossed to Long Island to take the North Country Road to the end of the North Fork where Greenport is now, and where in those days there was already a ferry to the Connecticut shore at New London. Often one had to wait several days for favorable weather, but the service was reasonably dependable. It was for Washington a hard, winter journey, for besides spending his twenty-fourth birthday (February) on Long Island he had his troubles on the way. Some very pleasant gentlemen whom he met on the road suggested a friendly game of cards, with the result that he lost so much money that he did not have enough to return home, and had to borrow from a friend in New York City on the way back. One of his negro slaves got drunk and knocked over a costly vase in one of the houses where Washington stayed—another expense he had not counted on. But the reason he took this Long Island route was that he would otherwise have had to swim or ford in midwinter those eighteen streams between New York and Boston.

In the latter city Washington found Governor Shirley kind and sympathetic. The governor had met the young Virginian before, because he had lost a son in the Braddock disaster, and Washington had been the one who had broken the news to him. So he heartily endorsed the appointment of George Washington as Commander of the Virginia troops, and the tedious journey was crowned by complete success.

With the unsurpassed harbor facilities of Greenport, it seems strange that no considerable town grew up there in the eighteenth century. Before there was even that village of "fifteen dwellings," large ships dropped anchor in the harbor, where they loaded up for the West Indian trade. Here along the North Road farmers came with their teams of oxen, bringing produce and cattle for the New York market and taking in payment coffee, sugar, molasses and rum.

The Greenport that one sees today, on either side of the motor highway, is pleasant and tempts one to linger. A traveler who wrote a magazine article on a trip to Gardiner's Island, sixty years ago, was quite scornful of the "modern and garish" aspect of this town—the houses were painted in gay colors in those days—but since that time the village has mellowed, and chaste white paint prevails, though there is a section of the town, near the railroad station, which looks as new as a suburb of Los Angeles.

What is most tempting about Greenport is the water front, that long, ragged fringe of wharves, boatbuilders' yards and sail lofts from which one looks out across the harbor to the wooded bluffs of Shelter Island. Of course, the whalers in these waters have long since become completely extinct, and those square-rigged ships that sailed from here direct to the West Indies for molasses are also long since dead and gone. Nowadays one would as soon expect to see a trireme come into the harbor as a square-rigged sailing ship. But there are schooners and sloops to keep alive for a while longer the fading tradition of the days of sail.

Of course we should not forget that it is Greenport from which our cup defenders have taken their skippers in recent years, and I was delighted to see, on a ramble along the wharves and ship-yards, standing grotesquely high in the air, the unmistakable hull of a racing yacht.

Beside another wharf lay a slender two-masted schooner, the

Philippe, with hull and spars glistening in aluminum paint. This is the vessel of the "Sea Scout Nautical School," whose Commodore, W. J. Marshall, takes crews of eighteen boys at a time out on two weeks' cruises. He told me that boys come from all over the country to Greenport to make these cruises. On this vessel

STIRLING CREEK

the Scouts learn real seagoing ways, "to hand, and reef, and steer." Everything is sailor-fashion, for this schooner has no motor power. Wherever she goes, even to sliding up to her wharf, she moves under sail, and makes her eggshell landings without any back kick of a screw.

To a masculine mind there is something fascinating about boatyards. The smell of fresh lumber, tar, varnish and paint combine most agreeably with the salt breeze, and perhaps there is something about the untidiness of these yards that is most appealing. There is no feminine hand here to clear up, for no New England housewife ventures into these sacred and smelly precincts. In a boatyard you can drop a piece of lumber, a fathom of rope or an empty paint pail and fifty years afterwards they are resting in the same spot, unless consumed by the elements.

SHIPYARD

Weeds, like the blue chicory, delight to flourish here and grow rank in all the corners. Perhaps it is this very reprehensible carelessness of shipyards that attracts the artist, because what other people call untidy he calls picturesque.

In and around these yards, too, are human figures that harmonize with the general happy-go-lucky scheme, wrinkled old gaffers, wearing long-visored fishermen's caps that make them look like a kingfisher on a limb, sitting motionless except for the gentle swing of their jawbones as they ruminate on a quid of tobacco. Apparently they move only when it is time to eat or go to bed. Sometimes these ancient mariners can be prevailed upon to talk. One, who with only slight encouragement had gone into autobiography, explained his single blessedness thus: "No, I ain't never had a wife. I'm married to my boat. She don't answer back, and she does what I want her to, that's more'n I'd git from any woman." He paused and spat. "Not that I ain't had my chances," he added reminiscently.

Other men, also in long-visored caps, are hard at work shoveling clams into baskets and swinging them into waiting trucks to be carried to New York. Greenport is also an important center for the oyster industry, all of which, added to its boatbuilding, makes a very respectable volume of business.

In a visit to the North Fork, Greenport is the logical base of operations, whether one spends a week motoring about, gamefishing or sailing, or tarries only for a single night. The tavern where the youthful Washington laid his head has long since gone, but hard by, on the other side of the church, stands a dignified house with tall pillars in front. This is Townsend Manor, a dwelling of the year 1803, now an inn, where a pleasant welcome, rest and goodly entertainment await the traveler. Down by the shore, in the rear, is the modern guesthouse of the Manor, with seats under the trees by the bank of Stirling Creek. There one may watch the small boats that come and go in waters that once reflected the hulls of whaling ships and West Indiamen.

On a summer evening by all means wander through the back streets and along the wharves before turning in for the night. The impression grows that the burghers of Greenport do not half appreciate the possibilities of their town to attract the summer resident. When George Whitefield, the evangelist, came this way on the same road that young Washington followed, he

THE ACADEMY, MILLER PLACE

tarried at a house and left as a souvenir the line scratched on a windowpane: "One thing is needful." That pane is still preserved. (Query: How did a poor preacher come to have a diamond or even to borrow one?) Some people say "the one thing needful" for Greenport village today is good advertising. But maybe the inhabitants don't want to be bothered by any more

TOWNSEND MANOR

summer people than they have now, and that point of view is readily understandable of course. Somehow one doesn't look for a Chamber of Commerce or a publicity expert in a place like Greenport. A century ago it had its boosters and dreams of a boom as a railroad and shipping center. Even before that (in 1824) the citizenry hereabouts petitioned to have canals dug, to connect Gravesend with Jamaica Bay, and another at Canoe

DISCOVERING LONG ISLAND

Place, to open into Peconic Bays, Sag Harbor and Greenport, so that there would be a landlocked complete waterway from the mouth of New York harbor all the way here. That grandiose idea, too, died aborning. In fact, Greenport woke up from all these dreams of affluence with nothing but a headache. Perhaps in these days it is quite content to be itself, and stick to its clams and oysters, weakfish, scallops and boatbuilding. That may be the wisest point of view after all.

CHAPTER IV

GARDINER'S ISLAND

FROM Greenport it is only five or six miles out to the end of the North Fork and Orient Point. After passing through East Marion, the road runs along a narrow strip of sand with Long Island Sound on one side and Gardiner's Bay on the other, both equally blue. The village of Orient itself lies on one of those lanes off from the main road. It is another of the placid, forgotten hamlets of the waterside so characteristic of the shores of Long Island.

A short way beyond the village is Orient Point, the very tip of Long Island's North Fork. The tipmost tip, however, is now private property, so, as a sign warns us, one may not drive down the roadway to the water's edge at Plum Gut.

The highroad turns a sharp right at this point to bring travelers down to the New London summer ferry. Plum Gut, which cuts off Plum Island from Orient Point, was in the early eighteenth century a narrow little stream at low tide, across which the settlers could drive their cattle, and the Indians told the white men that they remembered the time when a man could vault the stream with a pole and not get his moccasins wet. The difference today is eloquent of the constant change being made in Long Island's coast line by the sea.

The region hereabouts is not so picturesque as it was sixty to seventy years ago, when this tip of the Island was as remote from Broadway as Siberia is today, when there were more of the old houses and when there were still windmills whirling their arms on the sky line. In 1872 appeared two ponderous volumes entitled *Picturesque America,* edited by no less distinguished a person that William Cullen Bryant, and profusely illustrated by wood engravings made from sketches drawn on the spot by a number of artists, notably a young Englishman, Harry Fenn, who later became one of our leading black and white artists. In fact, it was largely due to Harry Fenn that the book was undertaken. The work became a landmark in the history of American illustration. Because eastern Long Island was one of the sections selected as "picturesque," it is interesting to see what Mr. Fenn saw fit to sketch in the area we are exploring now. He made a drawing of Orient, for example, which is a charming composition containing an old fishing sloop in the foreground, with a wide expanse of sea marsh around it. In the background rise a windmill, to the right, and to the left a square church tower. Not one feature of that sketch except the marsh grass is visible today. The Orient windmill was destroyed long ago; and as for that church tower, it was probably inserted there by the artist to balance his picture, for it is one of those "English Perpendicular" towers which Mr. Fenn remembered so well in his homeland but which was never seen on Long Island, at least not at this remote spot.

There was another picturesque windmill at East Marion, too, and it was still doing business as late as 1878, but that also has gone into the limbo of forgotten things. More's the pity, for a windmill here and there would relieve the sky line to great profit in this flat landscape. But, perhaps, as Whittier wrote,

> We lack the open eye and ear
> To find the Orient's marvels here,

for some painters have found much inspiration along this shore.

Beyond Orient Point is a still narrower strip of sand, so slender that one could not call it a "tongue" of land, or even a "finger"—shall we call it a "string"?—that trails out into the harbor, pointing backward into the Bay. This, only a few years ago, was known as "Long Beach," but it has now become a link in the chain of state parks which have already been mentioned as one of the glories of Long Island. A fine, hard roadway has been built on that string of sand, luring the motorist to Orient Beach State Park.

This, like the other park areas, has been intelligently planned to make the most of what the terrain can offer. A dense growth of scrub cedars has been utilized to provide welcome shade on a summer's day, where lunch benches and seats have been placed. There is a wide parking space, also bathhouses and playgrounds for children. A goodly margin of the shore is set apart as the bathing beach. It is all as orderly and speckless as the old New England "parlor." Not a scrap of newspaper nor a cigarette package on the ground offends the eye. How the untidy American public has been taught to behave in these parks is a mystery and a triumph. From the south beach we see the wide stretch of Gardiner's Bay, with the bluffs of Shelter Island to the right. Straight ahead, a distance of seven or eight miles, lies Gardiner's Island.

This is one of the most romantic and historic spots of all this Long Island region. In the summer of 1884 the author and editor, George Parsons Lathrop, accompanied by the artist, Harry Fenn, hired a catboat at Greenport and sailed over to Gardiner's Island. There they were entertained as guests of Mr. and Mrs. Gardiner in the ancient Manor House. Mr. Lathrop jotted down his notes,

Mr. Fenn made his incomparable landscape drawings, and the result was an article in the *Century Magazine* for December, 1885. But now strangers may not venture there without permission. For many years the island has been leased as a hunting preserve, first by the late Mr. Clarence Mackay, and at present by Mr. Winston Guest. The Manor House is now tenanted only by a caretaker, and very naturally, since the entire island is a game preserve, no trespassing can be permitted. So, while one may still hire a sail or motorboat at Greenport and circumnavigate Gardiner's Island, it is now sacred to the birds and the deer. Mr. Fenn's drawings, even more than Mr. Lathrop's text in that *Century* article, suggest an island of rare beauty, with heavy timber in the central part, and high, open sheep commons ending in bluffs fronting the ocean on the east.

In September, 1932, a group of one hundred members of the New York Historical Association were given the rare privilege of visiting the island under the guidance of Mr. Morton Pennypacker, who has made Long Island history his life study. The visitors tramped three miles over the island, and were greatly impressed by finding a forest of one hundred acres which had never yet known the woodsman's ax. Although the tropical hurricane of 1938 took its toll of many a noble tree, there still stand giant oaks and walnuts and elms, the like of which it would be hard to match for age and size in any comparable area east of the Rockies.

Though Gardiner's Island is not for the casual visitor to explore now, it has a history worth telling, and we'll imagine the reader sitting in the shade of a wind-bent cedar at Orient Beach, facing the south breeze and the wide blue sheet of the bay, looking at this distant island shore, and all set to listen to its story. For it is not an ordinary page of history. It starts with an English soldier of fortune. It includes pirates, notably the famous Captain Kidd, who really hid his treasure here, but took it up again. British invaders swarmed over it with fire and sword during two wars. A beautiful girl of the island married a President of the United States. All this and more make up the varied story of this narrow, crooked, seagirt isle, before it became the undisturbed refuge for wild life it is today. And from the first sentence of that history to the last this island has remained in possession of the same family. After three hundred years it is still "Gardiner's Island." It was the first English settlement in New York and, though the oldest, is the only one of these American feudal manors of colonial times which has remained intact.

The founder of the family and creator of the estate was one Lion Gardiner, a military engineer, who served in the Low Countries under the Prince of Orange, meeting in the Netherlands a Dutch girl who became his wife. In 1635 he came to Boston, having signed up to serve with a group of settlers who had received a grant of land at the mouth of the Connecticut River. There he built a fort which he named Saybrook. In Old Saybrook may be seen his statue today. He defended the colonists successfully against the savages,—he was once seriously wounded in Indian fighting—and displayed much wisdom and tact in dealing with the red men. It is said that if his advice had been heeded there probably never would have been a Pequot War.

In 1639 he bought from the Indians an island, lying at the eastern end of Long Island, a 3300-acre tract of land, nine miles long by about one and a half in width. He named it Isle of Wight. For this he paid the curious price of "ten coates of trading cloath," and some other articles of value approximating 20 pounds. In the same year he received a "patent" from the Earl of Stirling, confirming his possession under the King of England. Stirling, in a vague way, had been given by the King a large tract of territory, in and about Long Island, much of which was claimed by the Dutch. Gardiner, his wife, children and servants, together with some of his old soldiers, crossed over from Saybrook to this island patch of wilderness, settled down and began to cultivate it. There a daughter, Elizabeth, was born, the first child of English blood to be born in the present area of New York state.

It seems like a daring venture to go from Saybrook practically alone, with only his family and small retinue, to a distant island and to make there a home. It would have been easy for even a small band of Indians to raid the place and wipe out every soul, for there never was a fort on the island. But Gardiner had already made a reputation, not only as a resolute soldier but also as a man who dealt fairly with the Indians. So the tiny settlement on the island was never molested by the red men.

Before coming here from Saybrook, Gardiner had made friends with Wyandanch, later chief of the Montauk tribe. From him he had repeatedly received warnings of Indian conspiracies to attack the Saybrook colonists. Once Gardiner even gave himself up as a hostage while negotiations were going on between Indians and Englishmen. Later, when the chief of the Narragansets kidnaped the daughter of Wyandanch on her wedding night, Gardiner went in pursuit and succeeded in ransoming her and bringing her back to her father. The sachem in gratitude gave his friend a large tract of land, including the area where Smithtown is now, and when he died he left his son to the guardianship of Lion Gardiner and his son David. It might be difficult to find in American colonial history another such shining example of friendship between the white settler and the savage.

After some years Gardiner left his island to the care of the old soldiers he had brought with him from the mainland and whom

GARDINER'S ISLAND

he had settled as farmers, and he himself spent the last decade of his life in East Hampton. This was the scene of another rescue

LION GARDINER

(*From the statue by Partridge at Old Saybrook, Ct.*)

of a female. However, the woman in this case was no romantic Indian maiden but a toothless and wrinkled crone known in the village as "Goody" Garlich, the wife of the carpenter. She was employed as a nurse in the Gardiner home. One day she had some words with another woman, who accused her of being a witch. That was a serious charge in the seventeenth century. The elders of the church ducked her in the village pond, and sent her to Hartford for trial. No doubt she would have been hanged if Lion Gardiner had not interfered. He scoffed at the idea of witches and promised to be sponsor for her good behavior. Then he took the poor, terrified woman off to his island, gave her a cottage and looked out for her the remainder of her life. And if she made any more flights on a broomstick she was careful not to make any landings in East Hampton. Of course, no elder of the Puritan church could molest her further, for Lion Gardiner's slightest wish was the law of the Medes and Persians on Gardiner's Island. He came nearer than any other colonist to being an absolute despot, for the Isle of Wight—he spelled it "Wite"—was established by the deed as a feudal estate, and so it continued long after the system had been abolished in England. For when Charles the Second did away with English feudal manors, the decree did not affect the manors in America.

There were curious odds and ends of special privileges enjoyed by the heads of these estates; for instance, all property which caused the death of a tenant reverted to the Lord of the Manor. If a man broke his neck by being thrown from a horse, that horse was led to the manorial barn. Also, all stray property unidentified as to ownership was appropriated—wreckage and boats, sheep and cattle, etc. So, all in all, being head of a manor must have been profitable as well as pleasant.

But the full glory of the title did not arrive until Lion's son David reigned in his stead. To him, for a consideration, Governor Dongan of the English colony of New York gave a new patent which created the island both a lordship and a manor. This was in 1686, and the document is still preserved by the family. An odd stipulation was the annual tribute to the King of "one ewe lamb" (if required) on the first of May. How that lamb was shipped to Buckingham Palace, and whether it was ever served on the royal table, history does not say. One of the rights included in this patent was that of "advowson," meaning that the proprietor could appoint a clergyman for the island, thus becoming the spiritual as well as the temporal ruler.

So David Gardiner became "Lord of the Isle of Wight," not a bad title, and probably the only such a one in the American colonies. The tomb of David's son John is in the burying ground at New London, and this epitaph reads—beneath an impressive coat of arms—"Here lyeth buried ye body of his excellency John Gardiner, Third Lord of ye Isle of Wight." Lion Gardiner was buried in East Hampton, but there is a family cemetery at Gardiner's Island in which twelve generations of the family lie, beneath tombstones on which are blazoned their heraldic arms. In regular English fashion, the inheritance fell to the eldest son until 1829, when the eighth proprietor, "having no issue," left it to his younger brother.

It was in the time of the John Gardiner, who was "Third Lord of ye Isle of Wight," that Gardiner's Island was visited by the notorious Captain Kidd. In the late seventeenth century there was an outbreak of piracy in all the Seven Seas, and especially on the American coast. William Kidd, the son of a Scottish preacher, was at first an honest and able skipper, who did such good service against the local pirates that he was rewarded by a gift of £250 by the New York Assembly. It was then decided that he should go forth as a privateersman and attack the pirates in the West Indian ocean, particularly those who made their base on the coast of Madagascar. Some gentlemen of high station chipped in on shares in this enterprise, the Earl of Bellomont, then Gover-

DISCOVERING LONG ISLAND

nor of both New York and Massachusetts, the Lords of Oxford and Romney and the Duke of Shrewsbury. King William was to have a ten per cent cut on the profits, too. So, under these high social auspices, Kidd went forth. But when he got into the Indian Ocean the heat or something affected him strangely. Afterwards he said that his crew became mutinous and demanded that he turn pirate. Perhaps he was merely one of those sons of ministers who do surprisingly reprehensible things. Evidently he asked himself, in the words of the old hymn,

> Shall I be carried to the skies
> On flowery beds of ease,
> While others fight to win the prize
> And sail through bloody seas?

Certainly not. So he turned pirate himself. He shook hands and drank rum with the very Madagascar pirates whose heads he was supposed to chop off, and, in general, cut loose on his own account to see whom he might devour. Very soon he sailed through some bloody seas of his own and fought to win some handsome prizes. Chief of these was an Armenian ship having on board the trousseau for the daughter of the Great Mogul.

Kidd's successes brought out howls of wrath which were echoed so loudly in Parliament that the King felt obliged to offer a reward for the buccaneer's arrest. But the latter felt so safe with all his titled partners in the enterprise that he sailed boldly back to America. He knew that "Blackbeard" (Teach) had enjoyed the protection of Governor Eden of North Carolina and expected the same of the Earl of Bellomont.

On a June morning in 1699 John Gardiner was surprised to see a strange, armed vessel riding at anchor in Gardiner's Bay. After she had lain there two days without a sign of activity, John de-

GARDINER'S ISLAND

cided to go out and take a look at her. As he boarded the vessel he was met politely by Captain Kidd, who said he was on his way to see Lord Bellomont in Boston, and would Mr. Gardiner have the kindness to take ashore for him two negro boys and one negro girl to be kept there until sent for? Gardiner complied, and the next day Kidd sent ashore a request that Gardiner come aboard and bring six sheep with him. After that Kidd felt the need of a barrel of cider, which also the Lord Proprietor of the Isle of Wight supplied. Then Kidd produced a piece of muslin for Mrs. Gardiner, and parted with friendly compliments. As he sailed he fired four guns as a salute, and headed for Block Island. Meanwhile some vessels had come from New York and taken off a goodly part of his cargo, the part that might not look well to an officer of the law. Then in three days Captain Kidd came back, accompanied by another vessel, to which he transferred still more chests of valuables. His final consignment of treasure he turned over to John Gardiner, consisting of a box of gold and jewels, a bundle of quilts and four bales of goods. This Kidd concealed in a little dell not more than a mile from the Manor House, called "Kidd's Valley" ever since. A stone now marks the place and the occasion.

"If I call for it and it's gone," said he to Gardiner, "I will take your head and your son's."

However, he was gallant enough to make Mrs. Gardiner the present of a bag of sugar, a great scarcity in those days; and after she had had prepared for him a roast suckling pig at his request, he softened still further and presented her with a large piece of cloth—a silk fabric interwoven with a pattern of gold thread. This had been intended for the bridal dress of the daughter of the Great Mogul. The fabric was long treasured by the family, and was at last cut up and distributed among the heirs. A piece of it may still be seen on exhibition in the East Hampton library.

Kidd went on to Boston, perfectly confident that Lord Bellomont would protect him as soon as he knew what a rich cargo of treasure had come back from the Indian Ocean, but Bellomont had suddenly developed a great zeal against pirates. He promptly threw Kidd into prison and sent out a demand for all the deposits of the treasure. Orders came to John Gardiner, who hastily took up the stuff in Kidd's Valley and carried it to Boston. He made a careful inventory of it, which is still preserved in the family. Here it is in part: Three bags of gold dust, one of coined gold, one of silver coins. One bag of gems and rings, one of uncut stones, lump silver, gold bars, silver bars, 69 precious stones, "by tale," etc., besides the bales of cloth and other goods.

Gardiner thought he had made a complete delivery, but on unpacking his bag on his return he saw one large diamond roll out on the floor. He was going to send it back to Boston at once, but his wife interposed. "No," quoth she, "Captain Kidd owes me that for the worry and trouble he made me. I'll keep it myself." Another version of the story is that the diamond was discovered in a bucket of drinking water, from which circumstance Mrs. Gardiner argued that it was Captain Kidd's tactful way of leaving a guest present. At any rate, she presented the jewel to her daughter. The chaplain on the estate may or may not have seen it first, but soon after his arrival he offered his heart and hand in marriage to the girl. The couple eloped, taking the jewel with them, so, after all, Mrs. Gardiner's ill-gotten diamond did not stay long at the Manor House.

As the storage places of Kidd's treasure were all known and carefully cleaned, it is strange that later generations went so crazy over the idea of finding more. Tons of earth have been removed in this romantic but vain quest all along the Atlantic coast, although they do say that over a century afterwards, on the beach of Gardiner's Island, where Kidd landed his boxes and bales, someone kicked up in the sand a gold ring of ancient Spanish design, which probably was dropped on this visit.

As for Kidd, for all the rich prizes he had won on bloody seas, he was sent to London to be tried on five counts of piracy and one for murder. His claim, that his captures were legal because of certain privateer commissions, was denied. In due season he was carried to the skies, not on flowery beds of ease, but at the end of a rope. The peers who had invested in his ship did not appear at his trial, and the fruits of his piracy were confiscated by the government. The poor daughter of the Great Mogul never retrieved a single jewel or yard of silk from her trousseau.

Kidd's visit was a genteel afternoon call compared with those of other pirates who came to Gardiner's Island in the next thirty years. In 1728 a horrible gang of French, Spanish and mulatto cutthroats overran the island, stole everything movable, slashed the wrists of the proprietor and wounded many of his workmen before they left. They were outraged by the discovery that Mr. Gardiner had left his gold on the main island, and tore up all the paper money they found in his house. Ten years later Paul Williams, a Block Island boy who had taken to the black flag, fell upon his neighbors of Gardiner's Island and ravaged them of all their movable goods.

During the Revolutionary War, after the Battle of Long Island, the British were in full control east of Manhattan, and Gardiner's Island was in the most exposed position imaginable. In the winter of 1780-81 a British fleet under Vice Admiral Arbuthnot lay at anchor in Three-Mile Harbor, off Gardiner's Bay, and the commander-in-chief used Gardiner's Island as a convenient source of supplies. The officers sent boat parties ashore to help themselves to sheep, cattle, grain and timber as desired. Of cattle alone they slaughtered twelve hundred head. The officers of both army and navy came here also for hunting—Lord Percy, Sir William Erskine, General Clinton and Major André among them—all very fine gentlemen. But they made themselves unpleasantly free with the Manor House. They tramped on clean floors with muddy boots, and played quoits in the dining room. The marks of that game are still visible on the floor and walls.

During the war the invaders looted everything on the estate so thoroughly that by 1784 the Gardiners had practically nothing in real assets besides the land and the buildings, and no money to pay even the back taxes. The lord and lady of the isle were as poor as their humblest tenants.

Not all the scornful invaders returned home to boast of the fun they had. Here on the island some three hundred officers and men ceased from troubling and took their long rest. Others sank into Davy Jones' Locker. On the road map may be seen the name "Culloden Point," near the tip of Montauk. This was named for a British ship of the line, *Culloden,* which in January, 1781, being ordered out to intercept some French vessels, had barely got under way before she was overtaken by a fierce gale which drove her on the shoals at Shagway Point. After drifting westward a mile or two, she went down, with all hands, off the point that now bears her name.

Another war, a generation later, brought the English back to Gardiner's Island. The Commodore of this squadron, Sir Thomas Hardy, stationed his ships in Gardiner's Bay. Sir Hugh Pickell, one of his officers, landed from the fleet with an armed force, demanded supplies of the Gardiners and threatened to burn everything over their and their tenants' ears. In general the titled gentleman breathed threatenings and slaughter on the helpless

GARDINER'S ISLAND

family. Gardiner hastily sent his wife and children with the servants into the cellar for safety and kept them there. But when Hardy got wind of his subordinate's boorish conduct he sent Mr. Gardiner a letter of apology. Hardy had not forgotten the time he had been nursed through smallpox by an American woman in Huntington more than thirty years before.

Once a party of Americans from the squadron under Commodore Stephen Decatur, which was then blockaded in New London harbor, crossed the Sound in open boats and landed on Gardiner's Island. There they hid in the woods until a squad of British bluejackets landed, together with several of their officers. Then the Americans surprised them, took them prisoners and carried them to the Connecticut shore. Commodore Hardy, thinking that Mr. Gardiner must have had a hand in the business, sent a party to the Manor House all steamed up with indignation, and ready to take him prisoner to the fleet. But they found the master of the house in bed with medicine bottles massed about his pillow. "Sh!" cried his wife. "Mr. Gardiner is very ill!" The British officer in charge, knowing that the Commodore certainly wanted no sick prisoner, then demanded the Gardiner boy as hostage. But as he had gone away to boarding school the party finally returned to the fleet with no prisoner at all. After they were out of sight Mr. Gardiner recovered instantly from his critical illness!

Fortunately the War of 1812 lasted for only about two years and a half, and thereafter the nineteenth century was peaceful and eventful. Conditions on the island were more nearly feudal than anywhere in America, or even perhaps in England, at least where there was free labor. It was a self-containing, self-sustaining little community, ruled absolutely by the Gardiner family. The islanders had their own mill, smithies, looms, carpenter shops and so on. The children of the tenants and artisans used to come up to the Manor House and recite their catechisms to Grandmother Gardiner. In 1884, when Mr. Lathrop made his visit, he says that the windmill "supplies flour for the whole population," but he found, oddly enough, no wharf, so that getting on or off shore was a difficult matter.

The nearest land lay three and a half miles to the west of the Manor, at a spot still called "Fireplace" on our road map. On this strip of beach it was the custom to make a great fire of dried seaweed whenever anyone wanted a boat to come over from the island. On seeing the smoke, a boatman would row over for the visitor. If he was a stranger the boatman would demand his business, and if he was satisfied he would ferry the man over. This was the only means of communication. It seems an awkward way of fetching a doctor in a hurry, especially if the weather was stormy, and the mail service must have been very sketchy. In fact, it was not until Mr. Clarence Mackay leased the island and laid a telegraph and telephone cable that Fireplace ceased to be the island's one means of contact with the outside world. Naturally this was the only route by which the people of Gardiner's Island could go to their church at East Hampton on Sundays, for there never was a church on the island and no chaplain after the Reverend Mr. Green eloped with Miss Gardiner and Captain Kidd's diamond.

The traveler of today may readily reach Fireplace in his car, and if the weather is clear he can just descry two small, white patches against the dark woods, one the Manor House and the other the windmill. The Manor House dates from 1744, a fine, wide-fronted old mansion with a row of five dormer windows in the roof. In the century and a half of its lifetime additions have been made to the original Manor House, but it has kept its eighteenth-century character. The timber used on the building was all cut from the woods on the island, but the Gardiners imported their Carara-marble mantelpieces, with their classic figures and ornaments, from Italy. Behind the house are still standing the slave quarters (New York did not abolish slavery until 1827). Near by the house, lying in the grass, is a cannon with burst muzzle. This was used during the Revolution to signal to the shore the approach of British men-of-war.

In the house itself Mr. Lathrop found a hospitable welcome and many priceless relics of Gardiner history. But he adds, in his article, that the old manor is most certainly haunted. He and the artist Mr. Fenn, in their guest chamber, heard strange sounds all through the night, and they saw peculiar sparkles of light dancing about the room, and in the black, fireless hearth of their chamber saw "an uncanny ring of green flame revolving at midnight." Perhaps old Goody Garlich was putting on a little entertainment for the guests.

But they didn't mind their haunted chamber—or if they did they were ashamed to admit it—and were sorry to leave the island. "After the chafe and whirr, the sordid toil, and fallacious glitter of a city hibernation," Lathrop wrote in his genteel style, "how idyllic it seemed!" Probably in these days there is many an artist and writer to whom Gardiner's Island would seem just as idyllic and who would gladly apply for the post of caretaker thereon if the present one is tired of the job.

There is a romantic and mysterious story to be told about Gardiner's Island, one which, in its entirety, has never seen the light. This has for its heroine the beautiful Julia Gardiner, who was born in this ancestral manor. Most of her girlhood, however, was spent in the East Hampton home of the Gardiner family, although she often visited her cousins on the island by way of the ferry at Fireplace. Her father, David Gardiner, became State Senator for New York and rejoiced also in the military title of Colonel. Being a man of wealth, he was able to give his daughters the advantages of school in New York City and of travel in Europe. Julia and her sisters were received at court, both at Naples and in Paris, and were said to be "the sensations of the hour."

Naturally, as their father was an important man in the political world, they attended also state receptions in Washington. There President Tyler saw Julia, and, though he was having an unhappy time both with his own party leaders and with the opposition, and though he had been a widower not more than a year, he promptly fell in love with her. John Quincy Adams makes one of his characteristic acid entries in his diary to the effect that John Tyler "is making a fool of himself" playing the old game of "December and May" with the twenty-four-year-old girl, who was thirty years younger than her suitor. For a middle-aged widower he was quite romantic about it. For instance, since he could not leave Washington to woo her as he would like, while she was visiting in Gramercy Park, New York City, he ordered the Marine Band from the Brooklyn Navy Yard to go thither and serenade her.

In 1843 the nation boasted the first screw man-of-war in the world, the *Princeton,* and on board her were mounted two huge wrought-iron guns of a new type, Captain Stockton's invention. After preliminary tests he reported to the Bureau of Ordnance: "As a gun it is quite perfect. I do not think that *any* charge of powder can injure it." It was decided to give a public reception at Washington on board the *Princeton,* to show off its new gadgets, and fire the big guns as a piece of government publicity. So hundreds of invitations were sent out for a grand fete aboard ship on the twenty-eighth of February, 1844. The guests included the President, who had already accompanied Stockton on the trial trip of the vessel, members of the Cabinet, Congressmen and Senators, army and navy officers, ministers and ambassadors and other bigwigs with their wives. Among the ladies was the aged Dolly Madison. Of course the Honorable David Gardiner, of Gardiner's Island, and his daughter Julia were invited, too.

As President Tyler himself described the scene afterwards:

Never did the eye gaze on a brighter or more animated scene than that which the beautiful river exhibited during the forenoon of that fatal day. There floated the ship whereon had been concentrated so many hopes and anticipated joys. Decked out in trim array, there waved from every rope and yard some emblematic flag in token of our amity with the whole world, while proudly above them all floated at our mast head our own beautiful banner. Numberless barges shot out from every cove and point, loaded with their living freight and flew on the wings of hope and joy toward our gallant ship. There was but one person in that crowd who did not partake of the hilarity which so universally prevailed. . . .

That person was Ann Elizabeth Gilmer, wife of the Secretary of the Navy. She had received, she said breathlessly, a dreadful premonition of disaster and death, in which her husband was doomed to die, here on this very ship. The President did not know this at the time, but Julia Gardiner also had been terrified by a dream of the same dreadful import the night before. It was more real than any other dream she had ever had, she told her father. She described to him the warship's deck, in exact detail—she had never seen it—and said that in her vision two white horses came along the deck, and as they drew near she saw the riders as skeleton figures of death; but one of them, as he turned and looked into her eyes, had the face of her father.

So real was the vision that she begged her father not to go to the *Princeton,* that it might mean death for him. Naturally he threw back his head and laughed. "My dear," he cried, "a silly, bad dream. And you would give up for that the President's reception?" It took time and several hours to persuade her, but in the end she gave in, like a dutiful daughter, arrayed herself in the dress that had been specially made for the occasion and by the time they reached the Potomac she had almost shaken off the weight of that dream. But it all returned as she stepped upon the deck, for to her startled eyes she recognized what she had never seen before except in her vision, the quarter-deck of this steam-driven man-of-war. But she was soon overwhelmed in gay greetings of old friends, and the warmest welcome of all came from the hand and the smile of the President himself. It was for Julia Gardiner a time of happiness and triumph, for she was the undisputed belle of that brilliant occasion. Certainly there was no doubting the President's feeling toward her. He was all devotion and gallantry; matrons whispered to one another behind their hands and other young ladies looked on enviously from under the brims of their bonnets.

But through all this gaiety Ann Gilmer moved with a stricken face. "What can be the matter with her?" asked Julia of a friend.

"She says she had a dreadful dream—the silly. She's a perfect kill-joy. Look at her moping around!"

A dreadful dream? That was curious. For a moment Julia's own vision came back to her with a chilling touch, but she shook it off.

At one o'clock the *Princeton* had weighed anchor and steamed slowly down the Potomac to where a wide reach of the river gave safe room for testing the range of the big guns, and an hour or so later the ship rounded to for the firing. The great forward gun, the "Peace-maker," was then discharged with a tremendous bang, and the 200-pound shot kicked up a jet of water far down the river. Again, as the ship neared Mt. Vernon, the gun was fired as a salute in honor of Washington.

Then the guests assembled below decks for refreshments, or what in those days was called "an elegant collation." The affair had been a huge success already; everyone was enthusiastic about the new ship and the big cannon. At four o'clock the last course of luncheon had been served, and then there followed singing and more champagne. At this time word came from the quarter-deck that the big gun was to be fired again to please some of the guests. Immediately the people rose from the tables to go up on deck, led by the President and the Cabinet members.

When the Secretary of the Navy started to leave, his wife cried aloud in fear, and begged him frantically to stay below, clinging to him as if she would hold him back by her own strength. Gilmer was visibly embarrassed, but at last broke away impatiently. His wife dropped into a seat sobbing. People stared at her curiously and nudged one another as they went past her on the companionway. On deck the surgeon went about distributing cotton wads for the eardrums, and ordering all to keep their mouths open when the gun went off.

As for the President, it occurred to him that while the crowd was on deck he might have a few minutes of comparative privacy with the adorable Julia. So he slipped below, and sent a message to her to come down again and have refreshments with him.

"I suppose I'll have to obey orders," she laughed, and left the deck, accompanied by her father. John Tyler seated her at the head of the table and passed her some champagne. Someone called down from above, "Come, Mr. President, the gun is just about to be fired."

"I'm better engaged," he called back, but Senator Gardiner went up on deck. A moment later there was a loud explosion, and as smoke began to come down the companionway Julia turned to a young man at the table on the other side of her, saying, "Something must be wrong." He started up to see and, as he opened the door, turned back in horror. Someone cried, "The Secretary of State is dead!"

Suddenly to Julia the memory of that vision came back and her heart stood still. "Let me go to my father!" she cried, and ran to the companionway.

"My dear child," said one of the women, holding her back as she gained the deck, "you can do no good. Your father is in heaven." At those words Julia fainted, and did not recover until she was being carried off the ship in the arms of President Tyler.

A horrible thing had happened on deck. The great gun had burst with that last discharge, killing the men who stood nearest. Secretary of State Upshur, Secretary of the Navy Gilmer, Commodore Beverly Kennon of the Navy, Virgil Maxcy, late American chargé d'affaires at The Hague, and Senator David Gardiner lay mangled and dead. Eleven seamen were badly wounded, two of them in a dying condition, and the President's negro body servant was killed. Others escaped with burst eardrums and scorched faces, but at least two score were among the badly injured. One of the first to help with the wounded was the capable Dolly Madison, despite her years. In the midst of the dreadful scene stood the tragic figure of Captain Stockton, the man who had invented and built that gun. He had been so proud of his invention and this day had been the climax of his career. Had the President been in his own appointed place of honor he would certainly have been killed. As for poor Ann Gilmer, she wailed, "I knew it—I knew it! Why would no one listen to me?"

The tragedy drew John Tyler and Julia Gardiner together more closely. As he told her, she had saved his life by being there. In her hour of grief he was all tenderness and thoughtfulness, and he begged her to become his wife. The bodies of the victims were laid in state in the Capitol. Julia went to her father's coffin, and looking down she whispered, "Father, shall I marry him?" And she said afterwards, "Father seemed to smile, and I took that to mean yes." Four months after the *Princeton* disaster Julia Gardiner became the bride of John Tyler. The girl whose childhood had been spent in the remote quietness of Gardiner's Island and East Hampton, where the visit of a peddler from New York was one of the most thrilling events in a year, now found herself mistress of the White House, the leader of Washington society, the First Lady of the Land.

Strangely inexplicable as was that warning vision which came to both women before this tragic event, for Julia Tyler it was not the last. In January, 1862, she had another experience or dream of the same startling vividness. She saw her husband lying at the point of death in a bedroom in Richmond, where he had gone to attend the session of the Confederate Congress. This time she did not hesitate; she *knew*. Early in the morning she left her home, "Sherwood Forest," near the James River, and traveled as fast as she could to her husband.

He was much surprised to see her. "Are you feeling quite well?" she asked breathlessly.

"Perfectly, my dear," he replied smiling. "Did you hear that I was ill?"

Julia gave some confused explanation that made her look

foolish, as she knew. But when she entered her husband's bedroom she recognized the very bed she had seen him lying in when she had that vision, a bed she had never seen before. That same night John Tyler suddenly fell ill and never left that bed alive.

Today, as we look across the bay at this island, we see a spot more isolated from the world of human activities than ever since the Indians sold it to Lion Gardiner; even more so, in fact, for in those days there were aborigines living there and hunting and fishing throughout the year. Today the plows, the work benches, looms, forges, the windmill, are all gone or standing idle. The sheep and cattle that used to roam over the downs have vanished. Except for the caretaker living in the old Manor House, the island has reverted to primeval conditions of solitude. Of course it is an ideal place for a game preserve, since poachers can be spotted coming from any direction. Today Gardiner's Island is known among bird lovers as the home of the American ospreys, who come here in March, stay all summer and migrate in September.

Perhaps one of these days some future Gardiner, weary of mounting taxes in a not far-distant time, will gladly part with this island domain to the state. But let us hope that when that happens Robert Moses will still be Park Commissioner and will then add Gardiner's Island to his collection, not only keeping it as a sanctuary for wild life, but also making it accessible for the traveler, to whom such a spot, with its picturesque beauty and its romantic past, would be an island of enchantment.

CHAPTER V

SHELTER ISLAND TO SAG HARBOR

WHILE wandering along the wharves in Greenport and in checking with the road map, we discovered that Greenport Harbor is made by a large ragged island lying to the south. The Indian name for it was a mouthful, "Manhansack-Ahaquatuwamock," meaning "an island sheltered by an island." "This," says the writer in *Picturesque America,* "is as poetical and pleasing as it is geographically accurate." The briefer version in plain English is "Shelter Island." There was also an Indian word that described it as a place where much wampum was made, but that would probably be even longer.

At the foot of Greenport's principal street is a ferry to the island, and from where we stand waiting for the boat we see the horizon line lift to high sandy bluffs directly ahead, with the rest deeply buried in foliage through which pokes here and there a corner of the roof of some summer cottage. The whole contour is high and hilly as compared with all the surrounding district. Shelter Island, like Gardiner's, was a manorial domain, and it has its own present charm and historic past. What is better, it is not shut off from travel. In fact, it offers besides its own features the most direct route to the South Fork of Long Island.

About 1870 Shelter Island began to attract city people for their summer vacation. A steamer from New York came here every day, touching en route at Greenport and Orient and continuing to Sag Harbor. There was also the route by railroad from New York to Greenport, so the island was easily reached. Soon a great hotel arose and a rash of Queen Anne and plain Mary Ann cottages broke out all over the water front.

At this time Shelter Island was noted also for the annual camp meetings of the Methodists. Natives from both forks of the island and from Riverhead joyfully came hither to be converted every summer, amid picnic surroundings. Other sects held forth at

GREENPORT HARBOR WITH SHELTER ISLAND IN THE BACKGROUND

times. As Mrs. Hemans put it, the sounding aisles of the dim woods rang to the anthems of the Free-Will Baptists, too. The Free-Willers seem to have been a soft-shell variety of Baptists who didn't believe in predestination. But in the main this was the stamping ground of Methodists, and they say that when the exhorters were in good form and the wind in the right direction you could hear the hallelujahs distinctly in Greenport.

In and about Shelter Island there was another activity, around which hung an odor that was not the odor of sanctity and which produced an oil that was not the oil of gladness. This was the menhaden industry. Boats in the harbor let down their nets and hauled up millions of these little fish, called "moss bunker" or

SHELTER ISLAND TO SAG HARBOR

"menhaden," of about a pound in weight, which were valued for their oil content and possibilities for glue. Factories were established for the purpose along the shores, including Shelter Island, until the chorus of protest grew so loud that they had to be removed. Then the industry took to floating factories, which moved hither and yon along with the fishing fleet, spread their noisome odors on the air and covered the waters of the harbor with a black, oily refuse. That was going on when Harry Fenn and his colleague, Mr. Bunce, who did most of the description, arrived to write up Shelter Island for *Picturesque America,* and you may see what those floating "oil mills" looked like, for Mr. Fenn, holding his nose with one hand while he sketched with the other, made a picture of one. He drew also one of those huge spools that stood on shore for the drying of the nets. Some of them are still visible in remote corners of the shore, but the menhaden industry is now not what it used to be. Only one fish factory is left and that is busy making fertilizer out of menhaden at a spot with the incongruous name of "Promised Land," far removed from the nostrils of the summer colony.

The most vivid description of the fishery was written by Walt Whitman in "A Paumanok Picture." ("Paumanok" was the Indian name for Long Island.)

Two boats with nets lying off the sea-beach, quite still,
Ten fishermen waiting—they discover a thick school of mossbonkers
    —they drop the join'd seine-ends in the water,
The boats separate and row off, each on its rounding course to the
    beach, enclosing the mossbonkers,
The net is drawn in by a windlass by those who stop ashore,
Some of the fishermen lounge in their boats, others stand ankle-deep
    in the water, pois'd on strong legs,
The boats partly drawn up, the water slapping against them,

Strew'd on the sand in heaps and windrows, well out from the water, the green-back'd spotted mossbonkers.

There is talk at present of a bridge joining Greenport and Shelter Island. Natives—excepting those connected with the ferry—are all for it, since the federal government is expected to put up the needful cash. "But the summer people," said one of them to me gloomily, "they're agin it." There is such a thing as being too accessible, they think, and so the battle is on between the factions. For the present the ferry is the only way to Shelter Island for an explorer with a car. It may be added that the passage seems high. One dollar is the tribute exacted for a one-way trip, but it is $1.25 for a round trip, good, however, for only a single day. If you go on the hoof it is only fifteen cents, but you will find taximen on the other side who will take all you saved unless you are good for miles of tramping.

The present writer, touched with a thrifty impulse, left his car behind on his first visit, and sallied forth on foot to pay a call at Sylvester Manor. After trudging a few hundred yards uphill under a tropical sun he paused to ask a local citizen who was sweeping the sidewalk how to reach the Manor House. The worthy thus addressed looked blank. "Sylvester Manor? No, ain't never heard of it." Then he looked at me as much as to say, "There ain't no such place."

Just then an Angel appeared from somewhere, appropriately dressed in white. "I know the Manor," she said. "It's quite a long walk from here and hard to describe the route, but I can take you there in my car in a minute." So after proper and entirely perfunctory murmurs of protest, I entered the Angel's chariot and was wafted to a short cut to the estate just beyond a bridge over the entrance to Sylvester Creek, which goes inland from Dering

LILY POOL, SYLVESTER MANOR

Harbor. The blue-line road on the motor map shows how one could drive to the Manor gates, but it is much more roundabout. The short cut was a grassy roadway, bounded by dense shrubbery, winding up a slope for a few minutes' walk. A pool with pink and white water lilies lying to the left gave a pleasant intimation that I was approaching the estate itself. Soon the outbuildings

SYLVESTER MANOR, FROM THE REAR

were visible, and then the road came directly past an eighteenth-century formal garden with its boxwood-patterned borders, its Greek statue, stone bench, arbors and gay flower beds, including a sunken rose garden. Across and over a low white picket fence I could see the Manor House itself, a broad-fronted, dignified country residence of yellow clapboards with white trim, standing under magnificent elms. The house is not open to the public, but if the stranger were armed with a letter of introduction he would approach the front door past a great clump of bamboo and some boxwood bushes which are nearly three hundred years old. When the first bride came here to this isle in the wilderness she set out the same boxwood and here it survives, still faithful to her memory. It was a custom for generations that whenever an heir of the Sylvesters brought home a bride the foliage of the box plants was covered with gold leaf.

From the garden front there are driveways leading in and through the grounds. All around and overhead there are superb specimens of trees, many of uncommon varieties. There are copper beeches, for example, of magnificent size. And through these trees we catch a glimpse of the blue waters of Sylvester Creek. The reason for the presence of these trees is that Professor Horsford, the father of the present Lady of the Manor, was a close friend of Asa Gray, the botanist, who was his colleague at Harvard, and the latter delighted in bringing to Sylvester Manor specimens of trees to try out on the estate. He brought the copper beeches as a present on one of his visits. "Of course they won't last more than twenty years," he said apologetically. They are now well past forty. Professor Gray used to declare that the soil here and that in southeastern Japan were the absolutely ideal ones for plants, shrubs and trees.

Down on the water front of the estate stand some small weeping willows. The original ones have passed on long ago. One is descended in direct line from some plants which Lady Mary Wortley Montagu brought from the Euphrates to her friend, Mr. Alexander Pope, the poet, to be tried out at Twickenham Villa. Another is the descendant of a slip from the willow over Napoleon's tomb at St. Helena. To the left rises a dense grove of pines. These were planted at someone's suggestion to keep away malaria, and it is said there never has been malaria at Sylvester Manor since the pines first lifted their heads.

SHELTER ISLAND TO SAG HARBOR

A path bearing off from the driveway near the shore leads directly to a pool overshadowed by tall, deciduous trees on one side and the pine grove on the other. On its black-mirror surface float myriads of pink and white water lilies. It forms a dream picture. And there under a tree at the brink of the pool is a rustic bench where one may sit and drink in the beauty of the spot. There is no better place where we might pause and turn our thoughts back to the history of Sylvester Manor. For this is not one of those Long Island estates made overnight by a furious burst of buildings, the transplanting of big trees and acres of turf to obtain a quick effect. This, like an old English estate, has been mellowing for generations. Here famous men and women have come as familiar guests. Every rock and tree has its associations, and it still remains in the possession of the descendants of that Nathaniel Sylvester who first settled on this land in the year 1652.

There were in those days a number of English gentlemen who had invested in a sugar plantation in the Barbados. Being Royalists, they did not care to stay in an England ruled by Cromwell. They decided that they needed oak for making the hogsheads for shipping their sugar, and as Shelter Island had then a great growth of oak it was selected for the purpose and purchased. Very appropriately it was paid for with "1600 lbs of good merchantable Muscovado sugar." Nathaniel Sylvester, being appointed to take charge of the oak cutting on Shelter Island, came there to live, bringing his bride, Grissel Brinley, then only sixteen years old. Those seventeenth-century women must have been a stout-hearted lot, who thought nothing of going into a wilderness, making a home there, bearing and bringing up children. Grissel Sylvester was worthy of the best of them. Her husband built here a dwelling for himself and his girl wife, a house that stood for eighty years. Some of its timbers are still incorporated in the present Manor House. Sylvester's grandson, in 1737, built another home on the same site. Since his day there have been wings, porches and other additions which go to make up the rambling mansion as it stands today.

One of Nathaniel Sylvester's friends was John Winthrop, Jr., son of the first Governor of Massachusetts, a scholar and scientist, who helped found the Royal Society in London in 1664. There is extant a letter written by Nathaniel to John Winthrop asking advice about the care and feeding of an infant Sylvester, who was finding life very difficult.

In the year 1656, after four years' residence on the island, Nathaniel Sylvester heard of the persecution of Quakers in New England. He was not a Quaker himself, but he had a sense of decency and fair play, and a respect for freedom of conscience far ahead of his day. So he welcomed the Quaker refugees, and that kindly policy gave a new meaning to the name of his island. He encouraged them to stay by giving them lands for cultivation. There were not many of them in those early days who had the courage to stand out against the hatred toward the Quakers. One small boatload of pitiable refugees, including an ancestor of the poet Whittier, made its way to Shelter Island only to die soon after from their suffering and exposure.

Among the well-known Quakers who came here was Mary Dyer, who was welcomed to Shelter Island and might have stayed here in safety, but whose conscience drove her back to Boston to confront her enemies. And there the godly ones hanged her to a tree on Boston Common. Long afterwards Sylvester Manor was presented with the gift of a chair made from that tree on which Mary Dyer and so many of the other Quakers were executed.

The founder of the faith, George Fox, preached on these grounds to an open-air audience composed largely of Indians; and here came that fiery evangelist, Whitefield, whose eloquence once drew all the money out of Benjamin Franklin's thrifty pockets, as he describes in his autobiography.

In 1666 Nathaniel Sylvester was given a manorial grant for his island, and this was the first so established in the New York colony. Meanwhile he managed to keep the pace with both the Indians and the Dutch, and the families settled here grew and prospered under his kindly rule. The years, therefore, passed quietly and uneventfully as one Sylvester succeeded another as Proprietor. When 1775 came, dragging after it eight years of war, it found the Sylvester of that day a patriot, like his neighbor of Gardiner's Island, but, unlike the latter, he seems to have suffered comparatively little from those visitations of hostile fleets and armies.

As the visitor turns back toward the house he can see a stone causeway leading off to a creek on the left. That ends at a flight of stone steps that go down into the water. These are historic stones, for all visitors to Sylvester Manor, from earliest times, came by way of water and landed by boat or canoe at that stairway. The ship *Golden Parrot,* which plied back and forth between the Barbados and Shelter Island, dropped anchor here in the creek, and her boats made their landing at these steps in lieu of a wharf. These stones knew the tread of the Quakers, such as Mary Dyer and George Fox; the Methodist revivalist, George Whitefield—all these in sober garb. Here landed the erudite John Winthrop, Jr., in plain but rich Puritan dress; the Commissioners of the Dutch colony at New Amsterdam, arrayed in full uniform and high boots; Indian sachems, too, in deerskins and feathers; English Governors in high perukes and long velvet coats.

In less picturesque dress, during the nineteenth century, came a notable array of guests: President Timothy Dwight of Yale;

THE STONE STEPS, SYLVESTER MANOR

Ole Bull, the violinist; Henry Wadsworth Longfellow, Oliver Wendell Holmes, Helen Hunt Jackson, Sarah Orne Jewett, and James Russell Lowell. Here President John Tyler came on his honeymoon with his bride, Julia Gardiner. There is a rare collection of autographs written in pencil on a clapboard of the house near the front door and protected under glass. Here, too, came that same indefatigable Harry Fenn to make sketches of Shelter Island for *Picturesque America,* but he was then just a nice young man with a strong English accent and a fluffy beard, and not famous at all. Probably he was not asked to write his autograph.

There is a good story that among other notable visitors who visited the Manor before the custom of autographs began was the same Captain Kidd, who, as we have seen, gave the Gardiners of Gardiner's Island the benediction of his presence. Having run short of fresh meat, he landed at Sylvester Manor—no doubt by those same stone steps—together with several members of his crew. Seeing two pigs in the barnyard, he ordered his men to capture them. The squeals called forth an irate cook, who defied the whole pirate band in vigorous language. Kidd explained his need for fresh meat, and, taking the gold chain from his neck, he broke off a few links and gave them to the woman in payment. That satisfied her as an honorable business transaction, and the pigs went off to the ship. The sad part about this picturesque anecdote is that there is no record of the buccaneer's ever setting foot on Shelter Island.

Here, also, a century later, in August, 1784, a strange and romantic figure arrived, General Miranda of Venezuela, fresh from military service in Florida and all aglow with enthusiasm for liberty. He was just an overnight guest at Sylvester Manor, but the family records tell of a great picnic luncheon served under the trees in his honor. From here he continued his travels to Sag Harbor and East Hampton. Fortunately he left behind a diary of his American journey; and as he had been careful to obtain letters of introduction to practically all important people, he has left vivid comments, not only on the places he visited but also on our celebrities of the Revolutionary War era, from Washington down.

From America this soldier of fortune made his way to Russia, where he took his turn at being Gentleman of the Bedchamber to the Empress Catherine. Then he went to France, where, by some amazing twist of fortune, he became Commander-in-Chief of the French armies in the year of the Terror. Accused of treason, he narrowly escaped conviction and death by the guillotine.

Back in New York, in 1805, he gathered together an expedition to free Venezuela from Spain, and he solicited funds from his American friends for the purpose. To man his vessels he recruited some Americans who had no idea what he was up to. Two of these were boys from Long Island (Huntington and Sag Harbor), one of whom afterwards published a pamphlet describing in dreadful detail what the poor fellows suffered. For the expedition fizzled out in treachery, and though Miranda himself escaped, many of his followers were captured and decapitated, hanged or thrown into unspeakably horrible prisons.

Five years later, however, Miranda did succeed in entering Venezuela as a liberator, and for a brief time reigned as Dictator. Then his Venezuelan friends, becoming dissatisfied, turned him over to the Spanish authorities (for profit) and he finally died in the dungeon of the Inquisition at Cadiz.

In his life, spent all over the world, this man had tasted flattery, honor and power to a degree that few men have known, bestowed by alien peoples, only to be betrayed to his death by his countrymen. Of all the guest roll of Sylvester Manor this romantic knight errant in the cause of liberty stands unique for his adventurous career, and yet today he is almost completely forgotten.

Among the literary lions of the nineteenth century who came to Shelter Island should be included James Fenimore Cooper. At the time of his visit here he was simply a gentleman of leisure,

SHELTER ISLAND TO SAG HARBOR

not yet an author. He probably called at the Manor House to pay his respects, but there seems to be no record of his ever being entertained there as a house guest. But it was here on Shelter Island that Cooper began his career as a novelist. When he said once that he could write a better novel than most of those in circulation someone dared him to try, and here he squared away his elbows at a table, sharpened a flock of goosequills and went to work on his first novel. This was *Precaution,* an incredibly dull tale dealing with incredibly dull Dukes, Earls, Baronets, Admirals, Colonels and what not of the British aristocracy as he imagined them. He began it here at Shelter Island and completed it in Sag Harbor. His last chapter dealt with Quatre Bras and Waterloo, and right in the midst of his narrative of the clash of armies and fate of nations he pauses for a full page to moralize on war. Poor as it was, this book started him on his career.

The literary notables of the later generation, like Longfellow and Lowell, who came to Sylvester Manor were friends of Professor Eben N. Horsford, who, having married Mary L'Hommedieu Gardiner, daughter of the proprietor of the estate, had fallen heir to Sylvester Manor. Horsford himself was a distinguished scientist, finding time outside his professional duties to invent a formula for baking powder and an acid phosphate which became highly successful commercial products. He was also interested in early American antiquities and erected the well-known tower at Norumbega, on the Charles River, Massachusetts, to commemorate the arrival of Vikings centuries before the time of Columbus.

Sometime after these Viking discoveries of Professor Horsford, a summer citizen of Shelter Island put up a memorial there in the form of a bronze tablet on a boulder. This was dedicated with impressive exercises, including speeches and a brass band, and the monument may still be seen on the shore near the ferry to Greenport in the bathhouse yard. The tablet reads as follows:

> ON THIS SPOT JULY 11, 1508
> FELL PUTIKAOS
> LAST OF THE SIHAQUA INDIANS
> SLAIN BY THE NORSE VIKING
> RETAWERIF

That was a sad tragedy of course, but some skeptics raised a question as to the authenticity of this very ancient story. Whereupon letters came from antiquarians—one from as far away as Honolulu—declaring emphatically that the incident was genuine. The one from Honolulu explained that the Norseman Retawerif, though not a "Viking" in the usual sense, was a Scandinavian who had deserted from Henry Hudson's second expedition to the Manhattan area. That was circumstantial of course, but while the discussion waxed among the scholars, some one of those iconoclastic newspaper reporters poked his nose into what was none of his business and reported that the poor Indian who fell victim to Nordic rage had a singular name. If you read it backward it becomes "Soak it up." And applying the same test to the murderous Viking you get "Firewater." Alas, it is true that many a noble red man went to his happy hunting grounds slain by soaking up too much firewater. That much is certainly historic, but it does take the edge off our grief over this particular red man. To cap the climax, during the prohibition era a notorious speakeasy stood hard by this monument to poor Putikaos. What happened, evidently, is that an irreverent neighbor of Professor Horsford took this way of playing a practical joke, but it is strange that the hoax could have gone so far.

SHELTER ISLAND TO SAG HARBOR

Before leaving such glimpses as the traveler may have of Sylvester Manor from the roadway, he should not miss the old windmill of the estate, which may be seen from the road through a break in the trees. This was built across the bay in Southold in 1795, carried on a barge over to the island and then hauled by an ox team to where it stands today. It would seem as if it might have been much less trouble to import the workmen and build the mill on the spot, especially in view of the dreadful sand-rut roads of those days and the uphill grade from the shore. But moving buildings was very common in those early years.

If there is plenty of time the drives along the shore road and the country lanes are worth taking for views of the water and the shores of the North Fork. If you drive out to Plum Island, which really isn't an island, you will notice that the telephone company has obligingly put up a row of poles, parallel to the telephone lines, topped with small platforms. These are designed to tempt the fish hawks to build their nests away from the telephone poles and wires. Among the many services given by the New York Telephone Company this is unique, but doubtless, like the others, it is contributed "with a smile."

To reach Sag Harbor we must follow Route 114. It is none too clearly marked and makes unexpected right-angle turns; but you cannot get lost, for at the worst you would only come upon one of the roads along the shore and soon find your way back. The road runs through lush farming country with old houses, great barns, grassy pools, in which cattle stand knee-deep, and overhanging trees. These open up after a while and the road emerges into the sunshine again, right to the water's edge. Here is another ferry, seventy-five cents this time, to convey the traveler and his car to the smaller island that lies like a stepping stone between Shelter Island and Sag Harbor. This

Sag Harbor ferry was the inspiration for that delicious comedy of some years ago, *Salt Water,* featuring Frank Crane. Later the play was made into a movie, with Slim Summerville and Zazu Pitts.

The old seaport is not very impressive to the eye as the motorist trundles in past the usual filling stations at the entrance. All the fine trees on the business section of Main Street were sacrificed in recent years to widen it and accommodate the march of Progress. But it is clear that Progress was stalled somewhere and the trees might better have been spared. Later, many that Progress had overlooked were felled by the hurricane. The town wasn't any more impressive seventy years ago, for the writer in *Picturesque America* says: "Sag Harbor is old, quaint, and fishlike; it must remain a matter of taste whether the traveler should prefer its semi-decayed antiquity to the orderly and trimmed newness of Greenport." But a century ago Sag Harbor was an important shipping and whaling center, holding its head up even with New Bedford and Nantucket for its importance in the sperm-oil trade; but the same causes that made those cities to lose their chief means of livelihood killed Sag Harbor's prosperity, too, and the harbor sagged indeed. That depressing name, by the way, is a shortened version of the Indian "Sagaponack," which may be descried on the road map just to the south on both a town and a lake.

The dominating landmark of Sag Harbor is the Presbyterian church steeple. This started out respectably enough in the Christopher Wren tradition, but the architect cut loose on his own, and added strange ornaments derived from the Near East, with a touch of Egypt and a strong flavor of China. These flourish especially in the steeple, which was added sometime after the rest of the church was built. This steeple was made unusually tall for the rest of the building so that it could serve as a landmark for returning whalers, and despite its strange ornament it has an odd charm of its own like a demure parson's daughter in gypsy dress. The great hurricane of 1938 toppled it over, but it will surely be restored. This church, built in 1843, is a monument to Sag Harbor's climax of prosperity in the whaling era. It was known as the "Whalers' Church."

The finest dwelling left from the golden days of whaling is the mansion on the main street, one-half of which houses the Masonic Temple, and the other the Whaling Museum. This was the former home of Captain Benjamin Huntting, and is one of those stately Grecian temples that delighted our ancestors in the eighteen-twenties or thirties. It has noble proportions and was built with honest and loving craftsmanship. Such of the Sag Harbor houses as have survived the tooth of time can show inside beautiful woodwork in their trim and moldings. Those old sea captains, when they were loafing ashore after a long cruise, delighted in decorating their homes with fine wood carving.

James Fenimore Cooper tarried here for a time. Besides finishing his first novel here he wrote another in Sag Harbor (published in 1849) about sealing in the Antarctic. This was one of his last. He started off the first chapter with the year 1819, and the scene was Orient Point, "Oyster Pond Point" it was then. He used as his characters people of Sag Harbor whom he knew. In some instances he didn't even change their names. Meanwhile, in Cooper's time, the railroad had been extended to Sag Harbor, and this was among the many things which offended this truculent man of letters. In the preface to the *Sea Lions* he registers his protest in these words:

DISCOVERING LONG ISLAND

It is to us ever a painful sight to see the rustic virtues rudely thrown aside by the intrusions of what are termed improvements. A railroad is certainly a capital invention for the traveler, but it may be questioned whether it is of any other benefit than that of pecuniary convenience to the place through which it passes. How many delightful hamlets, pleasant villages, and our tranquil country towns are losing their primitive characters for simplicity and contentment by the passage of these fiery trains that drag after them a sort of bastard elegance, a pretension that is destructive of peace and mind, and an uneasy desire in all who dwell by the wayside to pry into the mysteries of the whole length and breadth of the region it traverses!

It does seem odd that, in a town where the men roamed from Atlantic to Pacific and from pole to pole in search of their whales or seals, Cooper should be worried about the railroads creating an "uneasy desire . . . to pry into the mysteries of the whole length and breadth of the region it traverses." There was nothing very mysterious about the railroad route between Sag Harbor and New York. But he was desperately afraid of the "bastard elegance" which the railroad dragged after it, ruining the "rustic virtues," and he was never reconciled to its presence. Perhaps as he sits aloft now he may feel sorry for his harsh words when he realizes how much money the Long Island Railroad is losing each year. What would he say to the "bastard elegance" that the railroad's enemy, the automobile, is now scattering over the rural scene? And he need no longer worry about imported elegance in Sag Harbor today, whether bastard or legitimate. The whales are gone; the seals, the fisheries, the trade with the West Indies and with China all vanished likewise. Nothing remains to take their place but the summer visitor. It looks as if the people of our Atlantic coast towns are reduced to taking in one another's

SHELTER ISLAND TO SAG HARBOR

scenery, from Eastport to St. Augustine. What we see in Sag Harbor is the identical picture all up and down the coast among the old-time shipping centers: two months of "summer folks," ten months on relief.

If Cooper went to the right church on Sundays he probably listened to the preaching of a certain Edward Hopper. Later this clergyman became famous for writing a hymn which is still popular, "Jesus, Savior, Pilot Me," with its nautical figures of speech so appropriate to a place like Sag Harbor. But like many another preacher, he grew gray in the service of the Lord. Like many another aggregation of deacons and elders, those of his church decided that Mr. Hopper was getting too old, that it would be nice to have a younger man who would appeal to the youth of the congregation, especially the girls. So they informed Mr. Hopper that he could go elsewhere.

Now most ministers who have had that experience—and they are legion—are compelled to take their dismissal lying down. They can't hit back. But this reverend could, for he had a sense of humor and wielded a mean pen. He was tickled to learn soon after his dismissal that the man the deacons employed to take his place was discovered to have dyed his hair to appear young. On the basis of this knowledge, Hopper (in 1869) published in pamphlet form a poem entitled *Old Horse Gray and the Parish of Grumbleton*. "Grumbleton" was Sag Harbor, streets and houses and all, and the characters were easily recognizable as members of his former congregation, notably those deacons. A girl who had been angry with her grandfather for helping to dismiss Mr. Hopper brought out a key to the characters, and was there a sensation in Sag Harbor! The town buzzed and rocked with delight, all except the people who had been imbedded in the poem like the famous flies in amber. They rushed all about town trying to seize and burn all the copies of the book. In this satirical poem Hopper himself was the "Old Horse Gray," and the poem shows that the people who had turned him out of the stable and purchased another had "settled on an ass" tinted with hair dye. The new preacher didn't like that at all.

Then it was that Mr. Hopper, having got his revenge, gave himself up to pious contemplation and composed the hymn that gave him his chief fame. He could write feelingly about "life's tempestuous sea," in which "unknown waves before me roll, hiding rock and treacherous shoal." Those were the deacons who were smiling to his face but who knifed him behind his back. And there were many in his former congregation who, looking upon their new minister with his dyed raven-black locks growing on an empty head, wondered if they had done well to discard a man who could write a famous hymn like that, and "settle on an ass."

There are not many relics in Sag Harbor today to recall the days of its glory. Mention has already been made of the Presbyterian church and the Huntting mansion, the only two that survive. The citizens like to tell you that Sag Harbor and New York City were both named ports of entry at the close of the Revolutionary War by the same Act of Congress, and in that act Sag Harbor was named first, if you please. In whaling days, those twenty to thirty years before the Civil War, there were about seventy Sag Harbor vessels in the whaling business alone and they brought back what was for those days fabulous wealth. Today in Sag Harbor's Oakland Cemetery there stands a monument representing a broken and splintered mast. This is a memorial to five young captains of whalers lost at sea. It may also be regarded as a monument to the old Sag Harbor, a city of the sea, which is no more.

CHAPTER VI

EAST HAMPTON

FROM Sag Harbor Route 114 runs through a dot on the road map marked "Hardscrabble," a melancholy name suggesting that the good old days here were not all beer and skittles. It was the name of a farm that belonged to the Dayton family in East Hampton, and in the mid-nineteenth century there was another farm near by that bore the equally melancholy name of "Toilsome." This survives today as the Toilsome Dairy. Such names suggest that farming in these regions was not too easy or lucrative. Hardscrabble is so small that the motorist can hardly see it with a naked eye when he passes through, and certainly there is no traffic light to give him pause. After a few miles of field and woodland on each side of the road he comes out on the street running into the heart of East Hampton.

Please note, Gentle Reader, that this municipal title is a two-word affair. Bridgehampton, Westhampton and Southampton succumbed and have become one word, like "Damyankee" in the South, but not East Hampton. The Postmaster General and the President of the Railway Express Company have issued formal decrees that East Hampton shall also become one word. But who or what are they? Is this country Russia, Italy or Germany that a dictator shall say how a town's name shall be written? A thousand times no, and all that sort of emphatic negation. The citizens of the place concerned ought to have the say-so in this important matter, and they have made it East Hampton forever.

And if you look at your road map you will see that the gasoline gentry have had the wisdom to recognize the fact. This, Traveler, is the first lesson to learn: "East Hampton."

The next important fact is borne upon us the moment we enter the main street: we realize instantly that this is a place to linger. We must turn right as we come in and drive slowly along that broad avenue under the elms to breathe some of the atmosphere of this unique village at the very first. Then as soon as possible find a lodging for the night, stable your car or turn it out to pasture by the roadside. There are four excellent small hotels to stay in, all of them adapted from East Hampton homes of over a century ago: the "Huntting," which is an expanded version of Reverend Nathaniel Huntting's parsonage of bygone days; the "Maidstone Arms," successor to the former Osborne House of ancient fame; the "Hedges," once a country boardinghouse of the eighteen-seventies and in recent years reopened as a delightful country inn with the flavor of an old home, and one of the famous hostelries on Long Island. Then, for those who like to be within sight and smell of the ocean, there is the "Sea Spray," also most comfortable and of high repute, standing on the crest of a dune in a bower of flowers. There the wayfarer from inland regions may sit at table in full view of the ocean. The other three are on the main street, but the Sea Spray is about half a mile south of the village green, directly on the shore.

These inns tend to serve the well-to-do, and some of them require a purse with the bulging outline of a dowager. For the wallet that has distinctly a girlish figger there are here, as elsewhere, modest "tourist accommodations," readily discovered, and some of them housed in ancient dwellings full of "atmosphere" and General Grant decorations. At any rate, no one can see East Hampton from a car. This is emphatically a village of

VILLAGE POND

EAST HAMPTON

such intimate and picturesque charm that it can be appreciated only by sauntering along its wide, shady avenue, pausing here and there to hang over a fence to gaze admiringly at some old house nestled deep in its flower garden.

Let us imagine, then, that we are beginning our stroll from a spot opposite the "Hedges," at the southern end of the village street where the Green begins. Here, in the middle, is the duck pond, with the roadways on either side joining to make the main street beyond the north end of the Green. "Green" is a highly appropriate word, for there is so much of that color reflected in the pond from trees overhead and trim lawns that run right into the water that from certain angles the pond looks like a huge plate of pea soup in which you half expect to see giant croutons afloat. There was a time when flocks of ducks and geese, especially geese, skimmed these waters and waddled up and down the bank. Later, when East Hampton became a noted summer resort, the plebeian ducks and geese vanished, and for a while lordly swans floated about and gave the Green an air of elegance. Apparently they didn't prosper, for the surface of the pond is broken now only by an occasional toy boat or the ripple from the nose of a muskrat.

As we begin our stroll we might follow the grassy margin on our left to lead us beside the still waters. On the other side of the pond we see the burial ground, shadowed by tall trees. Through a break in the foliage stands an old, gray windmill. As we walk farther we can see another windmill hard by, near two houses that are obviously very old indeed, and one of which we shall explore later, for it is the birthplace of John Howard Payne, author of "Home, Sweet Home."

From the first glimpse of the village street we have been struck with the breadth and the rows of gigantic elms that form a green roof above it. Near the spot where the Green and its duck pond come to an end stands a massive elm which drops its branches so low that the leaves are within reach of a person standing on the opposite side of the road. The main street itself where it begins at the end of the Green is about one hundred and fifty feet wide from sidewalk to sidewalk. (Williamsburg's famous Duke of Gloucester Street, considered a regal avenue in its day, is only ninety-nine feet in width.)

Overarching East Hampton's wide thoroughfare are superb giant elms, which spread their arms from side to side and touch fingers overhead. Since the oldest of them has not more than a century to its credit, we may hope that they will continue to spread and flourish for many more years to come. As that street stands today it has not its peer for a combination of spacious dignity and beauty among all the old towns of America.

The little brown library building on our left, with its open timber work, and the square, granite tower of St. Luke's Church on the opposite side give an English-village touch to this end of the street. And yet where in all England is there a village with such a vista as this? Certainly none with such elms. For the American elm is one of our finest natural possessions. Single specimens stand out best on a flat meadowland with a background of hills, as seen in the White Mountain region, but they also are magnificent as massed along our New England streets. One of the finest individual specimens here is the tree that stands at the corner of the long, low white building across the street from the library—the Guild Hall and Art Center.

Under these trees and along the sidewalks, for the most part rather deep-set from the street, are the houses that make up the ancient part of the village. These are typically New England in architecture. In fact, the whole street is of the Connecticut Colonial tradition carried to perfection—almost, that is. For perfection it needs a white New England meeting house with a graceful steeple pointing up into the blue above these elm tops, like the church at Mt. Sinai, or even perhaps a pink brick church of the Bullfinch tradition, with dainty pillars aloft and a little gilded dome, as the one in Peterborough, New Hampshire. The

TYPICAL EAST HAMPTON HOUSE, "ROWDY HALL"

"old church" on this site was torn down in 1871 when the present one was built. This was not happily conceived, and really doesn't belong on this street. Maybe Jupiter Tonans will yet smite it with a thunderbolt, or the Garden Club and Village Improvement Association will combine forces and purchase a church from one of these starveling small congregations on Long Island that can't keep theirs up, and reerect it on the site of the present one. Then East Hampton would be perfect.

As it stands, the village is a monument for the rest of the

country to study, to see what can be done by intelligent citizens. Its unique beauty is due to the two associations of public-spirited people, Garden Club and Village Improvement Association, which supervise not only the appearance of the town itself, but also keep off billboards and other eyesores from the roads of the whole township. The result is that in all its long history East Hampton never was so lovely as it is today. Proudly its residents declare that it is "the most beautiful village in America," and they may be pardoned their boast, for they have had much to do with making it what it is. At the same time, East Hampton is not a museum piece of antiquity. This is an age of drugstores, movie houses and garages, and we are obliged to have them, even in an old town, as well as eighteenth-century windmills and seventeenth-century houses. But here these twentieth-century conveniences are kept from being obtrusive.

Meanwhile we saunter along the walk, look over the white picket fences at the old homes and continue to marvel at the overhanging elms. After all, these are the real aristocrats among the trees; they stand there with such a conscious dignity, like the wives of Spanish grandees at a court reception, wearing their foliage as if it were a mantilla of green lace. There should be a memorial tablet somewhere on this street to the man who planted them.

When in our walk we come to the end of the village there stands another windmill, the "Hook Mill," in its own little green triangle of lawn. Behind it is another graveyard, but not so old as the one we caught a glimpse of at the south end of the street. Once there was a duck pond here by the Hook Mill, too, for evidently the East Hamptonians of two hundred years ago ran heavily to the cultivation of ducks and geese long before the "Long Island Duckling" ever appeared on a restaurant bill of

EAST HAMPTON

fare, and it took two ponds and two greens to accommodate them.

East Hampton citizens take pride in the fact that the village possesses three of its ancient windmills—one has been destroyed —but their arms are forever still. Nantucket has only one of her four left, but that stands on its highest hill for all to see, and in the summer when there is a fair wind the sails are spread and the arms whirl round. Inside, the machinery grinds corn—for sale to the tourist—and does a thriving business in the good old eighteenth-century windmill fashion. There's a deal of difference between a mill standing dead and one that comes to life with a good south breeze. Perhaps one day the Hook Mill may be seen waving its arms once more, just to delight the eye of the summer visitor anyway.

At this fork of the roads where the mill stands the village rather tapers off into obscurity on each side, but if we walk on a little way under the railroad bridge on the left we shall see one of the most typical and most ancient of the East Hampton homes. This is the "Dominy House," so named after the family that has lived here for generations. The building itself is about two hundred and fifty years old, and there is now an air of toothless and wrinkled old age about its fence with its broken gaps, where the pickets have fallen out, and the ragged shingles on the sides. Also, the grass grows rank about the front door. This entrance is an interesting example of the very simple old-time doorway before Greek pillars and fanlights expressed an age of greater prosperity. Around this door, as over so many of the East Hampton houses, grow two huge wistaria vines. These at the Dominy House writhe around and over the whole front door, the windows and eaves, like the two serpents with Laocoön in their coils. In the season of its bloom this ancient house must be a vision of beauty.

DISCOVERING LONG ISLAND

At this point we might do well to turn back and walk on the other side of the village street to our starting place at the end of the Green. And, imagining ourselves to have all the morning

DOMINY HOUSE

for exploration, we can stop and cross back and forth, as we see things that call for closer inspection.

For instance, on the west side of the street stands a curious small, two-and-a-half-story building with a bell cupola on the roof. This is Clinton Academy, a lamp of learning that burned brightly here about a hundred years—from 1785 to 1881. It was the first school on Long Island to prepare for college and belongs to the company of such oldsters as Phillips Andover and Phillips Exeter, which were not more than ten years its senior. From this tiny building boys went to Yale, Harvard and Princeton.

ELM AT CORNER OF GUILD HALL

EAST HAMPTON

Its highest peak was reached after the close of the War of 1812, with a roster of one hundred and fifty-six pupils, all of whom were taken in as boarders in the village homes at the rate of one dollar a week. Girls were admitted as day pupils, and though there were no colleges for them to go to, they kept on bravely with their Caesar and Virgil. The tuition was five dollars a quarter "to be paid in advance."

The Academy had a good reputation, but the growth of free schooling made it impossible for a private institution here to keep its head above water. At any rate, it died with dignity. It never offered cut-rate tuitions or gave football scholarships. For a while the building was the East Hampton Town Hall, and now it is a local museum. On the ground floor are numerous relics of the offshore whaling days, and upstairs all conceivable objects from a trundle bed to a Sunday-go-to-meetin' bonnet of 1830. One interesting item is the clockface from the tower of the old church which stood across the street. This clock has but one hand. In old East Hampton minutes apparently were of no importance.

Near Clinton Academy on the same side of the street is the modest but picturesque library building. This houses one of the most prized possessions of East Hampton. Its old, English aspect is due to the fact that the town was founded by settlers from Maidstone in Kent, who first called their community here "Maidstone," and then changed it later to its present name. To recall these English antecedents of East Hampton, the library building was designed as a modest copy of the one in the Old World Maidstone. It was built in 1912 as a gift to the town by Mr. and Mrs. Lorenzo Woodhouse. In 1930 an addition was made by other generous citizens, and here Mr. Morton Pennypacker moved from Kew Gardens his famous Long Island historical collection of eighteen thousand volumes, pamphlets and papers.

These are now housed in a fireproof wing of the building.

The interior of the library is most inviting. The rear windows open out on a charming "close" or cloister—you couldn't call any such spot a back yard—with its fountain and bronze child figure, stone benches and massed shrubbery. Naturally, this library is the place of historical research on Long Island, but there is much here to interest the casual tourist. Here among other relics is that fragment of the cloth of gold which Captain Kidd stole from the trousseau of the Great Mogul's daughter and gave to Mrs. Gardiner. Here are sheets of paper made in the old mill at Roslyn in 1790 by no less a hand than George Washington's. One piece, in honor of the celebrity himself, has the watermark of an eagle with laurel leaves, and the other, in honor of the owner of the mill, has "A. Onderdonk." There are samples of paper money from this mill, too, made with a red silk fiber by a secret process. The last important job for the old mill was the manufacture of paper boxes for thousands of chunks of wedding cake which President Grover Cleveland distributed to deserving Democrats and meritorious mugwumps at the time of his marriage.

There are many other objects of interest, which the visitor may pick out for himself according to his taste, such as the palette of Thomas Moran, a tiny little thing for a painter who covered such huge canvases. The library possesses a first-edition copy of Cooper's first novel, *Precaution*. There is a map of Long Island, dating from 1616; a copy of the first newspaper published on Long Island—of 1791, in its first issue. There is a painting by that Stony Brook artist, William Mount, first exhibited a hundred years ago. The list could run on indefinitely, and the exhibition case alone is good for a long pause. In brief, this East Hampton library is unique, and almost perfect. To make it quite

EAST HAMPTON

perfect somebody, or a group of somebodies, should give it the endowment it needs so much.

Directly across the street from the library is that long, low white building we noticed as we started our stroll. This is another cherished possession of the village, and this also represents the

THE MULFORD HOUSE

civic pride and generosity of certain citizens, particularly the same Mr. and Mrs. Woodhouse who gave the library building. This includes a summer theater, called the "John Drew Memorial Theater" in memory of the famous actor who made his summer home here for many years. It is such a theater as few summer stock companies—"straw hat," as the profession calls them—

have the pleasure of playing in, for though small, it is perfectly equipped. The building contains also three art galleries, one the "Thomas Moran Gallery," after the famous painter who lived and worked here during a great part of his life; the "South Gallery"; and a small exhibition room, named for the daughter of the Woodhouses as a memorial to her.

The grounds in the rear serve also as an ideal outdoor setting for exhibitions of sculpture. There are no such exhibition facilities elsewhere on Long Island this side of the Brooklyn Museum.

From here, walking south on the roadway that keeps to our left of the Green, we see, close together, two very old houses, to the rear of which rises a windmill. The first is the John Henry Mulford House, probably the most antique of the village antiquities, dating from the middle of the seventeenth century and looking pretty much—except for the wrinkles of age—as it did in the beginning. A Mulford still lives here. One of his ancestors was a Samuel Mulford who went to London in 1704 and again in 1716 to protest against unfair laws made by the New York governors. The story goes that he sewed fishhooks in the pockets of his homespun coat to discourage London pickpockets. Though at first he was laughed at for his odd clothing and provincial ways, he won his case. A waistcoat and cane of his are preserved in Clinton Academy.

The next house beyond is also a "salt box" of the seventeenth century, facing, like its Mulford neighbor, not on the road, but due south to get the benefit of the winter sunshine. But this one, in contrast to the decrepit Mulford House, is very orderly and trim. A flag hangs forth from an upper window, and a sign near the sidewalk tells us that this is the birthplace of John Howard Payne, the author of "Home, Sweet Home." Among all the antiquities of East Hampton this is its chief jewel. It has been restored, and now for a twenty-five-cent fee the visitor may enter and look about at the interior of a seventeenth-century house, and the collection of Payne letters, portraits and other relics on display.

For a long time there was a difference of opinion about which was the real Home, Sweet Home of Payne's song. When Harry Fenn came on his *Picturesque America* errand, he had pointed out to him quite another house, which he duly sketched for the book. Also when the Tile Club came here they were shown over the other house. But later research has established the fact that the present shrine was actually the house in which Payne was born. The confusion came from the fact that his father and mother moved about in the village. The father, William Payne, married a Sarah Isaacs, whose family lived in East Hampton, and here he moved about 1780. The Paynes at that time went into a house already one hundred years old. It is now pushed back some fifty yards from the street, and is known as the Nelson Osborne house. This was the cottage which was called the "Home, Sweet Home place" in the eighteen-seventies and eighteen-eighties. William Payne supported himself by teaching, and did well enough to encourage the idea of founding an academy here. When Clinton Academy was inaugurated Payne was one of the first faculty of two.

His father-in-law, Mr. Aaron Isaacs, owned a number of houses in town, and this in which the Paynes set up housekeeping was one of them. Professor William Payne evidently was not always on the dot in paying his rent to Papa Isaacs. Very likely he was often considerably behind, for his thrifty father-in-law saw fit to push him out of any house he could rent to someone else and settle him in one of the unoccupied properties. Thus the Payne family came to have several home, sweet homes in East Hampton, but the one we are now visiting happened to be the one which Mrs. Payne was occupying when, on June 9, 1791, their second son, John Howard, was born. This was her own childhood home, the Isaacs homestead.

Aaron Isaacs was, as his name suggests, of Jewish antecedents. He came here from New York City and married a daughter of one of the leading families—the Hedges—in East Hampton. Despite his name and race he was one of the strictest and most orthodox of the local Presbyterians. Perhaps at this time it is a pity to bring up Mr. Isaacs' ancestry, because as a grandfather of the poet he spoils the Aryan purity of the famous song. Presumably no homesick American exiled in the Reich may now sing " 'Mid pleasures and palaces though we may roam" without getting arrested for it, and causing international complications. There is also the legend that Mr. Isaacs did his bookkeeping in Hebrew so that no one could pry into his business affairs.

When the boy John was born the father was away trying to establish a new home in New York City. Thereafter, for some years, the Payne family moved from pillar to post, as they tried one place after another; but the East Hampton home of the aunts and the grandparents was the place to which the children returned as their home for long visits. So this is the house Payne had enshrined in his memory when he wrote his famous song. This fact has been so definitely settled that the village of East Hampton bought the house for sixty thousand dollars and is keeping it as a memorial of the town's most famous son. Everything else about the early history of that schoolmaster's family is so foggy that Payne himself never knew just when he was born. He often said it happened in 1792 instead of 1791, and is known to have given his birthplace as New York several times. Possibly as an actor he felt that he should use the name of some

"Home, Sweet Home"

EAST HAMPTON

place of importance rather than an insignificant hamlet like the East Hampton of the seventeen-nineties. This inaccuracy and confusion over the poet-actor's birthplace followed him to his grave, in Tunis, North Africa. The inscription placed there read that he died on April 1, 1852, and that he was born in Boston on June 8, 1792. The facts are that he died April 9, 1852, and was born in East Hampton June 9, 1791.

The same blundering devil of hit-or-miss followed all the poet-actor's financial affairs, too, for he was perpetually in trouble over money matters. He certainly did not inherit his grandfather Isaacs' gift for making money and holding it. In fact, while in London he knew the grim interior of a debtor's prison; and in Paris, at the time he wrote "Home, Sweet Home," he was, in his own words, "in a state next to starvation." For all the millions of copies of "Home, Sweet Home" that were sold, he received practically nothing.

The birthplace we shall presently enter is one of the oldest houses in the village, being of the same vintage as the Mulford House. Some suggest a date in the neighborhood of 1660. It certainly had more than a century to its credit when Payne was born here. The visitor steps across a grooved millstone at the door, and, turning left, begins his tour of the downstairs rooms. But the first thing he should do after paying his admission fee is to buy the souvenir booklet of "Home, Sweet Home." This is handsomely illustrated, and the historical narrative comes from the authoritative hand of Mr. Pennypacker of the library.

The interior of the house is a place of delight for anyone interested in American antiquities, as well as in John Howard Payne. The beams, doors, paneling, fireplaces, utensils, furniture, etc., are all of that era in which the poet was born, or earlier. The treasures that meet the eye on every side were collected by

Mr. Gustave H. Buek, who, thirty years ago, purchased the property and restored it, adding a wing, or "ell," on the rear and to the side, in order to make it livable, without harming the original character of the house. It was after his death that the whole property was transferred by purchase to the custody of the village of East Hampton.

All that the house contains is the fruit of Mr. Buek's zeal in collecting. Here are chairs of all the antique patterns: Windsor, ladder-backs, Chippendales, Hepplewhites, Sheratons and fiddle-backs. In the kitchen is every cooking utensil of the ancient days.

The next important single item in this exhibit is the collection of lusterware. This seems to have been Mr. Buek's special hobby. Here on display is one of the finest and most complete collections of luster to be seen anywhere. This luster process was invented, no one knows just by whom, or when or where. But the famous Josiah Wedgwood experimented with it for four years, and then in 1780 began to manufacture it. It is a process by which earthenware is covered with a metallic coating. It flourished until about one hundred years ago, when the electroplating method was invented. Meanwhile three types of lusterware were developed: copper or brown, gold or purple, silver or platinum. This last was one of the earliest uses of the metal platinum. Luster of all types and of all sizes is in this collection. There is also to be seen a handsome spode tea set with gold ornament, which tradition says was bought as a bridal gift for a girl whose wedding never came off, but who kept the china just the same.

On the walls are two portraits of the poet: one, of the romantic and handsome young actor in his early twenties; the other, of the middle-aged, bewhiskered man who was thankful to obtain a federal job though it took him to Africa. This picture was painted by Willard, the man who produced the popular "Spirit of '76." Mr. Buek discovered this portrait in a forlorn basement shop in Boston. Around the walls are numerous letters written by Payne, together with other personal items, which make this not only a treasure house of antiquities but a personal shrine.

The objection might be raised, in a reading of "Home, Sweet Home," that the poet must have had some imaginary English cottage in mind because of the line "Oh, give me my lowly thatched cottage again!" We never think of American cottages as being thatched. But the antiquarians say that the seventeenth-century houses hereabout were thatched, like their prototypes in England, and that when Payne was a child undoubtedly some part of the house roof was still covered with thatch. "Lowly" is a bit of poetic license for a house that stood two full stories in front—as high as any country house in those days—but he may also have been thinking of the north side in particular, where the roof slanted down so low that a boy could scramble up on top of it.

In the rear of the Home, Sweet Home house stands a windmill. This, when Payne was a child, stood on a slight knoll on the opposite side of the village pond, where now a tree flourishes. Mr. Buek bought it to preserve it and moved it to this present site, where it certainly makes a unique background for the old house and is also a little museum of ancient tools and implements.

Directly in front of the old shrine lies the property of St. Luke's. Here stands a charming stone church of the English village type. Just as the library across the green is an echo of the Maidstone one, so this building is a small copy of the Maidstone church. The beautiful bookplate for the library drawn by Mr. George Wharton Edwards—the original drawing is found hanging on the wall of the reading room—shows a view of the Maidstone church tower. The interior of St. Luke's is worth a trip inside and the door stands open. The darkness after the bright sunshine outside is intense at first, but it does not take long to perceive that this little church has been designed with exquisite

SAINT LUKE'S CHURCH

taste. Above all, we notice that all the stained glass is admirable in design and workmanship, a rare thing to be discovered anywhere here or abroad among modern churches.

The first Episcopal church was established here in 1855 with a lay reader whom we shall meet later, Mr. John Wallace, for he was East Hampton's man of mystery. Four years later a spired, red-shingled building was erected as the first St. Luke's of East Hampton, and that was succeeded by the present stone church in 1917. The first Church of England service was held here during the Revolutionary War. Dr. Samuel Buell, pastor of the local Presbyterian congregation, was asked to read the Episcopal burial service over the body of a British officer to be interred in the South End Cemetery. Buell looked the page over as it was handed to him and consented to read it provided he might leave out a word which he said was "tautological." The Englishman who had made the request agreed, and Dr. Buell read the service through, excepting that, when he came to the passage "In the sure and certain hope of the Resurrection," he struck out the tautological "sure," and made it, "In the certain hope of the Resurrection." He had to let these Englishmen know that in their church service whatever they had could be improved by a Scotch Presbyterian.

Out again in the sunshine, we resume our walk a few steps farther, and then enter the Old South Cemetery by a stile. Here the graves stand in irregular rows along the slight eminence that slopes down to the pond. This graveyard was originally a churchyard, for when the settlement began this was the site chosen for the erection of the first church. And the graves are laid so that the dead when they rise may face the light of the Great Day. But their pastor, the Reverend Mr. James, was buried heading in the opposite direction so as to face his congregation when they arose, as he was accustomed to do on Sunday mornings. This seems to have been a not infrequent practice among eighteenth-century divines. His inscription on a brownstone tablet may still be deciphered: "Mr. Thomas James dyed the 16th day of June in the year 1696. He was Ministar of the Gospell and Pasture of the Church of Christ." This gravestone lies near the broken-pillar monument in the Gardiner lot.

At the northern end of the burying ground, where we entered, is a common grave in which twenty-one men are buried: eighteen seamen, the captain and his two mates. These were washed ashore from the wreck of the ship *John Milton* at Montauk Point in February, 1858. A terrible northeast gale struck the vessel as she was trying to double Montauk Point. In the blinding snow the captain evidently lost his bearings. The next morning saw the wreck of the vessel piled up on the rocky shore about five miles west of the lighthouse. As an eyewitness described the scene, when the men of East Hampton finally broke their way through the drifts, "Ship, masts, spars, sails, officers and crew lay in a confused and frozen mass on the bleak beach." It was the opinion of many seafaring men that the disaster was due to the fact that Montauk Light had been changed only a month before from a steady beam to a flash. In the meantime a lighthouse with a steady beam had been set up at Ponquogue, thirty miles to the west. In those days there was no way of notifying mariners already at sea, and the skipper of the *John Milton* probably mistook the Ponquogue light for the Montauk one, and steered directly upon the rocks.

A public funeral was held in East Hampton for the victims. The pastor preached from the text in Job: "Terrors take hold on him as waters; a tempest stealeth him away in the night." After the service in the church a long procession, with carts and farm wagons drawn by young men, conveyed the bodies to their burial in this spot.

Continuing our walk through the cemetery, we will come upon various family lots, containing the remains of the first families of East Hampton, the Mulfords, the Gardiners, the Hedges, etc. The Gardiner lot is easily located by the tall, dark brownstone obelisk which marks the burial place of that David Gardiner who was killed on board the *Princeton* by the explosion of the gun.

Here, hard by, rises a broken pillar, a monument to John Alexander Tyler, eldest son of President John Tyler and Julia Gardiner. The brief story of his life, as given in the inscription, is worth reading. As a boy of sixteen he joined a battalion of Virginia artillery under Robert E. Lee, in 1861, and fought all through the war to Appomattox. Then he went to Germany to study mining engineering. As if four years of war were not enough, he volunteered as an Uhlan in 1870, and when that war was over he received a decoration from the hand of the Emperor William "for gallant and distinguished services." After that he came back to his native land, went out West, became a United States surveyor and inspector of Indian lands, and died, as the epitaph says, "in the full vigor and pride of manhood." The body of this gallant Virginian was brought back here to this little village in Yankee-land for his burial because it was the childhood home of his mother.

The concluding summary of the epitaph suggests what manner of man he was:

With the grace and manly beauty and captivating and polished manners there were united in him a warm and generous nature, a strong and cultivated intellect, a true and loving heart, a fearless and impetuous courage and an integrity of character which no danger could appall and no allurement weaken.

In an age when "everything you can get away with is O.K.," we could well use some more shining gentlemen like John

Alexander Tyler.

Another tomb to a Gardiner is the one to David L., interesting to the archaeologist because it is a copy of the sarcophagus to Scipio Barbatus in Rome, the oldest of the Roman tombs extant. It is appropriate here because there was something of the antique Roman about all these Gardiners. But the most important memorial of them all is the monument to the founder of the family, that doughty soldier and pioneer so aptly named Lion Gardiner. It is unhappily a "canopy" tomb of granite, done in what passed for Gothic style in the eighteen-eighties. Beneath the canopy is a recumbent effigy in armor, intended to represent the gallant old soldier himself. This memorial was designed by no less a personage than James Renwick, the architect of St. Patrick's Cathedral and of Grace Church in New York. Evidently, in honor of the knightly virtues of Lion Gardiner and in recognition of his proprietorship of Gardiner's Island, the architect decided to represent a knight in armor, such as one sees in English cathedrals. But there is a hiatus of two or three hundred years between the head and the feet. The helmet might be of the fourteenth or fifteenth century, and also, perhaps, the body armor and gauntlets, but the boots suggest the seventeenth. At any rate, Lion Gardiner never wore any such armor, unless he sent back to England for his ancestor's suit standing in the hallway and put it on at night to repel the attack of the famous Long Island mosquitoes while he slept. But that hypothesis has no historical foundation. Probably Mr. Renwick had very hazy ideas as to what sort of armor a gentleman wore in 1660, if any. Partridge's statue at Old Saybrook shows what the costume should have been, but here poor Lion Gardiner is represented as an anachronism in granite.

This monument was erected in 1886. Before that date the old

hero lay in a very modest tomb with a railing of cedar around it. There was even some doubt as to whether this was actually his burial place. To make sure, the grave was opened, and the skeleton was found in perfect condition after two hundred and twenty-three years. A physician who was present said that it belonged to a man who must have been six feet two inches in height.

On this occasion it was discovered that Lion Gardiner was buried, like his friend Parson James, with his head to the east. Unfortunately the men who set up this memorial placed it the wrong way, so that the head of the effigy now lies over the bones of the old warrior's feet. Curiously enough, one of the men who assisted in the excavation was a Montauk Indian named Wyandanch, a descendant of the Indian chief of the same name whom Gardiner had befriended.

The epitaph that runs all around the sides of this tomb is spelled in the style which is supposed to be appropriate to the seventeenth century, with "ye" for "the" and silent "e's" tucked on as many words as possible. However, it is worth noting that this is probably the only recumbent effigy of a knight in America.

Next to Lion Gardiner's memorial lies a very modest stone to his Dutch wife, Mary Willemsen Deurcant, who shared all his hardships and perils in the wilderness but received very little glory in life or death, as is the way of this thankless world.

Near by lie the graves of two of the former wives of John Gardiner, the "Third Lord of Ye Isle of Wight," whose bones, as already noted, rest in New London. It was this gentleman who had to play host to Captain Kidd. And so we may prowl around this graveyard and decipher other ancient or modern headstones *ad libitum*. Or we may stroll down to the honeysuckle-covered fence that separates the burial ground from the Green and look out over the placid surface of the pond reflecting the shadows of overhanging trees on all sides. This was the pool in which poor "Goody" Garlich was ducked—and nearly drowned—for witchcraft, before she was rescued by Lion Gardiner.

There's another ducking story connected with this "duck pond," too. A certain Ebenezer Dayton, who had been a privateer of questionable sorts during the Revolution, having been robbed by the Tories of all the booty he had collected, started out after the war to recoup his fortunes as a peddler. On a Saturday evening he arrived in East Hampton with his pack, ready to do business the following Monday. But he came bearing on his face the unmistakable pink evidences of measles, and the following day his landlady begged him to stay indoors. However, in those days, going to church was the simplest and easiest way of advertising to the whole community that he had arrived with his wares, so he insisted on attending Divine Service, measly rash and all.

When his condition was observed, there was so much wrath in the congregation that he decided that it would be wiser to depart, and not stand upon the order of his going. But some young men overtook him as he fled, rode him on a rail back to the village and ducked him in this same pond. Despite this treatment the peddler recovered, but he gave the measles to a hundred people, old and young, several of whom died, and from East Hampton the epidemic spread over the rest of eastern Long Island.

Nothing daunted by what he had done, Ebenezer sued the informal posse of youths for his ducking. He hired a young lawyer, not famous then but destined for some notoriety in after

DOORWAY OF DOMINY HOUSE

EAST HAMPTON

years, a certain Mr. Aaron Burr. And so ably did this legal gentleman handle the case that Ebenezer won his suit and an award of one thousand dollars, a fortune in those days.

The duck pond has brought us back to where we started our

AFTER THE HURRICANE

morning's walk, which has been on both sides of one village street. There are other pleasant streets and lanes to be discovered and explored, running east and west from this. A short drive south and east will bring us to the bathing beach, the golf links, the Maidstone Club house and the handsome shore estates of the modern part of East Hampton. But all these wisely keep their places as twentieth-century features, and do not intrude. It is the old-village aspect that gives the place its unique charm and makes it unforgettable. We have tarried for a whole chapter sauntering along a single street. Our next stroll must be down that other quiet lane of its long and honorable past.

POSTSCRIPT. The foregoing description of East Hampton was written in the summer of 1938. A few weeks afterwards the tropical hurricane of September 21 fell upon the village, and while the loss of life was fortunately small, the devastation wreaked upon the trees was heartbreaking. The broad Main Street became an impassable mass of tangled trunks and branches. Of those magnificent elms which made that street so beautiful probably seven of every ten crashed. A few were hoisted back in place in the hope that their roots had not been injured beyond recovery, but most of them were done for. So great was the mass of wreckage that, even after four weeks, some of the estates on the street still looked as if they had been in the line of barrage fire.

But there is no necessity of altering the description as written on a day when those elms were in their glory. Although dismayed at their loss, the citizens of East Hampton began immediately not only to clear away the wreckage but to replace the fallen trees with new ones as large as could be obtained. Nature comes to the rescue after such a disaster, and the newcomers to East Hampton will still find it has arresting beauty, even though the noblest trees are gone. The description and the accompanying sketches that were made before the hurricane shall stand, if for no other reason than as a memorial to the village as it looked before the catastrophe, and as it doubtless will look again.

CHAPTER VII

OLD TIMES AND OLD-TIMERS OF EAST HAMPTON

IN the introduction to this record of exploration the reader was presented to the Tile Club who, sixty years ago, made an excursion to Long Island for the compelling reason that "nobody goes there." In the course of their wanderings they came to East Hampton. Already the village was becoming known as a summer resort. Only a few years before, Mr. Bunce and Mr. Fenn had written and sketched here for that *Picturesque America* whose trail we have come across more than once already. The former wrote that the town "consists of one wide street, nearly three hundred feet wide [a slight exaggeration]. There are no hotels, no shops, no manufactories. . . . It is rapidly becoming a favorite place of summer resort, visitors at present finding no accommodation save that offered by private families; but," he adds mournfully, "its growing popularity makes the erection of hotels almost certain, and then goodbye to its oldfashioned simplicity." Mr. Bunce had just seen with dismay the new hotel on Shelter Island, and the trippers it had attracted from New York.

But when the Tilers came trooping in they found the "old-fashioned simplicity" still flourishing. "The town," wrote their scribe, "consisted of a single street and the street was a lawn. An immense tapis vert of rich grass, green with June, and set with tapering poplar trees, bordered on either side its broad expanse by ancestral cottages, shingled to the ground with 'shakes' —the primitive split shingles of antiquity. . . . Not the Warwickshire landscape," he adds with an artist's appreciation, "not that enchanted stretch from Stratford to Shottery, which was Shakespeare's lovers' walk, is more pastorally lovely."

The chief difference between the East Hampton of sixty years ago and now lay in the rows of Lombardy poplars lined up like a regiment on each side of the street. Between these grew the young elms which, in their maturity, were the glory of the twentieth-century village. A greensward extended from one sidewalk to another, through which ran the ruts made by the occasional farmer's cart or the carriage of the summer boarder. In that day there was none of that perfect trim to the lawns, the Green and the picket fences which greets the eye today, for Village Improvement Associations and Garden Clubs were unheard of then. The grass grew rank beside the pond and tall weeds lined the walks and fences. But at that the Tilers could not remember seeing such a village street even in England.

Naturally they sketched here with great zeal, not only along the street but also on the beach. The musicians (honorary members) loafed about and posed for their friends as quaint natives and old salts, whenever such figures were needed. The Tilers called at the old Nelson House, then known as the birthplace of Payne. They spent their first evening with the reigning head of the Mulford clan in the Mulford House, and found him "a fine, obsolete gentleman with a becoming and handsome sense of personal and family dignity sitting on him." And most interesting of all, they met a charming old lady, who had been "my little Rosalie" and "my little Sweetheart" to John Howard Payne. He was old enough to be her father, but he cherished a sentimental memory of her as a pretty child in East Hampton. He wrote her many letters, some of which the old lady read to the young artists. She spoke of her own memories of him and

OLD TIMES AND OLD-TIMERS OF EAST HAMPTON

of how much, despite his fame, he suffered from poverty. "Mr. Payne used to say," she added, "that he employed more intrigue to conceal his poverty than all the diplomacy used at Washington."

At first they had been inclined to scoff at the Payne legend, but after the visit with "Rosalie" they returned to their lodging in a reverent mood. They found that there was a good piano available in the parlor. The violinists tuned up their strings, and the "Barytone" (David Bispham) stood up to sing. There, that still June evening, to the accompaniment of piano and violins, he sang all the stanzas of "Home, Sweet Home," his superb voice warm with the emotion of the place and its memories. The club members declared afterwards that they had never heard Bispham sing so magnificently, and that they never realized all that lay in those words until then. Perhaps it has never been sung so well before or since.

It was probably through these members of the Tile Club and their articles in *Scribner's Magazine* that word spread abroad regarding the artistic attractions of East Hampton, for within five years of their visit the village was being written up as the "American Barbizon." Mr. Thomas Moran made his home here, and when he wasn't painting Rocky Mountains and Grand Canyons he devoted his brush to the more intimate scenes that lay just outside his East Hampton studio. Summer art classes flocked here, especially a large group of ladies of the newly formed Art Students' League of New York. But they did not paint in smocks and slacks. They were still ladies, though art students, and contemporary pictures show them at work in tight corsets, trailing skirts, and bustles. For a while the place became something of a fad. *Harper's Magazine* published a serial, entitled *A Romance of East Hampton,* in which the young hero—"Captain Forsyth of the Royal (late Bengal) Engineers"—wore a full beard prettily parted in the middle.

But for some reason the American Barbizon did not last. These summer art colonies suffer much from infant mortality anyhow; and when Mr. William M. Chase, another one of those Tilers, started his summer art school near by in the Shinnecock Hills, the art students migrated thither. Thereafter the village children could once more sit on the grassy bank of the pond without getting vermilions, ultramarines and cadmiums on their panties.

The appearance of East Hampton when the Tile Club arrived was probably little different than it was when Mr. John Tyler came riding in on his horse to pay his respects to Miss Julia Gardiner some thirty-five years before. At that time, however, it was more than a farming and fishing town. It was the heyday of deep-sea whaling and boys left the village to ship on board whalers at Sag Harbor in high hopes of a "greasy voyage." Many an East Hampton boy forsook his books and the ancestral plow as soon as he could to sign up for a whaling cruise, for the average earnings, even for the "lay" of a foremast hand, were much better than those of a farm worker.

One of the Mulford boys, for example, followed the path of the sea instead of the furrow, not entirely to the liking of his parents. In the East Hampton library are preserved some letters that passed between young Harry Mulford and his father, dated "North American State of New York," 1831. One letter expressed the wish that Harry would come home and help his father on the farm now that he was getting along in years; it gave him good advice, prayed God to protect him, and was signed, "Your affectionate father, Jonathan Mulford." A letter from this same Harry in 1836, written off the coast of Brazil, suggests that the boy might have tarried to advantage in school before listening to the call of the sea, for he writes, "I havent hurd a thing from hum . . . i shod be glad to receve a letter from sum of you." . . . There is a photograph of Harry Mulford, taken in his old age, standing by the fence of his East Hampton home, which is the "Home, Sweet Home house" of today. In his latter days, fearing that the matter would not be properly attended to after his death, Mr. Mulford purchased his own tombstone and had the inscription made thereon, excepting only the date for his demise.

But deep-sea whaling was on its last legs a full decade before the Civil War, and that phase of profit and adventure faded out. Before the days of deep-sea whaling, offshore whaling had been a great source of income to the inhabitants of these eastern Long Island communities. The business goes back to very early Colonial days, for the Indian taught the white man how to hunt and kill the whale and cut him up for profit. East Hamptonians are still complacent over the fact that in 1672 the Nantucketers sent an offer to hire one James Loper to come and teach them the art of "whale-citching." By that time offshore whaling on Long Island had been a recognized business for twenty years. It seems that Mr. Loper declined the offer, for he had just married Elizabeth Howell, granddaughter of Lion Gardiner, and she would not leave East Hampton for Nantucket.

Whaling was very profitable but a messy and smelly business. The oil would be "tried out" on shore and a favoring wind would carry the fumes into the doors and windows of every house within miles. Even the Long Island mosquito quailed before it. And the young men of Amagansett, Bridgehampton, East Hampton, towns famous for their offshore whaling, would come ashore, frequently splashed all over with the blood of their victim. Then it was *de rigeur* to wear the bloody clothes about town for the girls to see, because this was the red badge of courage which bowled the ladies over.

Today, any kind of whale is almost as scarce as the sea serpent. The Norwegians now hunt them down in far-off waters with steamships and harpoons shot from a cannon. By an odd chance a right whale was actually taken off East Hampton on February 22, 1907, but that was a curiosity. The Natural History Museum of New York City desired it as a specimen to exhibit, but nobody knew just what to do with it. It was a huge mass of flesh getting more obnoxious every minute. But a young man named Roy Chapman Andrews tackled the job without any experience whatever, and after infinite trouble succeeded in mounting it with perfect success. It still hangs from the ceiling of the Museum for all to see, a monument to a young man's toil. It may also serve as a memorial to that adventurous industry which for two hundred years meant so much to the lives and fortunes of the men of Nantucket and the coastal towns of New England and New York, but which is now as completely dead as the poor old whale himself.

Between the date of the founding of East Hampton, 1649, and the present year of grace, the history of the village is not a matter of events but of men and women. In the era of the Revolutionary War the outstanding figure was the pastor of the church, that Reverend Samuel Buell who struck out a "tautological" adjective in the Church of England burial service, as noted in the previous chapter. When the British came hither with ships and troops, he found himself in a dilemma. He was an ardent rebel, but instead of fleeing to Connecticut, as so many did, he conceived it to be his duty to stay in East Hampton to do what he could to soften the rigors of war for his flock. So he remained

Hook Mill

OLD TIMES AND OLD-TIMERS OF EAST HAMPTON

and established friendly relations with the enemy officers by going on hunting expeditions with them. By this means he was able to intercede for the village people with considerable success, though he made no secret of his patriotic sentiments, and once told a British officer to his face that he was "the devil incarnate." But Dr. Buell created such pleasant relations between the British admiral Arbuthnot, whose squadron lay in Gardiner's Bay, and the citizens of East Hampton that Arbuthnot gave a dinner to them on board the flagship *Royal Oak*. And Dr. Buell responded to the occasion by reading a poem entitled "The Royal Oak." This, in particular, roused the indignation of the Long Island patriots in exile on the Connecticut shore, and after the war the reverend gentleman was branded as a Tory, much to his grief and wrath. But this did not in any way alienate his congregation from him and he continued to serve his people until his death.

Among his good works was his share in the founding of Clinton Academy. He conducted the opening of that temple of learning, in January, 1785, with an impressive program. He himself led off with "psalms, prayer, and sermon." Then, to quote a contemporary, "Mrs. Fanny Rysam, with more than usual elegance, pronounced the 'Messiah' by Mr. Pope, and was succeeded by Mr. John Gardiner [a youth evidently] who with a dignity and eloquence superior to his age pronounced the following oration." . . . And this was pretty long, too.

But the old gentleman must have been a man of rare force of character combined with goodness of heart. Even now, after one hundred and fifty years, Dr. Buell's name is still green in East Hampton.

East Hampton's most famous son, however, was John Howard Payne, born here in 1791. He started out in life as a romantic actor, and had a record of considerable success in the principal cities of America, from Boston to Charleston. In the former city he once acted in a benefit performance with and for an actress, Mrs. Poe, who had a ten weeks' infant at the time, named Edgar, who later became famous on his own account.

In January, 1813, friends of Payne raised a fund of two thousand dollars to give him a year's stay in Europe; but his introduction to England was a two weeks' imprisonment in a Liverpool jail. This was because Great Britain and the United States were then at war. However, the following June he was able to appear on the English stage in the romantic part of Norval in the tragedy *Douglas*. Later he played Romeo and Hamlet. He acted in Ireland, made a visit to France and Italy, returned to England and, in 1818, made his last appearance there as an actor. Thereafter he turned to playwriting. But this proved to be a weak support to lean on, and the year 1821 found Payne languishing in a debtors' prison. A break of luck enabled him to get free and he returned to Paris. There he rented a small apartment in the Palais Royal, which he shared for a time with Washington Irving, and wrote a number of plays. One of these was *Clari, or the Maid of Milan*, a play with songs, in which the famous Mr. Kemble was expected to act.

This unusual name was taken from that of a girl cousin, Clare Isaacs, who was about his own age and with whom he had been a constant playmate in East Hampton. The child had died at the age of eight, and he had always enshrined her in a special corner of his memory. For this play, with the title so suggestive of childhood days in East Hampton, he wrote the song, "Home, Sweet Home."

He told a friend afterwards that the form of the stanzas was suggested by the music. While in Italy he had heard a peasant girl sing the melody. He asked her to sing it over again for him and jotted down the notes. When he sent his song to his music collaborator, Bishop, in London, he was delighted to learn that Bishop knew the air himself and had no difficulty in fitting it to the words. Bishop suggested a few changes in the lines, which Payne accepted, and which, in fact, were improvements. On May 8, 1823, *Clari* was given its opening performance at the Theatre Royal, Covent Garden. From the first the song was a hit, and though *Clari* is occasionally revived still, this "incidental" ballad is the only part of that play which has survived in popular memory. Needless to say, the song swept the English-speaking world. Even to our sophisticated age the language and figures of speech so typical of the Romantic Era have not banished it from popularity. It stands fast, together with Burns' "Auld Lang Syne," for those occasions when we do not feel ashamed of being sentimental.

In 1832 Payne returned to America after nearly twenty years in Europe. He tried this and that, had "benefits," but the money slipped away. In 1842 he was enabled to obtain from President Tyler the post of consul at Tunis. Perhaps Mr. Tyler was glad to help a fellow townsman of his wife, as well as the author of the famous song. So away the actor-playwright-poet sailed for Africa, this time as an amateur diplomat. Mr. Colt, the famous pistol manufacturer, gave him a gold-mounted sword to wear with his full-dress costume. This is among the relics to be seen now in Home, Sweet Home.

At any rate, in his new post he made such an impression on the Bey of Tunis that the latter caused "a huge new palace" to be built for him, one that was "finer than his own," so people declared. It was said that Payne could fling a cape over his shoulder and tap the hilt of that gold-mounted sword with the manner of D'Artagnan. He was always the actor, and his dramatic gestures and speech deeply impressed the Moorish potentate.

In 1852 Payne died, and his body lay buried in the little English cemetery there in Tunis for thirty years. The English residents put a memorial window to him in their church, and English tourists used to go to his grave under the impression that he was an Englishman. In 1883 his body was brought back to his native land, but not to the Old South Graveyard in East Hampton. He was reinterred in the Oak Hill Cemetery in Washington, as one who belonged to the whole nation.

Handsome, emotional, generous and impractical, he was always in debt until middle life, when the Government gave him a regular income and a sinecure. He was probably annoyed at the necessity of writing occasional statistical reports to Washington, but though he was a long way from East Hampton and all his old friends he doubtless enjoyed the satisfaction of being the central figure of a great Moorish palace, with a retinue of turbaned servants bowing to the floor, and of being known all over Tunis as a close friend of the Bey himself. " 'Mid pleasures and palaces"—well, it was not half bad for a man with a romantic temperament, and though an "exile from home," perhaps he rather fancied the "splendour" that "dazzles in vain." When his remains were buried in Oak Hill Cemetery, the coffin was followed to its final resting place by a cortege of notables, officers of the army and navy, members of Congress and President Arthur himself. Payne would have liked that, too. It was a good curtain for his last act.

When Dr. Buell rested from his labors his place as pastor of the Presbyterian church was taken by a young minister named Lyman Beecher, only twenty-four years old. Later he was said

OLD TIMES AND OLD-TIMERS OF EAST HAMPTON

to be the "father of more brains than any other man in America." Five of his lively and precocious offspring were born here in East Hampton. Then when the Lord continued to send additions to the family but no additions to his pay, Beecher moved from East Hampton to Litchfield, Connecticut. The trustees of his church felt that four hundred dollars was a plenty for any preacher.

What shifts the pastor's wife was put to in order to feed and clothe her expanding family can well be imagined. From memoirs written by men and women who could remember what a day's schedule was like during the first half of the nineteenth century, we can get a picture of a woman's life at that time. It was not only cooking, baking, washing, sweeping, scrubbing and mending, but spinning and weaving, curing meats, putting up preserves, preparing family remedies, homemade wines and, worst of all, the making of tallow candles and of soft soap. When the housewife found time to sleep is not clear. Every year, as a rule, she would have to lay aside her work for a brief recess to have a baby, or perhaps twins. That was her only vacation. Then when she got up again, always too soon, she had to try to catch up on the spinning, weaving, candles and soap. No wonder these wives and mothers lay down early in the churchyard, the only place where they could be sure of a good rest. In the Sag Harbor cemetery is a lot where a man lies with five consorts parked around him. Evidently he outlived them all, for the inscription on his headstone starts off with:

> Stranger, perceive as you pass by
> How thick the partners of one husband lie.

Lyman Beecher himself had three partners of his bed and board and they bore him thirteen children.

The first Mrs. Beecher had a yearning for the aesthetic which could not be quenched by howling infants and tubs of candle grease. At the beginning of the century there were no carpets in East Hampton. Sanded floors were the rule. Mrs. Beecher determined that she would have a carpet. Accordingly she bought a bale of cotton at a "vendue," spun and had it woven and stretched the fabric out on the attic floor. By the next schooner to New York she sent for crude colors which she ground and mixed with oil. Then she painted gigantic roses in the middle and a pattern on the borders. Finally the work of art was spread on the parlor floor.

The first caller was Deacon Talmage, who paused at the threshold in wonder.

"Come in, Deacon," said Beecher.

"Can't, 'thout steppin' on it."

"That's what it's for," said the proud possessor.

The Deacon then picked his way delicately across the masterpiece, his eyes fascinated by the pink roses. At last, turning to Beecher, he said reprovingly, "D'ye think ye can have all that and Heaven too?" In Harriet Beecher Stowe's reminiscences she says that her earliest memory is of those roses in that carpet.

It is hard to believe that this same indomitable Mrs. Beecher found time to start a boarding school for girls besides, and taught them all the elegant accomplishments, especially painting and embroidery. No wonder she died young.

There was another Beecher born in East Hampton not nearly so famous as her sister Harriet or her brother Henry Ward, but a very considerable person in her day, and that was Catherine. All the Beechers projected righteousness; some exuded it gently and sweetly, through every pore, like Henry. He did this so well that he packed his church to the doors every Sunday.

Others bristled it like the fretful porcupine; the females tended to do it that way, and the most bristly of all was Catherine, the eldest of the Beecher children. In an era of strong-minded women she dared more than any other of her grenadier sisterhood, for she dared to differ even from them. A photograph of her in her last decade shows a bespectacled eye and a mouth and jaw that would make a top sergeant of marines quake in his boots.

When she was nineteen she became engaged to a young professor, Alexander Metcalf Fisher of Yale. He, poor fellow, was lost at sea. Since he had not been properly "converted," according to her father's theology her lover had gone straight to hell from his watery grave, there eternally to dwell "in adamantine chains and penal fire." Very well, then, argued Catherine, if that's what it says, to hell with such a theology; only, of course, she was too much of a lady to use such an expression. So she became the one heretic of the Beecher family; in fact, she eventually joined the Episcopal Church. Yet for all her independence as a feminist she didn't think much of votes for women; and, though she opposed slavery, she disliked the Abolitionists as troublemaking fanatics.

Her chief idea was that the prevailing education for girls was contemptible trash. I am afraid she didn't think much of the curriculum of her mother's female seminary in East Hampton. But it would be edifying to hear her opinion of a modern "finishing school." At twenty-two, after her lover's death, she started a girls' school according to her own ideas in Hartford, and another one, ten years later, in Cincinnati. And while running her schools she wrote books, ten or a dozen in all. These were most edifying. Modern housewives should certainly read *Miss Beecher's Domestic Receipt Book Designed as a Supplement to*

Her Treatise on Domestic Economy. That ran into three editions. On page 240 she discusses the problem of the male at a dinner party:

When men become so refined and cultivated that they can supply wit and good sense instead of the overflows induced by the excitement of wine, diluted by the stupidity resulting from excess in eating, a housekeeper will find the giving of a dinner party a very different matter from what it ordinarily is found to be. . . .

Catherine must have had some dull dinner partners. "All the wit and brilliancy obtained," she adds with a vinegarish touch, "is the simple product of *vinous fermentation.*" After Alexander Fisher's death she seems to have had very little use for persons of the male gender outside her own family.

Chapter XXXII of this work is entitled "Words of Comfort for a Discouraged Housekeeper," which ought to find a responsive echo in these days. And there is also a chapter for "Domestics," in which the author tells them to be sure to read the Bible daily and keep the Sabbath Day holy. How the poor creatures could do that, with a huge Sunday dinner to cook and clear away, Catherine does not explain.

So she wrote her books, bristling with sharp but lofty opinions, and loaded to the gunwales with pious advice; all were once very popular but have long since been forgotten. Today nobody even remembers that there was a Catherine Beecher.

A month before the Tile Club came gaily into East Hampton, wearing wide, farmer straw hats, laughing and singing, and wisecracking, as we should call it now, Catherine died, full of years and righteous works, and with a Five-Foot Shelf of books to her credit. She probably would not have approved of these

SOUTH CEMETERY AND THE MILL

young painters and their musician friends. They were not dignified, they didn't attend any church while in East Hampton. Further, they delighted in frivolous jesting, which the Apostle Paul distinctly told the Ephesians was "not convenient," and which she would have darkly suspected was the simple product of vinous fermentation. Yet there's another verse in Proverbs which the Tile Club might have flung back at her, "A merry heart doeth good like medicine"; but the boys would probably have been too rusty in their Sacred Studies for that, and they would certainly have been scared to death of her. Catherine Beecher was representative of a Victorian type of woman as extinct now as a dinosaur, but once a great influence. Perhaps it is just as well that Providence cut off Alexander Fisher in the bloom of his youth. It would have been impossible for any man to live up to Catherine Beecher.

One more character of East Hampton must be noted before this little procession of old-timers is brought to an end. This is the Mystery Man, the Unknown, the "Man in the Iron Mask" of East Hampton.

In 1840 a stranger, attended by a servant, arrived in the village and put up at the tavern. He was evidently a gentleman of means and culture, and he spoke with a Scottish burr. He gave his name as John Wallace, and would gratify the curiosity of Hamptonians no further. After five years at the inn he found a welcome in the home of some warm friends, the Huntingtons, and lived with them for twenty-five years or more, in the house still to be seen four doors south from the Presbyterian church. His Scotch servingman left him to go West.

Nor were the Huntingtons his only friends by any means. His generosity, kindliness, courtesy won him everybody's affection. And what a wealth of Old World contacts he brought into this Long Island hamlet! He had been a friend of Jeffrey, editor of the *Edinburgh Review*. He had known the famous writers of Scotland and England. What a treat on a winter's evening to sit with him before the fire and start him talking!

Every now and then, through a labyrinth of banks, a letter would come to him. He explained that these came "from my lady friend in Edinburgh." Books and magazines—money, plenty of it—came through the same roundabout route. The inevitable gossips of East Hampton were eaten up with curiosity, but they could not break through by either force or guile. Some said that John Wallace was a bishop gone wrong, or a titled criminal fleeing for his life, and so on. But he was so devout, so noble in his life it was impossible to believe evil of him. He was a giver of both money and time. Boys eager to be prepared for Yale and backward with their Latin would come to him to learn. Books were rare in the village and Mr. Wallace was generous in lending his large supply. At first he used to make the trip to Sag Harbor every Sunday in order to reach an Episcopal service. Later he was the prime mover for the erection of the Episcopal church in East Hampton and the largest contributor. He became its first lay reader, and may well be called the father of St. Luke's. For more than thirty years he walked the village streets, living a blameless life and beloved by all. He seemed perfectly content to stay in East Hampton, and when he died, on the last day of the year 1870, he was buried in the South cemetery, where a plain marble slab may still be seen with the name he bore, "John Wallace."

The friends with whom he had made his home for a quarter of a century felt that some word about his death should be sent to the one person who had kept in touch with him all these years. Accordingly they addressed a letter to "Mr. Wallace's

OLD TIMES AND OLD-TIMERS OF EAST HAMPTON

Lady Friend, Edinburgh," and sent it back through the chain of banks. After a long time a brief reply came back, very cold and formal, signed "Mr. Wallace's Lady Friend."

Years afterwards persistent search revealed the fact that "John Wallace" had once been High Sheriff of a Scottish county and lived in Edinburgh. He was a bachelor of fifty and high in the regard of his fellow citizens for his good works, being tendered once a public testimonial for his philanthropy. Suddenly he was accused of a grave and mysterious crime. The Lord High Advocate passed on to a mutual friend the tip that next morning a warrant would be made out for his arrest. That night he fled the country, attended by one servant. He told his friend that he was innocent of anything worse than an indiscretion, but he could not face the disgrace of a trial. And so, in search of a new life, peace, and security, he found his way somehow to East Hampton. Probably he could not have discovered anywhere a spot better adapted to his needs than this Long Island hamlet. At any rate, save for his Sunday trips to Sag Harbor, he seems never to have wanted to leave. Here he found no brilliant society of wits and statesmen like the one he had left behind in Edinburgh, but he did meet with friendship, understanding and respect for his secret. He grew old contentedly, satisfied that his final bed should be made for him in the South burying ground. East Hampton had proved for him not only a refuge but a home. To this day his real name has never been divulged.

These were some of the old-timers of East Hampton. But we should not omit at least a mention of certain distinguished figures of a later generation who came here to make their homes, at least as summer residents. The name of Thomas Moran, the landscape painter, has already been noted in connection with East Hampton. He came here first as a member of that Tile Club excursion. He lived and worked here, and is buried in that graveyard on the village green. Another famous artist, both of the brush and the etcher's needle, who made his home in East Hampton was the late Childe Hassam. John Drew, the foremost figure of the American stage in his day, was a resident here; and, as said before, the beautiful theater in the Guild Hall was dedicated to his memory. In one of the older houses lived Percy Hammond, the dramatic critic. Ring Lardner, the humorist and master of the short story, had a house on the dunes overlooking the ocean. Many another artist or writer might be mentioned, and the list could be extended to the present-day journalists, poets, illustrators and painters, to whom East Hampton holds the same charm that it had for those young men of genius, the members of the Tile Club, when they made their memorable visit here six decades ago.

In leaving this tranquil spot we may turn once more to the words of Payne himself. He used to refer affectionately to East Hampton as the "goose heaven," because of the flocks of geese that waddled along the streets and splashed in the pond. There were still plenty of them left for the Tile Club to laugh at when they came half a century later. But in the *Democratic Review* of February, 1838, he has these words to say of his birthplace: "Many an eye wearied with the glare of foreign grandeur will, ere long, lull itself to repose in the quiet beauty of this village." A century afterwards, "quiet beauty" is still the phrase to express the charm of East Hampton.

CHAPTER VIII

MONTAUK

AMONG the many pleasant features about a sojourn in East Hampton are the varied and delightful drives of exploration that one can take. The folders of the hotels inform the visitor about the facilities for golf, surf bathing and fishing, but neglect to tell him that he can have a good time poking into the back country along the small blue lines of his road map. For instance, it is a delightful run of only five or six miles out to Fireplace, where we can get the closest view from land of Gardiner's Island. Here is that beach where for many years the big bonfires were built to call the boatmen from the island shore. And we can return, by taking some crosscuts, via Three-Mile Harbor Road, for the sake of a look at that body of water where once the boats of a British fleet came ashore for supplies during a year of the Revolution. All this region is now more empty of life and habitation and shipping than it was when Admiral Arbuthnot first clapped eyes on these shores. Farms that once were being cultivated, like Hardscrabble and Toilsome, have long since sunk back to jungle. Even the villages have "gone native." Hereabouts is the site of the deserted hamlet of Northwest. Nothing remains now but its cemetery and the roadway once leading there, still called the "Old Northwest Road." Other villages indicated on the map, like Kingstown, Springs, Barnes' Hole—it's impossible to avoid the lure of that name—have a very low visibility.

If you turn your car in a southwesterly direction, toward

Wainscott or Apaquogue, you come upon the very modern summer colonies. Divinity Hill, for example, won its name because of the many summer homes of clergymen from New York. Here, they say, the reverend gentlemen relaxed; they stayed away from church on Sundays and said "damn" all they wanted to, and went back greatly invigorated to their pulpits.

Speaking of names, what could be more enchanting than "Promised Land," lying to the east, not far from "Lazy Point"? The road map shows a dot for the former place, and the traveler expects to see, perhaps, another East Hampton, all elms, hollyhocks, salt-box houses, gardens and white picket fences basking on the shore of Gardiner's Bay. Alas, there is nothing to see in Promised Land but the last remaining menhaden fertilizer factory. Once an Alsatian pianist, being without visible means of support in his native land, came to America. He expected that instantly a recital would be arranged for him in Carnegie Hall, that rich old ladies would stuff his pockets with hundred-dollar bills and young heiresses make proposals of marriage. And when all this did not happen at once he concluded that America was a dull, money-grabbing country with no feeling for Art, after the time-honored fashion of our foreign, nonpaying guests. So he sat, brooding morosely, on a bench in the Battery, having slept there the night before, and being exceedingly hungry. But his eye caught a poster, advertising that men were wanted for work at "Promised Land." This pianist knew enough English to appreciate the significance of that name. What could be lovelier? So he signed up and was sent with the gang, only to be landed at this fertilizer factory, where for a considerable space of time his five finger exercises were with fish scales only.

We have already run across the menhaden industry as it used to flourish at and around Shelter Island. This present use of the fish for fertilizer is the oldest of all, for the Indians taught the settlers to bury two menhaden on each side of every sprouting corn hill. But even the tough-skinned pioneers who could call the fragrance of whale-oil fumes "a good healthy smell" just couldn't stomach the whiff from cartloads of all-too-mellow menhaden, and they abandoned the custom. On my visit to this fertilizer factory in Promised Land, however, I caught no smells whatever—perhaps the business has become refined—and the workers therein most courteously gave a drink to my thirsty radiator.

The countryside hereabouts also does not live up to its poetic names. There is another place, called "Devon," which contains the pleasant golf course of the East Hampton Club, but do not expect it to remind you of Devonshire. In all this area the land lies flat and rather drab, except where we catch glimpses of blue water. Farther east, for a mile or two on a sandy road treated with oil, the route leads on to a place with a still more attractive name on the road map, Lazy Point. Here a nubble of land sticks out into the water with Cherry Point on the west and Lazy Point on the east.

As we came upon this region there was nothing to be seen except a row of fishermen's shacks along the low bank that overhangs the beach. These were slapped together with all kinds of material, after the fashion of this school of architecture, with a liberal application of tar paper. Here and there a stray dory lay high and dry upon the sand, and boards, oars and lobster pots rested in a jumble amid bayberry bushes. Over all hung stillness. "Fishin' don't pay no more," is the cry, for nowadays, they say, the middleman, who never saw a net or a dory, gets all the profits. So Lazy Point was living splendidly up to its name. Not a soul was stirring, not a curl of smoke from a stovepipe or chimney gave a sign of life. The only person at work, as the eye swept the horizon, was Mr. James Preston, the illustrator, who had come with me from East Hampton, and who, in beret and Byronic collar, was busily sketching the fishermen's huts. As Longfellow says in the "Village Blacksmith,"

> Thanks, thanks to thee, my worthy friend,
>   For the lesson thou hast taught!
> 'Tis only artists who work for the love of it,
>   And they don't get paid as they ought.

The last two lines may not be quite accurate as quoted, but the fact stated is beyond dispute.

The finest excursion from East Hampton, however, is to Montauk Point. The best way is to start off in the dewy morn, planning to make a day of it, and not return until the dewy eve. Today an elegant state boulevard takes the motorist in luxury directly to the State Park at the tip end of the Island. In the old days it was no such easy jaunt. There are photographs still to be seen of the narrow, sandy, rutted avenue of agony that used to be known as the road to Montauk. Bone-breaking carts and carriages made the journey, crawling and lurching inch by inch, like tortoises crossing a plowed field. In the "Hither Woods" the passenger had to stoop to prevent the branches from sweeping his hat off, and all the way, in summer months, he would be pursued by swarms of man-eating mosquitoes. That long strip on the map, Napeague Beach, was particularly famous for them. But men and women made the journey in those days, nevertheless. A certain Mr. Charles Parsons, a mere "city feller" from New York, with two friends tramped the whole length of Napeague Beach to Montauk Point in the year 1870 and came back the same way, writing up his experi-

Montauk Point, Winter

MONTAUK

ence for *Harper's Magazine*. Anybody who knows what it is to hike through miles of sand will salute him. Fortunately for him, he made the trip in October, when the mosquitoes had retired for the season, and he was able to do it in two days.

He took four days for his round trip, but, much as we may be

FISHERMAN'S SHACK, LAZY POINT

tempted to emulate his noble example, we intend to get back to East Hampton for dinner the same day. So off we turn our car on Route 27. This has its half-mile moment of beatitude and ecstasy as the Main Street of East Hampton, and then it just becomes the same old state highway. But it does pass through another ancient village, Amagansett. Although she looks like a less beautiful sister of East Hampton now, she once vied with her in the whaling business, and also in the lucrative matter of wrecking. This doesn't mean that the people here actually lured ships to their doom by false lights, as in more iniquitous parts of the world—far from it. But if the Lord wrecked a ship on their beach, especially one with a goodly cargo, who were they to shun their blessings? Every man, woman and child welcomed a wreck as a dispensation from Heaven.

The custom was to mark a piece of castaway stuff with one's initials and then run home for a horse and cart. Even a stray spar was saved and taken to the village. Once a large consignment of calico came ashore, all of the same pattern. Shortly after, the females of this part of the Island blossomed forth in dresses of the identical material. And another time a cargo of children's copper-toed boots and shoes came to rest on the sands of Amagansett. After they were sorted for sizes, all the youngsters suddenly appeared in them, until they became known as "wreck shoes," and other children would jeer at the wearers.

In December, 1922, the *Madonna V* went aground near Montauk with a cargo of choice liquors. The year was, needless to say, in the era of prohibition, but needless also to say, all hands from the villages worked mightily to save that cargo.

As for the whales, how plentiful they used to be two hundred years ago may be suggested by the fact that a woman traveling between East Hampton and Bridgehampton in the year 1700 once counted thirteen whales that were stranded on the beach.

Although there are some fine old houses in Amagansett to be seen from the principal street (which is Route 27) one should switch off toward the sea and make the small jog that can be seen on the road map for a glimpse of the dunes and the shore. There is a poet who makes his home in East Hampton, Mr. John Hall Wheelock, and some of his finest poems were inspired by the seashore here. Here is a bit from "Noon, Amagansett Beach":

MONTAUK

Loneliness—loneliness forever. Dune beyond dune,
Stretches the infinite loneliness—pale sand and pale sea grass,
Pale beaches, mile upon mile. . . .

That expresses the beach and the dunes. But back on the Amagansett highway there is no loneliness, for this route is exceedingly popular for motor travel, especially in vacation season. And as long as it is so well managed, we should not complain.

Where Napeague Beach narrows to a slender neck of land between the Bay and the ocean we enter another of those delightful state parks, "Hither Hills." Shortly after coming into this area of hills and woods the motorist has his choice of taking the drive to the right, which runs along the bluff of the South Shore, or to keep to the main highway. The proper way is to take one route one way and the other on the return. From this point of our excursion, by either way the explorer begins to understand why people go to Montauk Point, for here is superb scenery, as viewed from the high bluffs and hilltops. The land rises steadily as we go east, and the traveler is delighted by infinite stretches of sea and sky, with rough moorland and wind-twisted trees in the foreground. *Picturesque America* called this the "finest sea drive in America. . . . The hills," the writer goes on to say, "are like the open downs of England. . . . The heart expands, and the blood glows under the sweet, subtile stimulant of the scene [note the alliteration] even while the delicious calm and contentment fill the chambers of the mind." That was literary style in the eighteen-seventies. Mr. Charles Parsons, who hiked out to the Point with his friend, says it had been his fortune to "visit the coast of Italy, to ramble on the heathery hills of Scotland, and to visit Newport, Nahant, Cape Ann and Long Branch [this does seem like an anticlimax], but the two days' tramp along the beach and the ride over the downs of Montauk on that memorable October day stand in strong relief above all other similar experiences."

So when the Tile Club came out of the Hither Woods they "came on a scene of freshness and uncontaminated splendor such as they had no idea existed a hundred miles from New York." At the highest crest of the road there is a place set apart considerately for the motorist to turn aside his car and take in at his leisure this vision of "uncontaminated splendor," and let "the delicious calm and contentment fill the chambers of the mind."

Beside the roadway in the Hither Hills Park the driver sees a sign warning the motorist to drive carefully to avoid hitting the wild deer. Probably it isn't often that a deer strays out upon the parkway, but it is pleasant to know that the creatures are roaming freely and safely in the thickets on either hand. When the settlers first came these same woods were noted for their wolves.

In time we come to a place where an office building sticks up in a very perpendicular, sore-thumb fashion, and where restaurants and filling stations line the road. Here, too, is a crossroad, where we may turn left and drive to the village of Montauk, sitting on the wide shore of Fort Pond Bay. This is a sort of capital for fishermen. Once it was very important for commercial fishing, but in these years it exists primarily for sport. In fact, Montauk has been called "the greatest sport-fishing center on the Atlantic coast north of Florida," and this activity goes on the year round. The whole area here is clustered with ponds large and small, offering some fresh-water fishing as well, but the prime attraction is the sea. At the close of the nineteenth century Nova Scotians came here to fish for profit during the summer, going back to their home ports in the fall, but since that practice has been outlawed by more recent legislation many of these Canadians have remained to make their home in Montauk.

Another profitable enterprise of Montauk used to be rum-running in the days of prohibition, but this, too, has vanished, with all its excitement, risks, great profit and even greater losses. One vessel was seized off Montauk with a million-dollar cargo of liquor.

Continuing our journey by the main parkway, we find that the drive becomes increasingly beautiful. Ahead appears the lighthouse which marks the end of this long peninsula of Long Island. We shall roll down a gentle slope to a wide space where we can park the car temporarily. Then we shall walk on up to the lighthouse, which we have had as a center of interest in our landscape for several miles already, with its tall shaft of white crossed by its black belt.

Entering the government reservation about the lighthouse, we are informed by a notice that visitors are admitted to the tower only from eleven to twelve and one to three on weekdays. This cuts out the Sunday tripper and gives the keeper and his assistant one day of rest, which no doubt they greatly need during summer months. As it is, eighteen thousand visitors a year wish to climb those spiral stairs with their one hundred and thirty-six steps. But you can't blame the traveler who has come all this way for wanting to make the ascent. There's no doubt about it, that view from the top of the lighthouse on a crystal-clear afternoon is well worth the knee action required. In the immense panorama before the eye we can see the Connecticut shore at Stonington, and the various islands that lie between: Block; Fisher's; Plum, just beyond Orient Point; and, right under our lee, Gardiner's. But even the traveler who is rather inclined to weight and poor wind need not repine, for he can stand on the crest of the bluff—"Turtle Hill," they call it—and get a view as beautiful, even if not quite so extensive, as that from the top of the lighthouse.

Of course before making the trip here one should arrange the right kind of day, when there is a bright sun overhead, a cool breeze from the ocean in our faces and the sound of surf below. Before our eyes stretches a blue expanse, flecked with whitecaps and the sail of sloop or schooner and spreading as far as eye can reach to where it makes a sharp line against the paler blue of the sky. It is worth coming far to enjoy that view.

Just a hundred years ago a plump little woman, in a large bonnet, with tight flaxen curls bobbing over each ear, came down the sandy road in a cart toward this lighthouse This was the poet, Mrs. Sigourney, "the American Hemans," "America's Tenth Muse." Despite her forty-six years, her tight corset, her voluminous skirt—under which she doubtless wore six petticoats, as a perfect lady should—she had undertaken this rough journey in search of fresh inspiration for her pen. She was always looking for something to write about, and before she joined the choir invisible, in her seventies, she had published a staggering total of sixty-seven books, prose and poetry. She could manage to turn into poetry almost any subject—almost any person, except her husband. He kept a hardware store in Hartford, and not even the Tenth Muse could squeeze any poetry out of him.

Mr. Sigourney's idea of good poetry was the stanza from a good old Puritan hymn:

> My soul is but a rusty lock:
>   Lord, oil it with thy grace;
> And rub it, rub it, rub it, Lord,
>   Until I see Thy face.

MONTAUK

This combined religion with the hardware business.

Now, Mrs. Sigourney had heard of Montauk Point, and here she came to get material for another poem. So out she stepped, arranged her skirts, took her pencil and note book from her reticule, with this result:

>Ultima Thule of this ancient isle,
>Against whose heart the everlasting surge,
>Long traveling on, and ominous of wrath,
>Forever beats! Thou lifts't an eye of light
>Unto the vexed and storm-tossed mariner,
>Guiding him safely to his home again.
>So teach us mid our sorest ills, to wear
>The crown of mercy, and, with changeless eye,
>Look up to heaven.

It was quite in Mrs. Sigourney's best style, and she must have felt well repaid for her trouble in making the journey. Since this poem, with its neat moral tag at the end, was in the edifying tradition of William Cullen Bryant's "Thanatopsis," naturally it was quoted with approval in Mr. Bryant's *Picturesque America*.

Another poet, Walt Whitman, with whiskers streaming in the wind, and exceedingly baggy clothes, came to Montauk at a later day. He was moved to write also, and these are his lines:

I stand on some mighty eagle's beak,
Eastward the sea absorbing, viewing,
  (Nothing but sea and sky)
The tossing waves, the foam, the ships, in the distance
The wild unrest, the snowy, curling caps—that inbound urge and
    urge of waves,
Seeking the shore forever.

There was no moral tag to this one, and Mr. Whitman was not very popular among the literary pundits of the day. Hence

DISCOVERING LONG ISLAND

Walt's "Montauk Point" did not appear in *Picturesque America*. But his lines describe the scene rather better than anyone else has done, though he did forget to mention the lighthouse.

Down to the right a path leads to a cove with a stony beach. Directly south, on the next headland, we can see a house in the

ON MONTAUK

old tradition with sloping roof and wide chimney, snuggling under the arms of a windmill. This is a private summer home, and the wide acreage all about is strictly fenced off against trespassers. But though the house is an imitation Colonial, that windmill is a genuine one. It used to grind flour and corn meal in Southampton, having been erected there in 1763. Later it was moved to Wainscott, near East Hampton, and in 1921 it was dragged somehow all the way out to this present sight. The combination of windmill and house is not only a joy to the owner but a delight to the tourist's eye. How easy it would have been to erect something else on that bluff which would have been a deformity!

Whether the tourist climbs the lighthouse stairs or not, he may demand some statistical information. Accordingly, be it known that this lighthouse was built here in 1796. It is a hundred feet high, having been enlarged twice, and still burns kerosene oil; originally it was a steady light, as mentioned in the story of the wreck of the *John Milton,* but was changed to the flash in 1858. It carries now a steady red light also, visible only to the northwest. In 1853 the French government, by some impulse of generosity long since obsolete, presented to America a beautiful lens. Through official idiocy—not in the least obsolete now—the Collector of the Port was not told about it, and he allowed it to lie in a warehouse until it was sold at auction for seventy dollars. Later, the man who bought this lens sold it to his Uncle Sam for nine hundred dollars, not a bad profit, and the government sent it to Montauk. That lens served here for fifty years.

When in 1792 a site was chosen for this beacon, the present spot was selected to "be perfectly safe from the encroaching sea." In that year it was 297 feet back from the edge of the bluff. The distance is now short of 140 feet.

Another important fact to be noted is that one comes "on" Montauk and goes "off" Montauk, exactly as if it were an island. Indeed, in earlier days, it was even more isolated than any of the principal islands on the coast. You had to learn to walk if you lived here. A lighthouse keeper, for example, took a pleasant January day in 1856 to walk off Montauk to Bridgehampton on an errand, and then stopped in at East Hampton to see some friends, and walked "on" Montauk again. That was just an ordinary stroll. One of the Montauk Indians here known as Steve Talkhouse, used to charge twenty-five cents to take letters from the lighthouse to mail in East Hampton, going afoot both ways and with astonishing speed.

In the early days there were many Indians living on the Point. Wyandanch, who was the friend and the "blood-brother" of Lion Gardiner, became chief of the Montauk tribe before his death. But here as elsewhere the red men rapidly dwindled away. Lyman Beecher went out occasionally from East Hampton to preach to the pitiful remnant of the Montauk tribe that existed in his day. But he found them not at all interested in the state of their souls.

When the Tile Club continued their pilgrimage as far as Montauk they were delighted to learn that there was still a chief of the local tribe, with the impressive name of "King David Pharaoh," and that he lived in the neighborhood. They decided that they must pay their respects to His Royal Highness and, following directions, they tramped down to a small cabin beside a pond. The house was of unpainted clapboards, and under the eaves hung salted eels and weakfish put out to dry. This was the palace. A colored woman admitted the young men to the royal presence.

"Here," writes the scribe of the club, "on a clean bed lay an invalid figure that compelled them [the club] to reverence. King David Pharaoh was lying as still as a marble image. Off went the hats, we remember, for the first thing." The young men had come for a lark and a good joke to tell about when they returned to New York. It needed no one to inform them that this emaciated figure in an incongruous striped sport shirt and trousers of coarse bagging—a man only forty years old—lay dying of consumption.

Someone suggested a hymn and a member started off with a litany in Latin, in which several others joined. "Thank you," said the dying man, "but I don't understand it very well." David Bispham was standing in the back of the room, and as the others turned to him to sing something at this point, he came to King Pharaoh's pillow and in a low tone sang, in English, Fauré's "Les Rameaux." At the chorus of "Hosanna" the others joined him. The Indian whispered that he enjoyed that song very much. Then the visitors said good-by and filed out quietly. "The Barytone" afterwards sang to brilliant audiences all over the world, "before crowned heads," but here was an impromptu recital that was unique and unforgettable. His audience was a dying Indian chief—a "King"—his head on a hard pillow, his limbs motionless and his black eyes fastened on Bispham's face. It was the white race singing a requiem for the red man they had exterminated. A few days after the Tile Club's visit, King David Pharaoh had slipped away to his Happy Hunting Ground.

For the better part of two hundred years Montauk Point was used for grazing, both for sheep and cattle. There were three houses set up to shelter the men who were the herdsmen for these flocks. "First House" burned down long ago; "Second House," at the head of Fort Pond, is still inhabited; "Third House," near the highway, is standing but has had no occupant for ten years and is falling into decay. This was the one which served as a sort of guesthouse for the people who used to come on Montauk for hunting, fishing and adventure. There in a book the visitors used to jot down their names, and sometimes long poetic effusions besides. The Tile Club were entertained here, too, on June 16, 1878, and they left not only their names but small sketches. Here at Third House, twenty years later, Colonel Theodore Roosevelt and some of his officers stayed when the Rough Riders came back from Cuba.

That was the occasion of tremendous activity at Montauk. On August 9, 1898, the first detachment of nearly 30,000 soldiers was landed in Fort Pond Bay, back from Santiago. The breakdown in our medical, sanitary and supply system had been almost as bad as that of the British army in the Crimea. The result was that a large number of these khaki-clad men had to be brought ashore on litters, some with yellow fever, and more with typhoid. And in harmony with the rest of the blundering story the men began to arrive before there were proper facilities to take care of them. Soon, however, there was a field hospital set up and the doctors and nurses were busy. The soldiers who were well were detained here until all danger of carrying infection was eliminated. The encampment was named Camp Wikoff after Colonel Charles A. Wikoff who was killed at Santiago. Forty years later, on the anniversary of the arrival of the first transport, those who were left of the Rough Riders gathered at Montauk Point, again under the auspices of the Montauk Historical Society. They held exercises in memory of their beloved commander and chose a site for a monument to him.

Supposing, after considerable walking about the Point, we are ready for an early lunch, we shall find, very handy to the roadway and the parking area, a modest place of refreshment under the auspices of the Park authorities. Here we may eat, according to wind and weather conditions, either indoors or out. It is particularly enjoyable to sit at a table sheltered from the sun by a wide blue umbrella. From here we can enjoy a view that is as fine as any on the Point. On a clear day the Connecticut shore can be seen faintly on the horizon, and as we look around to the lighthouse itself and the wide expanse of moorland and sea we must rejoice that this beauty spot has been spared the usual billboards advertising cigarettes, laxatives, chewing gum, motor oil and what not—also "hot-dog stands," "barbecues," souvenir shops and all the rest of the ruck and rubbish that commonly afflict the eye. This beauty belongs to the American people and is safeguarded by the State of New York. Someday, perhaps, the Natural Bridge of Virginia, also one of America's beauty spots, will be rescued from a vulgar commercialism that has carefully built a high board wall to make sure that no motorist may catch a glimpse of the Bridge without paying the demanded tariff.

There is further room for thankfulness that certain big ideas for Montauk were never realized. One of these was to develop Fort Pond Bay as a transatlantic port of entry for New York, to avoid the congestion of New York Harbor and to build up here a great summer resort. The father of this idea was Mr. Austin Corbin, then the able and energetic President of the Long Island Railroad. He had other dreams, too, which have since come to realization, such as the tunnels connecting New York with the Jersey shore and with Brooklyn; also the bridge over the Hudson where the Washington Bridge is now. But his pet idea was the Montauk port.

It was in 1885, more than fifty years ago, that he published his plan for the first time. He was then building a steamship line to ply between Milford Haven in Wales and Fort Pond Bay in Montauk. But the grandiose scheme dragged. In 1894 a bill was introduced in Congress to make Fort Pond a free port, and authorized the owners of the land to go ahead with dredge and masonry to build harbor facilities. But it slept in committee. Two years later Mr. Corbin was killed in a runaway, and a few months afterwards Congress decided that a free port was unconstitutional. The phrase "free port" meant that cargoes could be transshipped for reexport without going through customs. Nevertheless, some building was begun—new roads, a pier, a small hotel. Others took up the plan as it had dropped from Mr. Corbin's hands. Then came the World War as a quietus.

After that was over, the idea was revived, and in 1931 a squadron of battleships was sent here to demonstrate how safely heavy-draft vessels could navigate in Fort Pond Bay. This was at the orders of the gentleman who was chairman of the House Naval Affairs Committee, which caused many people to wonder why our fleet was being used to help advertise a real-estate project. Since then no one has brought forward the scheme. *Requiescat in pace.* The New London ferry makes Fort Pond Bay a modest port of entry, anyway.

While this plan was developing a new one was proposed. In 1926 Mr. Carl G. Fisher, the man who promoted Miami Beach in Florida, sailed to Fort Pond Bay, afire with another Big Idea. He was going to make Montauk another Miami, the former for summer as the latter was for winter. Forthwith he and his associates bought ten thousand acres with nine miles of water front, built a hotel, "Montauk Manor," an office building, a golf course, a yacht club, a polo field, and a pier in Fort Pond Bay, costing half a million, and so on. Money was poured out in torrents, land prices jumped to fantastic figures, but trouble came. The real-estate bubble in Florida burst, and the hurricane came on top of the remains. Three years later, the New York stock market blew up and introduced the depression. The Montauk Beach Development Corporation has been seriously restricted in its operations ever since. Montauk village has now wakened from its dream of being another Miami and is, instead, developing its one unquestioned gold mine, sport fishing. With all due deference to the energy and abilities of Mr. Fisher, we can be thankful that Montauk is not another Miami Beach.

When Mr. Robert Moses came out here to establish some more of his parks, there was violent opposition at first from the very people who welcomed the idea of another Miami Beach. They thought that the landscape would be ruined, that the trippers would make themselves obnoxious, that the moors and beaches would be littered with tin cans, Sunday papers and lunch boxes. On the other hand, Mr. Fisher himself cooperated with Mr. Moses in his acquisition of land here, both at the Point and farther back in the Hither Hills; and Mr. Moses drove his plans through the opposition in his characteristic style. Now, as we lounge under our blue umbrella and look about, we can be grateful that we are not sitting on the edge of a port of entry for New York City, and that Montauk is not another "Myammer" Beach. Instead, this spot of glorious sea and sky and rolling downs has been saved for ourselves and for generations to come.

CHAPTER IX

THE OTHER HAMPTONS

IN the previous chapter it was suggested that we make a day of it, exploring the Montauk region, returning in time for dinner at East Hampton. But if the calendar is right, the traveler can add an unforgettable picture to his album of memories by taking his dinner on Montauk Point and seeing the moon rise out of the ocean, drawing its train of sparkling silver reflections across the water. However, sooner or later, we are back again at East Hampton, ready to take our way to the westward, like the well-known course of empire. This time we shall head for those other Hamptons—those one-word Hamptons, who have pusillanimously succumbed to the postal authorities and the Express Company—and begin to get acquainted with the South Shore of Long Island.

To continue our journey we turn our car back on Route 27. Soon we are passing through Bridgehampton, another of those pleasant seaside villages which need not detain us unless one has a hankering for old windmills. There is one here, on a private estate on Ocean Road, not far from the Civil War monument. This old mill was built over a hundred years ago at Sag Harbor and moved here. There was something strangely restless about these Long Island windmills, for not many of them stand where they were originally built. They were moved hither and yon, especially yon, over miles of sandy roads, up hills, and even across the bays, before they settled down for keeps.

FIRE ISLAND LIGHT

THE OTHER HAMPTONS

Just beyond Bridgehampton we enter the town of Water Mill, and as we pass the Green we see another windmill which has been preserved by the local "Improvement Association." This one, also, was built in Sag Harbor, in the year 1800. In 1814 it was dragged hither by a team of twelve oxen. Heaven only knows how many weeks or months it took to make the trip, or how it got by the overhanging trees all along the route. But here it arrived and set up business for the local farmers, and here it still remains. The Great Hurricane made the cap and arms a mass of wreckage, but scarcely had the wind died away before the Improvement Association set about repairing it, and it looks now as fine as ever.

Here in the heart of the windmill country, and perhaps at the door of this particular one, might be posted a very ancient and curious little poem which was, and maybe still is, affixed to an old millpost in Sussex, England:

> The windmill is a couris thing
> Compleatly built by art of man,
> To grind the corn for man and beast
> That they alike may have a feast.
>
> The mill she is built of wood, iron, and stone,
> Therefore she cannot go aloan;
> Therefore to make the mill to go,
> The wind from some part she must blow.
>
> The *motison* of the mill is swift
> The miller must be very thrift,
> To jump about and get things ready
> Or else the mill will soon run empty.

In England, by the way, the destruction of the old mills was even more ruthless than here. Thirty years ago practically the only ones to survive in good condition were those that had been converted into teashops. Finally, a special "Windmill Section" was created by the Society for the Protection of Ancient Buildings.

The name of our village, however, has to do with another mill which lies just off our highway to the right, this side of the railroad track. This, as a building, is not so picturesque as the windmill, particularly as whatever water wheel it had is no longer in existence. It just sits by the stream, angular, erect and gray, like one of the old-time Quaker schoolmarms. But you can still see, under the roadway, the waterfall tumbling through its square cement outlet, and a placid stream flows lazily under a rickety, Japanesy, little footbridge into a tidal creek. In an article written for *Harper's* in 1878, "Around the Peconics," the artist Smedley made a sketch of this water mill, and it is interesting to note that in the fifty years since then the scene has not changed in a single detail except for the big sign of the "Tea and Gift Shop" on the mill.

From Water Mill the road leads straight ahead a few miles to the most famous of all the Long Island summer resorts, Southampton. This community has long been noted in annals of lawn tennis and golf, and in the society pages of New York papers. Here is the Meadow Club, which for more than fifty years has held invitation tournaments that brought the greatest tennis players to its courts. Here also are the famous Riding and Hunt Club, the Sebonac Yacht Club, the National Golf Links of America and the Shinnecock Hills Golf Club—the first in America.

Southampton is even more noted as one of the summer capitals of society. Here for decades the wealthy have come to build their "stately pleasure domes," enjoy their vacations elegantly and expensively. Here at the Beach Club or Riding Club they

THE OTHER HAMPTONS

have been photographed for countless rotogravure sections for the edification of the rest of us.

It takes only a glance to show that Southampton is very different from East Hampton. If the latter is a "hamlet," the former

THE WATER MILL

is certainly a townlet. It puts on quite citified airs in its streets; and the rush of summer visitors long ago swept away almost every vestige of the old Southampton, which dates back to 1640. Only rarely, here and there, as we drive through the residential section can we see some little old cottage with lean-to or gambrel roof which serves as an example of what old Southampton must have been. The rest is exceedingly brisk and modern.

Here are smart shops displaying the latest word in fashions. We recognize the names of well-known Fifth Avenue emporiums over the doors of very modern-looking places of business, with fancy glass, colored tiles and gleaming stainless steel.

The residential Southampton is outside the village, along the beaches and the waterways. To see this we should turn left toward the shore at the traffic light, and continue toward the sea. It is worth while to drive along the roads that run between these summer homes of the rich—great, fenced-in estates, in the midst of which stand palatial villas of the pre-Hoover era. They are very handsome, but, Reader, envy not the men and women who built or bought them, and now have to own them. Yonder mansion, for example, with its fifteen chimneys, has also its fifty thousand headaches, for which there is no effective aspirin. This whole magnificent array of summer palaces is only a herd of insatiably hungry white elephants. The upkeep of all this architecture and landscaping increases yearly, and the taxes climb steadily higher.

So we, plain citizens in the poor but fairly respectable station in life to which God has called us, need not repine. Rather we should drop a pitying tear for Mr. and Mrs. Croesus, who live inside those châteaux, leaning sadly against their society columns and shivering over their Social Registers. One after another, these great estates seem doomed to fall into the hands of the banks and the tax gatherers, to be cut up into bungalow lots or transformed into charitable institutions.

To add insult to the injuries of Southampton, a New York newspaper columnist recently declared that she had lost her preeminence as a society resort—that, indeed, her modest neighbor, East Hampton, is now considered "smarter"! That will be bad news if true. Imagine the Russian Grand Dukes, Polish

THE OTHER HAMPTONS

nobles and Hungarian counts, who used to infest Newport first, and then Southampton, looking for free lodging and a rich bride, now crowding into beautiful, unspoiled East Hampton! *Deus avertat!*

Next to the Beach Club of Southampton and rudely sticking its elbow into it sits another elaborate building that also looks like a clubhouse. This, they say, was erected by someone who had been denied membership at the Club. But, having plenty of money, he bought a lot alongside and put up his own private clubhouse with its swimming pool and everything. "That's that," said he, and so it is. Indeed, his towering brick walls spell "exclusive" even more emphatically than the Club itself, which is quite dwarfed by comparison.

Although the Southampton of today is utterly modern, it had an interesting and honorable past. The little "Hollyhocks House," as it is called on picture postcards, which is probably as old as the "Home, Sweet Home house" of East Hampton, if not older, sits in the midst of its twentieth-century surroundings as a reminder that Southampton was once a very different place. The "Terry Tavern," which we can see on the highway, as an adjunct of the Irving House, claims for itself a great antiquity, but it has been so much altered that no one would guess the fact. For some reason it advertises that it is situated "8000 miles from China," whatever comfort that may mean to a traveler.

No less distinguished a writer than Mr. James Truslow Adams has published a history of Southampton. From its pages we learn that this town, like its neighbors, went through the hard experiences of two wars with Great Britain, enjoyed the profits of a whaling era and had its share of shipwrecks. One Spanish vessel in 1816 came ashore on Southampton Beach, and as the waves burst over her sides, streams of silver dollars poured out into the surf. On that occasion there was no lack of willing hands for rescue.

It is hard to realize that this large and fashionable and modern resort by the sea claims to be—despite Southold—the oldest settlement on Long Island. To go to its Plymouth Rock, so to speak, we should turn north from Southampton on the North Sea Road. Following this to North Sea Harbor, about five miles, we find a huge boulder sitting alone in a field beside the water. On this is set a bronze plate with this inscription: "Near this spot in 1640 landed colonists from Lynn, Massachusetts, who founded Southampton, the oldest settlement in New York State." This site is called Conscience Point, for the legend is that when a woman stepped ashore from the small boat in which they had made the wretched, seasick voyage, she cried, "For conscience' sake, we are on dry land once more!" There is one thing to remember about those noble pioneers who stuck it out in the wilderness—anything was better than making the journey back again.

To continue our tour westward, we can return by way of Tuckahoe on a new and elegant boulevard to Suffolk Downs and Canoe Place, or follow the older Number 27 highway to the same spot. This latter road, when it gets into the Shinnecock Hills, shrinks to a reprehensibly narrow strip of cement, roughened by wiggly marks of tar, as if some giant had tried automatic writing here just for fun, and didn't have much success with it.

But it does wind in and around the Shinnecock Hills, an attractive bit of the peninsula, with rolling country, and with valleys covered with a variety of growth, especially pines and cedars, through which in any direction we can see blue water.

THE OTHER HAMPTONS

William M. Chase was so delighted with the region that he built a cottage here, and in 1891 established a summer art school. Chase, by the way, was one of the most active and enthusiastic members of the Tile Club. To accommodate the students a cluster of cottages called the Art Village sprang up about three miles from the Chases' home. There are many gray-haired men and women who can remember those days. "I was a student under Chase," they still say proudly, for he was a great teacher as well as painter. It was his pupils who commissioned Sargent to paint a portrait of him, the one which now hangs in the Metropolitan.

Those were happy summers in the Shinnecock Hills. The students used everything for their sketching; besides trees, beaches and blue water there were the Indians from the reservation near by, who were glad to make an honest dollar by posing for Mr. Chase's classes. One artist told me that the mosquitoes were pretty bad sometimes, but that the students used to slap them onto the canvas with a swipe of the brush to use as "accents." There's nothing like making the best of everything.

The Hills are just as beautiful now as they were forty-five years ago, but the smocks, camp stools and sketching umbrellas have vanished, just as they did from East Hampton two decades earlier. In fact, the last Shinnecock class was held in the summer of 1902.

As for Lo, the Poor Indian, he poses no more, for there are no painters who want him. In this vicinity, a short way out of Southampton and before we reach the Shinnecock Hills, is a squarish peninsula of about 800 acres, comprising the present Indian reservation, in which about 170 remnants of the Shinnecock tribe still live as wards of the government. Some road maps do not even mark this area, though they give every flying field and state park on Long Island. The Shell map indicates it as a pink patch, but shows no roads in it. However, a mile or so outside the center of Southampton on the main

IN THE SHINNECOCK HILLS

route there is a metal marker telling about the reservation, and at that point a dirt road leads off at right angles to the south. If the traveler is curious to see one of the most pathetic spectacles of racial decay in all the eastern section of his country, let him turn down this dusty, washboardy lane.

It is a wide, flat, almost treeless plain that comprises the reservation. On either side of the road the weeds stand rank and high. There are a few cabins here and there, most of them looking dilapidated, with broken windowpanes and patched sides. The scene reminds one of a negro settlement in the back

THE OTHER HAMPTONS

country of Georgia, except that even there the cabins would have vegetable and flower gardens around them. Here it seems as if a plow or even a hoe had never disturbed the ground.

The scene looks still more like the deep South when we pass the inhabitants of the reservation, for these "Indians" have kinky hair and African features. They are palpably negroid. There is an old-fashioned one-room schoolhouse, presided over by an intelligent teacher, who seemed to have more of the Indian in her face than any of the others whom I saw. But the children might well have come straight out of Harlem or Alabama. Next to the schoolhouse was a church; this, the teacher told me, had been floated across Shinnecock Bay and moved to its present site. It had a large hole in its roof and looked old and disconsolate. There seemed to be nothing else to the reservation. The weedy plain stretched drearily away, dotted here and there by little decrepit cabins.

With the loss of their racial purity these descendants of the Shinnecock tribe have forgotten all their Indian arts and customs. In the summer of 1938 the community organized (under guidance of friends in Southampton) a two-day powwow in order to raise funds to build a community house and renovate their decaying church. In their entertainment program they featured tribal dances, but these were performed by visiting red men, because the Shinnecocks had forgotten their own. The visitors, incidentally, took one-third of the wampum for their services.

Leaving the reservation, we continue our course on through the Shinnecock Hills to a spot in Hampton Bays called Canoe Place. It is so named because here was where the aborigines of olden time used to drag their canoes across from Shinnecock Bay to Great Peconic Bay, or vice versa. Now we cross a waterway of sufficient depth for pleasure craft to make the transfer by water. At the left of the road stands a huge wooden figurehead, a bearded person, with a lion's skin twisted about his stomach. This is Hercules. He is a long way from home, for he was carved in Athens, doubtless by some descendant of Phidias, and presented to the United States by the Greek government on the occasion of the visit of an American squadron. It was accepted, despite the classic objection to the "Greeks bearing gifts," especially in the line of wooden sculpture, and affixed to the bow of the ship of the line, the *Ohio*. Since that vessel was broken up in the waters of this neighborhood, the figurehead came to rest here, facing a famous inn across the road. In front of the figurehead is a stone bench, and at the base is a piece of what was intended to be verse, telling the legend:

> This is the strong god Hercules
> His mighty tasks he did with ease,
> One yet remains, mankind to please.
> The maid who kisses his mighty cheek
> Will meet her fate within the week,
> The one who presses his forehead
> In less than a year will wed
> No maid, no matron, ever taunted
> Him with refusing what she wanted
> Though hewn with wood and patched with tin,
> To all the gods he is akin.
> And the spirits of them all
> Hover over his pedestal.
> So whisper what you wish the most
> Fair maid it's yours and—the cost.

Who wrote it, or when, nobody seems to know, but the reluctance to use the word "damn" in the last line indicates a time way back in the reign of Queen Victoria.

THE OTHER HAMPTONS

Opposite Hercules is one of the most renowned places of refreshment on Long Island, "Ye Olde Canoe Place Inn." Although the present building dates from 1921, there has been a tavern here from the very beginning of English settlements in these parts. In fact, it was dispensing ale and strong waters to both white man and red twelve years before East Hampton was founded. When the predecessor of this inn was burned down, the old sign was saved; a replica of it swings in front today, bearing the couplet:

> This is the welcome I have to tell
> Ye are well come, ye are come well.

The chief interest about the Canoe Place Inn is that it was the summer stamping ground for generations of New York politicians. Here came Federalists and Republicans in the early days of the republic. These were followed by the Whigs, and when the Whig party passed out on the issue of slavery, the Lincoln Republicans took their place. But in the twentieth century the Inn became the rendezvous of the Tammany chiefs of Celtic origin, the McCarren, McCooey, Murphy crowd of New York and their successors. Near by, at South Jamesport on Great Peconic Bay, Boss McLaughlin, the ruler of Brooklyn, built a summer home; and the faithful henchmen who used to come to beg favors or take orders flocked to the Canoe Place Inn. More and more this region about Hampton Bays became the favorite locality for the New York state and city Democratic politicians to build their summer homes and enjoy the fruits of their labors for civic righteousness.

From Hampton Bays or "Good Ground," as it was once called, we can turn north, to the right, on Route 24 to Riverhead, which lies attractively located at the head of Great Peconic

Bay. The chief attraction there is the Suffolk County Historical Building which treasures, among other interesting relics, the "John Hulbert Flag." This, you will be informed there, is absolutely the first stars and stripes ever flung to the breeze. It was sewn and flown six months before Betsy Ross even threaded her needle. John Hulbert's flag is unique in that his thirteen stars have six points instead of five.

But with that gesture in the direction of Riverhead we hold to our course back along the South Shore toward Quogue. In this area we enter the land of the Long Island duckling. And in the presence of this industry which advertises the name of Long Island all over the world we should pause to do reverence. In the small waterways all along this part of the southern shore are raised and slain annually more than three million ducks. Riverhead, which we just mentioned, is the hub of this duck business for the North Fork, as Eastport is for the South Fork. The duck country embraces the triangle of which Riverhead is the apex, Eastport the west corner and the Quogues the east. There are in all about ninety duck farms. Here, by the small creeks and ponds, ducklings are incubator-born and bred. At the tender age of six weeks the duckling is allowed to learn to swim. Thereafter he leads a short but happy existence of fattening. At the age of ten or twelve weeks the bird, alas, meets a sudden and tragic end. His remains are then turned over to women—as Vergil says, "Ducks femina facti"—who pluck off the feathers by hand. These are then dispatched to Speonk—that name itself sounds like the dying cry of a duck—washed and sold. The naked corpse of the duckling is cooled in ice water, then packed with others of his unhappy brethren in apple barrels filled with ice, and off they go to the chefs and the steam tables the country over.

THE OTHER HAMPTONS

The Long Island duckling, it may be added, is of one breed, the White Pekin, which was introduced from China in the eighteen-seventies. Its plumage is such a pure white that at a distance one of these duck farms looks like a field where patches of March snow have not yet melted. But he is something of a whited sepulcher, for all his angelic plumage. Each little White Pekin is a most active fertilizer factory, and when the wind is right not all the perfumes of Araby could sweeten this little land of duck farms. But the dwellers hereabouts seem to think of this fragrance much as the old-timers did of the whale-oil try pots, "It's a good, healthy smell." At any rate, a great source of revenue is the Long Island duckling, and one of those products, which, like the Blue Point Oyster and the Long Island potato, carries the fame of this island into the uttermost parts.

But one must not think of Quogue entirely in terms of the duck industry. It is a fair and placid summer resort with a broad street in the middle from which lanes lead off right and left. One of these from the center of the town wanders down toward the bay and after crossing another street becomes a driveway leading to a large, wide-fronted house of gray shingles facing the sea. This is the home of a famous historian, the late Admiral Alfred Thayer Mahan, U.S.N. He was the naval officer who fifty years ago published a book called the *Influence of Sea Power on History*. He called attention to a fact that landlubber historians had underestimated; namely, the influence of navies in the past. He became world famous for this work, and the rest of his life he devoted to expanding his idea. Unhappily for the world, the Kaiser, Wilhelm II, read the book and was greatly impressed. Hitherto the German Emperor had not bothered much about navies. "Now," said he, "our future lies on the sea," and he ordered every officer in the Imperial Navy to buy and read that book. From this sprang the new German navy, one that threatened the supremacy of Great Britain on the sea and led directly to the World War. In fact, the high-minded American naval officer had thus unwittingly more to do with bringing on the worst war in the history of the world than any other man.

Bird lovers will be interested to look up the various "sanctuaries" on Long Island. We have already visited the one near Theodore Roosevelt's grave at Oyster Bay, and noted the protection of bird life on Gardiner's Island. Some of these sanctuaries are private and others are public, maintained by township or state. Here at Quogue is a privately owned refuge, chiefly for waterfowl. It is supported by the Southampton Township Wildfowl Association, as "Sanctuary Number One." Here are 1000 acres of land and 235 acres of water, sacred to the birds. In 1935 this sanctuary won first honors in a national competition among 235 such reservations representing 44 states. Visitors who wish to see how a first-class, privately managed bird refuge is conducted are welcome to inspect this one at Quogue.

We will leave Highway 27 at this village and take a pleasant road to Westhampton Beach. This was formerly known as one of those resort communities where the well-to-do built their summer homes and which newspaper reporters love to call "exclusive." Then, in September, 1938, it became the center on Long Island of the most extraordinary storm disaster the North Atlantic coast has ever seen, at least as far as any historic records show. Here and there in this narrative of travel this catastrophe has been alluded to, but since Westhampton Beach was its chief victim, here we may well pause to sketch the story.

THE OTHER HAMPTONS

The Weather Bureau had reported a hurricane moving north from the Caribbean and sent warnings to the east Florida coast. Even a party of relief workers was dispatched there. But later word came that the hurricane's course had been deflected away from Florida, and the relief workers were recalled. It was expected then that the storm would blow itself out in the north Atlantic as these September hurricanes usually do. Somehow it got lost at sea for a while.

Later the report came that the storm seemed to be heading more to the northwest; but this did not mean much to the public who read about it in the newspapers or heard it over the radio. The next day, September 21, the Weather Bureau's storm signals spelled to all mariners warning of the hurricane from the southeast. Vessels promptly scudded to shelter in the nearest port.

A high wind that began in the morning of that day rapidly grew in intensity. It had been raining for five consecutive days. The sky, at first hazy, again became overcast with scudding black clouds which dropped sudden torrents of rain. But there was nothing to distinguish the oncoming storm from any other severe southeaster. No warnings were sent to the coastal towns and villages of Long Island or New England; no relief parties were dispatched to their shores. Hurricanes just didn't happen in this region.

But this one did. Instead of dissipating itself hundreds of miles out in the ocean, the storm veered to the west, driving straight through Long Island, Connecticut, Rhode Island and Massachusetts. On Long Island the center passed directly over this summer resort of Westhampton Beach. Of course, any ordinary gale drives the water before it and raises the tide above normal levels, but this wind broke all records for intensity.

The height of the storm coincided with the flood tide, also, and the result was a rapidly rising mass of sea the like of which was probably never known in the three hundred years white men had lived on Long Island. An eyewitness said to me, "The water in the bay seemed to suck out to sea and then it came back and didn't stop for nothing; just went over the whole place." The result was called a tidal wave, but it would be more accurately described as a "storm wave."

Breakers of appalling size rolled in over the beach, then in over the protecting dunes. Bridges, wharves and cottages near the sea were crumpled up like paper and flung in pieces, end over end, through the air and water. Still the wind increased as the afternoon wore on, and the sea rolled in over the low coastal plain as if some ocean dam had burst and let loose another deluge. No one could face the wind; no one could even stand against it. On came the tossing waters, filled with debris, foaming on toward the main village, which lay half a mile from the beach. The summer houses here were not beach shacks, but substantially built, many of them luxurious and handsome summer homes of the well-to-do. Some had been closed for the season; others were still occupied. And yet the tempest grew in fury and the surf was soon pounding on these houses set far back from the normal coast line. One after another they broke apart; roofs and walls fell into the boiling surf, or were caught up in pieces by the hurricane and sent flying off through the air.

There had been sufficient warning to enable most of the residents to escape, but there were others who were trapped. One man was on his thirty-two-foot cruiser when the blast struck and carried his boat along before it. There was nothing for it but to stick to her, and let her run before the wind, steering her as best he could. When the keel grated at last, the boat had gone a full half mile from the anchorage over what was normally dry land and found a haven in the lee of the Westhampton Beach telephone offices.

During the height of the hurricane, a couple managed to join forces with their next-door neighbors; but before they could escape, the sea rolled in over the first floor, rising rapidly to the second, and driving all to the attic. Here the refugees collected, the group including two of the servants—one, a housemaid, had already been killed—and their dog. As the timbers quivered under the blows of the sea and the wind tore at the roof overhead, these people awaited the end. The crash came at last; but by a freak of luck, the whole attic floor broke off from the rest of the house and floated away like the Ark, containing its six people and the dog still unharmed. The southeast wind drove it out into the tossing waters of Moriches Bay, while the survivors clung desperately to the flooring to keep from being washed off. Then, as the hurricane advanced, the wind shifted to northwest and drove the raft back over the flooded fields to Quogue, where it grounded at last in four feet of water and against a mass of wreckage in front of the home of Admiral Mahan, the lower floor of which was also under water. It was as if the storm god enjoyed his little joke on the "influence of sea power." In this hospitable home the castaways were taken in; despite their terrifying experience, all had escaped unhurt.

Meanwhile, at another Westhampton home was the wife of the French consul general in New York. When the hurricane struck, her first thought was that there was an earthquake, because the walls of the house shook and swayed. She picked up her two-month-old baby, wrapped her in a blanket and started to leave, accompanied by the cook and nurse. As they stepped out into the tempest the water was already swirling about the house. Boards and tree branches and other wreckage went hurtling overhead, or tossing by in the waters. As the party of women set their course for the nearest neighbor's house on higher land, half a mile away, they soon found themselves in sea water up to their waists. They had not struggled far when they heard a crashing roar behind them that sounded above the tumult of the rain, wind and water. They paused for a moment to look back and saw their wide, rambling home collapse into the flood like a house of cards. However, they managed to reach the house they were struggling toward, where were collected fifteen or twenty of their neighbors. There the butler went out into the storm and rounded up three young men. These four, linking arms, helped the refugees struggle through the waters to other houses farther inland. All the while, the baby clasped so tightly in her blanket against her mother's breast was untroubled by wave or wreckage. The picture of the mother holding that infant and struggling through the roaring hurricane, rushing waters and flying wreckage suggests, as an appropriate caption, that line from Ecclesiastes: "Many waters cannot quench love, neither can the floods drown it."

The next day when the ocean had receded it left a scene of desolation. Out of one hundred and twenty-five houses along the Dune Road only six remained standing; smashed pleasure craft, wreckage and debris of all sorts were spread over the shore. Where homes had been, there lay only heaps of timbers and planks. When the rescue workers had completed their work they reported twenty known dead and others missing. The Westhampton Country Club, where not so long before had

THE OTHER HAMPTONS

been given the last dance of the season, was transformed into a morgue. Even a month after the disaster took place the whole area was still a scene of devastation. High on telegraph poles and on trees and bushes hung the rubbish that marked the unprecedented height of the sea. A fine new cement bridge leading to the dunes had one end smashed by the wreckage and driven by the storm wave.

Of course, the hurricane was not restricted to Westhampton by any means. The entire South Shore was overwhelmed. At Fire Island, for example, six hundred small cottages were swept away, but fortunately there were only two deaths. At Fort Pond, Montauk—the harbor that was to have become the port entry of New York and "a second Miami Beach"—the entire fishing village had been washed away. However, the manager of the Montauk Beach Company, having been the victim of several Florida hurricanes, realized what was coming and sent a truck to collect and bring to the Montauk Manor Hotel the two hundred or more people who lived in the village, so that all were rescued in time. From Westhampton the storm swept down through Southampton, destroying many fine summer places along the shore, and struck East Hampton, as already noted, with frightful destruction to its magnificent elms. On Shelter Island whole groves on the Sylvester Manor estate were laid flat like wheat by a scythe. Everywhere in this part of Long Island countless trees were brought down, and on those that remained standing every leaf was stripped away. There was no autumn foliage on eastern Long Island that year, for after the twenty-first of September the trees were as bare as in January.

From Montauk the hurricane leaped to the Connecticut shore, concentrated its fury on Rhode Island, flung itself across the middle of New England and then disappeared into Canada, leaving behind ruin that ran into hundreds of millions, and a death total of about seven hundred lives.

One other tropical hurricane on Long Island is recorded, for September 23, 1815, but no special data are available. At any rate, no such wind on our coast had ever been measured before. At Harvard's Blue Hill Observatory, one anemometer blew to pieces when the velocity of the wind passed a hundred miles an hour, and a later gust registered the incredible figure of one hundred and eighty-six. Seismographs made their wavy-line record for that day as if a major earthquake were on, for the ground was actually throbbing to the terrific pounding of the sea.

After the tale of desolation and death was complete, anecdotes of a lighter sort cropped up. For instance, a fisherman on Great Peconic Bay, who had been saving for years to buy a good boat, discovered around his house, when the waters went down, five boats, one of them a small yacht. A householder on Shelter Island reported that his five hens had vanished into space when the twister struck, but after several days they returned. They were badly storm-beaten, but they had brought back with them in triumph a cock, starved and bereft of his gallant plumage—"shorn tail, provisions lost, and only not a wreck," as the hymn puts it—but happy to find any port in time of storm. Like the Canadian Mounties, these hens had got their man.

Perhaps the best anecdote is one that was printed in the *New Yorker,* a fact that should vouch for its authenticity. It concerns "a man on Long Island who had satisfied a life-long ambition by ordering an expensive barometer from Abercrombie and Fitch. It arrived the morning of September 21st. Eagerly he unwrapped it and was disgusted to find the needle stuck at 'hurricane.' After shaking it in a vain attempt to start it working right, he sat down, wrote a very stuffy letter to A. & F., and went right out to mail it. When he returned, his house was gone, and the barometer with it."

That old saw about an ill wind was illustrated by a negro workman, busy with fallen trees along the road. "It sure was terrible," he said to me of the hurricane, "but it gave a lot of us poor fellows work, and God knows we needed it."

So came and went the Great Hurricane of September, 1938. As fast as possible all vestiges of the destruction were cleared away, though this was a matter of months, and Westhampton set herself in order, with new cottages rising to take the place of the old. Only those who were residents here before the disaster can still point out to strangers where the ocean cut new channels through the Dunes, destroying sections of the famous Dune Drive and changing the whole front of the shore.

The more one studies the map, or looks about him on the spot, the more difficult it is to understand how the sea could have wreaked such destruction in this place. For, with an ocean beach stretching parallel to the shore for two-score miles as a breakwater, all the bays and inlets in this region seem as placidly landlocked as could be imagined. And yet such is the way of a West Indian hurricane that nowhere was its fury more terrific than at this sheltered summer resort which happened to lie directly in its path.

CHAPTER X

THE SOUTH SHORE

THE lazy tidal inlets of Quogue and Westhampton Beach with their fringes of sea marsh and low sand dunes have already introduced us to the South Shore landscape. It makes a striking contrast to the North Shore, with its continuous front of high bluffs, shaggy with woods, reaching from the western end of the Island all the way to the neighborhood of Southold, where they gradually slope down to the level of the beach. But on the South Shore the land has been ironed out flat to the water's edge.

Although this is the ocean front of Long Island, there is no open sea to toss its breakers on the shore. Rather, the whole coast line is a series of great, landlocked bays, bearing different names on the map, but making up altogether one huge saltwater pond some eighty miles long, with an ocean barrier formed by a narrow breakwater of sand. This runs all the way from Southampton to Fire Island before there is an important inlet, and then the same formation continues as far west as the Jones Inlet. According to legend, all that lies between the ocean barrier and the shore was not so long ago, counting by centuries, a sea meadow. The Indians told the settlers that even Great South Bay was, in the time of their ancestors, a saltwater marsh, over which it was easy to walk safely in any direction. Altogether, the South Shore landscape is flat and bare compared with that of the North Shore, especially as we have seen it in that area between Roslyn and Port Jefferson.

THE SOUTH SHORE

The result of this difference of terrain is that there are two opposed camps of Long Islanders, each scornful of the other. If the Northerners point to the irregularity and beauty of their shore, with its deep indentations and beetling cliffs, the Southerners reply that they like flat country better because they can see farther; and as for beaches, they have stretches of smooth, velvety sand, whereas the North Shore people, when they go swimming, bruise their feet on stones the size of cobbles. Fortunately, the Pine Barrens lie as a no man's land between these two hostile camps, or there might be another Armageddon of North against South—a sort of War between the Estates.

As the map shows, there are second-class roads which will take the motorist along near the shore, but it is worth getting back on the Montauk Highway for the sake of seeing the most bizarre human creation on all Long Island. This is "Casa Basso," lying left of the highway, close to where the road from Westhampton Beach joins it. There our astonished gaze is arrested by a miniature castle of yellow stucco trimmed with red. Under the castellated turret is the entrance, shaped as a Moorish arch. Guarding the driveway stand two twelve-foot swordsmen of concrete, painted in brilliant colors, their swords thrust out at each other. They look as if they had stepped out of a Gargantuan scene from some grand opera by Verdi.

The driveway leads to a modest one-story building in the rear, which is a well-known restaurant, and if the visit can be timed for lunch the guest can wander about and examine the castle grounds at leisure. The two pugnacious cavaliers at the entrance are only an introduction to the display of what is sometimes called a "sculptuary." In the center grassplot is a prancing horse, once gilded, but now turning green. Near the restaurant is a nest of horses' heads with bright-blue eyes. There is also a "Roman lion," a Psyche (she was blown upon her nose during the hurricane) and so on, but the most impressive monument of all lies in an alleged "park" alongside, called "Pine Wold." Here is a life-size group representing a scene from *Quo Vadis,* in which Ursus is fighting the Aurochs (a bull), on the back of which is tied a young lady Christian martyr. She is a perfect thirty-eight; and though quite devoid of garments, her expression suggests that she is rather enjoying being the center of attention in the coliseum. Round the base of this group are arrayed, in ringside seats, gigantic turtles and crabs.

When I paused to admire this work of art it was after the hurricane, and one of the pines of Pine Wold had fallen across the Aurochs with disastrous effect, knocking off all the plaster on his port side and revealing the chicken wire beneath, which formed his brisket. For the sculptor worked out all these creations of his fancy on the spot. Some of the figures, like the swordsmen, were hewn out of solid concrete; others were made of plaster, over wood or wire forms.

From the cover of the restaurant menu it may be learned that all this strangely grotesque medley of objects, from the castle to the Aurochs, is the work of an American, named Theophilus Brower. As a young man he traveled and studied art in Spain and Italy, and returned so imbued with the Latin spirit that he turned himself loose to build on Long Island a castle like one he remembered near Seville, and then he adorned the grounds with romantic sculpture. All this was more than thirty years ago, and Theophilus is no longer living.

The name Basso, which fits so well into this operatic setting, comes from the family that now owns and occupies the property. Although the interior of the castle is not open to the visitor, it is interesting to know that the rooms are circular, one above

SAGTIKOS MANOR

the other, as befits a castle. Besides copying the Spanish prototype, the artist added flourishes of his own, quite unknown to the medieval fortress. He built, for example, to the top of the central tower and outside stair, a ladder, which can be seen from the ground. In this the posts that hold the railing represent be-

CASA BASSO

spectacled owls, rabbits and other strange creatures which would surprise and perhaps please Don Quixote himself.

During the night of the great hurricane Mrs. Basso filled her castle with refugees. Among them was a family of Polish children rescued from a cabin on the bank of the creek near by. "Oh," sighed a little girl gratefully, as she said good-by the next day, "I'm glad the hurricane happened, because now I've been inside a real castle! And I never expected to."

Perhaps if she had said "unreal castle" she would have come

nearer to describing its effect on less romantic travelers. But perhaps the phrase "Castles in Spain" will have more meaning after Casa Basso. It isn't often that a man can, or dares to, give full rein to his fancies as did Theophilus, and we will salute his shade as we go on our way, for the courage of his imagination if not for the artistic success of his performance.

Next beyond Westhampton is the place already singled out for mention among the notable nomenclatures of Long Island—Speonk. It rather surprises one to see how cheerfully the village bears up under that name. They say the word is Indian shorthand for "high land above water," but that doesn't seem very appropriate here. One could wish that for the benefit of the traveler the ladies of Speonk who pluck the feathers of millions of ducks, as mentioned already, might be exhibited somewhere along the highway working with flying fingers and flying feathers at their unusual profession. It would be such good publicity for the Long Island duckling business, too. But, unfortunately, this denuding process is carried on far from vulgar eyes, and we drive through Speonk seeing nothing to distinguish it from other South Shore villages of its size.

On this route, as along the North Shore, the main arteries of travel are dull, and deformed by road signs. The wise traveler who would see the real South Shore will branch off into the roads that lead toward the sea. One of these runs through the exceedingly attractive village of Brookhaven. On its outskirts, not far from where the road branches off the Montauk Highway, is a good resort in which to have lunch or afternoon tea, the Brook House. Behind the one-story tile building is a sheltered spot on the margin of a brown forest stream, on which busy ducks go scuttling to and fro—altogether a place that tempts one to linger over his tea.

THE SOUTH SHORE

The village of Brookhaven is associated in the writer's memory with a call on Mr. James Ford and his sister many years ago. The two were keeping house in one of those attractive white cottages on the main road, in a manner like Charles and Mary Lamb. Mr. Ford was a brilliant journalist in his day. I had just read his *Forty-Odd Years in the Literary Shop* and was delighted at the opportunity to meet him. At the time of my visit, however, he was literally dying by inches of diabetes—there was no insulin in those days—with both legs amputated and his fingers going one by one. But he still contrived to manage his typewriter somehow. As he talked he sparkled with fun, remembered delightful anecdotes about famous writers, artists, actors and newspapermen of London and New York with whom he had been associated. "By the way"—he fished with difficulty in his pocket—"here's a letter just come from George Arliss," and it was the sort of letter that Mr. Arliss would write to his old friend. Mr. Ford chatted cheerfully about his plans for more literary work as if he had fifty years ahead of him. A blind man, if he could have been present at that interview, would have envied Mr. Ford's apparent vigor, as well as his wit and gift of anecdote. Yet, as his visitor knew, and Mr. Ford himself knew, the sands in his hourglass were down to the last grains.

There is great charm in Brookhaven, in its shaded streets, its old houses of the New England type and its wide blue water front seen through the trees; but the name suggests to one traveler at least the presence there of the bravest human spirit he has ever had the honor to meet.

Just beyond Brookhaven is Bellport, once known in the seventeenth century as Acombamack, but fortunately designated so no longer. Once this was an important place for fishing and offshore whaling, because there used to be a cut in the ocean barrier at this point, one that some storm over a century ago filled up, leaving the town desolate.

Its chief distinction now, from a geographical aspect, is that it stands farther above high watermark than any other town on the South Shore. In the ironing-out process done by the last glacier one wrinkle was left at this spot. Osborn's Bluff, for example, is actually several feet above salt water, and can look down its nose east or west without seeing a hillock or a bulge to compete with it.

As a municipality, Bellport is up and coming in a way to make to blush many a sleepy and shabby neighbor. The village fathers issue a booklet that at first glance might be mistaken for the catalogue of a fashionable boarding school. "The Charm of Bellport," says the opening sentence, "is all pervading. It is savored by the richness of its historical interest and the character of its inhabitants." True, it is one of the oldest English settlements in this southern area, though in the better part of three hundred years, as far as can be learned by casual inquiry, nothing astonishing was ever known to happen here. As for the "savor" you get from "the character of its inhabitants," perhaps one has to stay a while to become acquainted. Just what that character is, the handsome booklet does not explain, but no doubt it is delightful. Anyhow, Bellport gives the impression of a smart and pretty summer resort by the sea. In the winter it goes in for "scooter" races on the bay, and for other ice sports. "Visit Bellport," says the booklet, "and we believe that you too will consider this beautiful village 'Nature's Gift Garden.'" We will cheerfully leave it at that.

When one reflects on the nationwide fame of Blue Point oysters it is surprising and disappointing to discover that the place they are supposed to come from is relatively so insignificant. As a matter of fact, more than one visitor has labored under the impression that Little Neck clams and Blue Point oysters were so called because of their anatomical peculiarities. The aforesaid clams, we used to think, were slender about their medulla oblongatas, and the oysters possessed a blue decoration on the shell. Apparently nobody is quite sure about the clams. Some hold that "Little Neck" does describe the clam, while other savants declare that the name comes from Little Neck, Long Island. All seem to agree that the oysters derived their name from the village of Blue Point here on the South Shore. But it is now a registered trade name for the oysters taken along the shore between Amityville and Smith's Point. At the same time the skeptic may be pardoned the suspicion that Blue Point is the name now used for any small, round oyster.

There is considerable sameness noticeable about the South Shore route and the towns which the highway runs through; that is, as the motorist sees them it is usually while going from one main street, with its drugstores, filling stations and movie houses, into another like it. The real character of these villages, like Patchogue and Sayville, is only to be seen in their lanes and byroads, especially as they wander down to the bay. Then you begin to understand not only why people spend their summers in these places but also why many of them with business in the big city contrive to winter here as well.

In passing through Sayville we might recall the shipwreck of the three-masted schooner *Louie V. Place,* which occurred just off the town on Fire Island shoals forty-odd years ago. It is still one of the worst marine disasters on the Long Island coast in the memory of man. The schooner was bound to New York from Baltimore in January, 1895. A great gale struck her, and as the waves broke over her they froze instantly on sails, decks and rigging. The sails and running gear were soon frozen into an immovable mass, and the schooner was driven helplessly past New York Harbor until in the early-morning hours she was hurled upon the shoals of Fire Island. The lifesaving station could not get a boat through the breakers. When they shot a life line to the schooner the wretched crew were too numb to bear a hand. They climbed a little way into the rigging. All the following day the storm raged at its height, and one by one the crew dropped into the sea. On the third day a boat was launched and the two surviving men were taken off; one died soon after, and the other never recovered from the effects of his suffering. By a tragic circumstance the body of the captain came ashore far to the east of the scene of the wreck, at Hampton Bays, the very place where he had his home.

At Islip (pronounced "Ice-lip") every motorist should pause to give a grateful salute to the memory of a local girl who made good. With her husband she did more than any other person in history for the cause of good roads before the birth of the motorcar. This heroine of the highways was Gloriana Margaretta Nicoll, born in Islip in 1759, to be exact. Her father was a leading citizen. He helped to found King's College (Columbia) and the New York City Library. His home was known as Nicoll Manor. In 1770, a boy of fourteen, John Louden McAdam, came there from Scotland to work for his kinsman. The roads here on Long Island were wretched in those days, and in his duties John trudged over them many a weary mile. As he did so, the idea of making good roads dawned in his mind. He often talked over the idea with Gloriana after she had consented to marry him.

THE SOUTH SHORE

In 1783, the war being over, he returned to Scotland with his bride, and there he succeeded in getting himself appointed Commissioner of Roads. Then John and Gloriana traveled to study roads together. They covered thirty thousand miles in their work, and for the expenses incurred the wife willingly spent her fortune. At last John worked out the structure of the famous "McAdam Road." When this had proved its virtues, Parliament voted the McAdamses not only the expenses they had incurred but also a handsome bonus, and offered John a knighthood besides. But all this achievement would have been impossible if Gloriana Nicoll had not been an enthusiastic partner in the work. Never before or since, perhaps, has an American girl's dowry been spent in so good a cause in a foreign land. The State Highway Commission should put up a tablet to her memory somewhere in Islip, alongside the road.

The vogue of Long Island towns as summer resorts began about 1870, but long before the Civil War New Yorkers started fishing and hunting camps along the South Shore, and Islip was a favorite rendezvous. When news of Sumter came in 1861 most of the towns burst into a display of flags, but one village near Islip remained colorless. A New York camper coming to the village store found a sullen crowd seated or standing about the premises. "Why don't you hang out the flags?" asked the city man.

"Flags, eh?" retorted one of the village solons. "Flags, and clams a dollar a thousand!" The conviction, in which they were all agreed, was that Mr. Lincoln's first business was to raise the price of clams, and until that happened there'd be no flag waving.

These early fishing clubs usually began with dues at one dollar a year, and when because of increasing luxuries the rate soared to ten dollars a year some of the richest members resigned in protest. For years there was a constant warfare between the club members and the farmers. The former brought accusations of poaching, and the latter retorted with indictments of chicken-stealing. Probably both were right.

Just beyond Islip is Bayshore. This faces the widest part of the Great South Bay. If the traveler is minded to go out to see that narrow thread of sand known as the Great South Beach, and visit the famous Fire Island Light, surrounded by a state park, here in Bayshore is the place to leave his car and take the passenger ferry. It was in this strip of beach between the lighthouse and Point O' Woods where the hurricane of 1938 wrought such havoc among the summer cottages.

As we drive on toward Babylon we begin to see more of the large country estates that suggest wealth. One of the most attractive of these, standing beside our highway about two and a half miles east of Babylon, is the great grandfather of all the rest. A state historical marker calls the wayfarer's attention to it, "Sagtikos Manor." Although the place is not open to the public, one may stand at the entrance and take a good look at the house and such of the grounds as are visible from the front. Here is another of those great manorial estates on Long Island, like Sylvester Manor and Gardiner's Island, which were founded in the seventeenth century and have continued in the possession of the family ever since. The present Manor House —the one facing the street—dates from the late eighteenth century, but it is unfortunately dwarfed by a white elephant of a modern addition in the rear. Shut off from the gaze of outsiders is a walled-in garden with bronze peacock fountain and wide lawns shaded by great oaks. Originally the property of the Van Cortlandts, it soon passed into the hands of the Thompsons, who held it for more than two centuries. The present owner is a Thompson descendant, but he also possesses the name and lineage of Lion Gardiner of Gardiner's Island.

In this house slept Governor Tryon, the last Royal Governor of New York, and General Sir Henry Clinton of the British army. Since the Squire Thompson of this period was a Whig, the General made frequent use of Sagtikos Manor, without waiting to be invited. His men also frequently camped on the grounds and made free with what they found. Once Mr. Thompson narrowly escaped being killed by a body of seamen, from a British man-of-war, who raided the house.

The most welcome guest in Sagkitos Manor was President Washington, who slept here on his tour of Long Island in 1790. The room which he occupied with its four-poster bed is still preserved as a shrine to the Father of His Country. And that is why on the gateposts is affixed the shield of the United States, and on the front lawn two small cannon of the Revolutionary War, indicating that this estate is not merely a residence but a historic monument. Nor is the spirit of public service restricted to its sufferings in the seventeen-seventies and eighties. When the new parkway system came to the Sagtikos Manor estate, the owner gave a large tract of land to the Park Commission for the use of the public. In recognition of this gift there is to be a "Sagtikos Park."

In the town of Babylon itself there is a large permanent population of those businessmen who daily commute to New York. This gives the place an air of suburban sophistication. A generous citizen, J. Stanley Foster, presented the town with a War Memorial Park of great beauty, surrounding a lake. But it would still be interesting to know why the founders of the place chose Babylon for a name.

DISCOVERING LONG ISLAND

In the early days when it was just another fishing village on the South Shore, an unexpected visitor landed on the beach. Commodore David Porter had been taken prisoner by the British in Chilean waters during the War of 1812. By arrangement with the English captain Porter and his men were sent to New York on parole in a small ship. Off Sandy Hook he was detained by the blockading squadron. Feeling insulted at this, he renounced his parole and, getting into the whaleboat with a crew, rowed away into a convenient fog, which covered the Americans from pursuit. They kept on rowing until they came ashore sixty miles from Sandy Hook, right at the doorstep of Babylon.

At first the inhabitants mistook Porter for a British naval officer—in those days there must have been no unmistakable British or American accent—but when he succeeded in proving who he was, the patriotic Babylonians put the whaleboat on wheels, hoisted him inside of it and then drove him in this triumphal chariot all the way to the Brooklyn Navy Yard.

It must have been a quaint spectacle to see the Commodore sitting on a thwart, his face lobster-red under the heavy black cocked hat and the July sun, as he was jolted unmercifully over the miles of sandy roads between Babylon and Brooklyn. And all the while he might have ridden comfortably inside a stagecoach!

David Porter was not a person of sweet temper, either. When courting the girl whom he married he became annoyed by her brother—as has often happened in courtships—and without wasting words he picked up the offending brother and flung him out of the window.

At any rate, however much the Commodore cursed and swore —to himself, let us hope—on this hero's journey, the citizens

THE SOUTH SHORE

of Babylon and all the farmers' children along the route enjoyed it enormously and felt very patriotic.

Just before entering Babylon we paused for a moment at Sagtikos Manor. After leaving Babylon and, passing by the "Merrick Road" or Montauk Highway, through the welcoming

TRYON HALL

and friendly atmosphere of Amityville—we come upon another eighteenth-century residence in the grand tradition, also, like Sagtikos, standing near the present highway, on the north side, with its windows looking out on the Bay. This is popularly known as "Tryon Hall." For years those windows were shuttered and boarded up like blind eyes. The front lawn was a jungle of tall weeds, and the whole a picture of desolation and decayed grandeur. More is the shame and pity, for this old house is redolent with historic associations. Like its neighbor, Sagtikos Manor, Tryon Hall was a manorial estate.

The original house, built here in 1696, was a small brick dwelling with a steep roof and chimneys at the end. There was nothing "manorial" about it at all, but it served as a home and refuge for Major Thomas Jones, an Irishman who fought for his king, James the Second, and when James was beaten, decided that he'd rather live in a new country. He came first to Oyster Bay and there fell in love with a Townsend girl of that generation, bearing the oddly immoral name of "Freelove." The father-in-law gave the Major a huge tract of land on the South Shore and here, in 1696, the couple started their married life in a brick cottage. Small as it was, a brick house was such a rarity on Long Island that for years it was known as *the* brick house." The Joneses were proud of it, and lived happily ever after, raising a fine flock of seven little Joneses and being highly regarded by all their neighbors.

In 1713 the Major answered his last roll call. Thereafter, the story goes, the brick house acted very strangely. Unaccountable noises were frequently heard, and one end window, flanking a chimney, absolutely refused to stay closed. There was no use bolting shutters across it, for some invisible hand would draw the bolts back and open the casement. Then a sash window was put in, but that was tossed out as soon as it was in place. Boards were nailed across, but they met the same fate. Finally, in exasperation, the heir sent a mason to brick up the window. But, as soon as the bricklayer had finished his day's job, out flew all the bricks and mortar to the lawn beneath.

After that, the Joneses moved out. If the ghost of the old Major insisted on staying in his house and playing jokes, he could have it all to himself. And so the brick cottage stood

THE SOUTH SHORE

empty for a hundred years or more, the most famous haunted house on Long Island.

Later, as the eldest son made a fortune for himself, he built, in the year 1770, on the same land and near the old house, a handsome thirty-room mansion. That is the dwelling we still see today. Here, before the house was a year old, grand entertainments were held, rivaling those of Sagtikos Manor. Hither, with flunkies and outriders and state coach, drove Governor William Tryon, and such a magnificent reception was accorded the distinguished guest, and so charming did he prove, that the name "Tryon Hall" was adopted for the house at once.

When, a few years later, the troubles began between the colonies and the mother country the master of Tryon Hall, David Jones, took sides with George the Third as his father had done for a Stuart king. He died in 1775, but his son, Judge Thomas Jones, was even a hotter Tory than his father. Now it happened that the British had captured, in Connecticut, General Silliman, and they would not exchange him except for someone of equal prominence. So some enterprising Connecticut patriots crossed the Sound, marched to Tryon Hall and kidnaped Judge Jones, carrying him with them all the way back to Connecticut to the home of Mrs. Silliman, where he was something between a prisoner and a guest. The exchange, then, was duly effected. Silliman and Jones had known each other at Yale, and the upshot of this experience was a warm friendship between the two families. When the two men met on a vessel for the exchange, Mrs. Silliman sent a fat turkey for them to dine on. But being a Tory, Judge Jones had to flee to England as the war came to a close, and his estate passed into the possession of his nephew Floyd, who added the Jones to his name with a hyphen. And "Tryon Hall" became "Fort Neck House," thus dispensing with any association with a Royal Governor.

In 1837 the ghost-ridden brick cottage was at last torn down. In 1906 the family gave up living in the Manor and rented it to outsiders. Five or six years ago it suffered the unhappy fate of being tried out as a roadhouse. For this purpose the interior was disemboweled of its walls and paneling. That venture failed, and since then vandals have smashed windowpanes and ripped away anything that could be carried off. Steps have been taken very recently to rescue the old mansion; and the good news is that it will soon be repaired and reoccupied, to everyone's satisfaction. Meanwhile, the local police, are keeping an eye on it so that there will be no more wanton destruction. I had not been sketching the old house fifteen minutes before a courteous officer of the law drove up merely to make sure that I was doing no mischief.

There is another place of interest to be found on this Merrick Road in Babylon, "The Duck Shop." Indeed, it is a safe hazard to claim that this modest manufactory is by all odds the most original place of business in all Long Island. Touring husbands who always step on the accelerator when they see, looming ahead, the danger signs, "Antiques" and "Curios," may safely slow down here and come to a full stop. For this shop is different, and one of its distinctions is its appeal to the masculine taste. It is not a "shoppe," but a little wooden-duck factory.

This Duck Shop is conducted by Mr. John Lee Baldwin, a native of Babylon. He is the proprietor, foreman and man of all work, combined under a single black derby hat. But do not imagine this to be a place of toil. A large white signboard on an inside wall of the shop reads in bold black letters, "The Duck Workshop—Ducking Work My Specialty—John Lee Baldwin [this in big capitals]—Originator and Founder." And, in the big-

THE SOUTH SHORE

gest caps of all, "NEVER WORKED AND NEVER WILL." Another signboard reiterates the idea: "This Is No Workshop, Only a Place Where the Brain Relaxes. John Lee Baldwin Specializing in Comfort." Could anything be more alluring? That is the point. Mr. Baldwin wants the world to know that when he sits down to a piece of white pine and starts to shape it with his clasp knife he isn't working—perish the thought! —he is just having fun.

What he does is to whittle out wild ducks of all sizes and in all poses of flight or repose. Curiously enough, he has never hunted ducks, and yet he makes the finest decoys in the world. For sportsmen who like the idea of making their own decoys he carves and paints heads, which they can attach to the bodies of their own handiwork. Besides the full-size canvasbacks, mallards and so on, and the other game fowl, such as geese and snipe, to be used as decoys, he makes six-inch models of the birds in action. These have gone out from this little shop to adorn the rooms of sportsmen, not only to every section of this country but also to many parts of the Old World.

As the caller enters the shop he sees ducks everywhere, from the door knocker to an expansive wire netting on which two hundred little mallards are fastened, flying in their V formation. Scattered about the room are also curious souvenirs of the time when Mr. Baldwin used to frequent auction sales and bring back all sorts of objects from a stuffed South American sloth to a Currier and Ives print.

This Duck Shop is notable as one of those rare instances of what Emerson had in mind when he said that customers beat a path to the door of the man who makes a better mousetrap. Mr. Baldwin does not advertise because he doesn't need to. Visitors beat a path to his door from many states of the Union.

And they say in Babylon that mail-order customers need to put on their envelopes only this delightful address: "Never Worked and Never Will, Babylon, L. I." The letter carriers know just where to deliver it.

From Amityville the highroad continues west into Freeport, a place renowned for its game fishing, but at this point we should be reentering the part of Long Island which is distinctly suburban. Instead, our itinerary will turn north toward that wide central area of the Island which so far has been ignored. But there is one point of interest so close to our "Merrick Road"—only a mile north of Amityville—that it must be included in this day's jaunt along the South Shore. In its way it is as absurdly out of keeping with the Long Island landscape as Casa Basso, with which this chapter began. It is Frank Buck's "Jungle Park," a real, honest-to-goodness zoo of wild animals. Twenty-five cents will suffice for admission to the premises, but another quarter should be invested in *Frank Buck's Souvenir Booklet*. The cover shows the intrepid explorer himself engaged in deadly combat with a python. The serpent has made two turns about Mr. Buck's left arm and is beginning to swallow him whole, starting at the wrist. However, the hunter is shown reaching for his trusty revolver with his disengaged hand, and you know he will speedily subdue the giant reptile. But such a picture puts one in the proper shuddery mood for inspecting Mr. Buck's denizens of the jungle, and as we turn the pages we see exciting photographs of these creatures taken in their native haunts.

Movie addicts will not need to be reminded that it was Mr. Buck who filmed *Wild Cargo, Bring 'Em Back Alive* and *Claw and Fang*. Of course, Very Superior Intellects, who cannot stoop to looking at lions and tigers, may go on past this Jungle Park.

But the rest of us will pay our quarter and gaze with delight at all these wild creatures, from pachyderm to peccadillo (if that is the right word). You may think you have a respectable knowledge of jungle animals, but do you know, for instance, the Agouti and Paca from the region of the Amazon? Or the Sooty Mangabey and the Blue-faced Drill of Africa? Or the Spectacled Langur of Malaya? Or the Seladang of India? I thought not. Well, here and now is your time to learn, for all those mysterious fauna are here in Mr. Buck's park and duly labeled.

After the thrilling picture of the python on the cover of the souvenir booklet it is disappointing to view the captive specimens. These creatures always seem to be wrapped around themselves in a trance as motionless as one of those chairwarmers you see in the corridors of a federal office building. Rudyard Kipling's "Kaa" in the *Jungle Books* was certainly more up and coming. Perhaps Mr. Buck can think of some way to make his pythons put on a better act.

The lions and tigers, however, are a grand lot and most satisfying. They look sleek and healthy; they lick their chops, and pace up and down with the stealthy swagger you expect in a man-eater. If the expression they cast upon us humans speaks ineffable disdain, it may be because they have to listen all day to a loud-speaker on the radio at the restaurant building across the way. At the time a Bengal tiger was looking down at me as if I were a leper of the pariah caste, a female crooner was bawling, "There is rith-um in my haht for yoo-oo-oo."

At all events, there is collected here such an infinite variety of bird, beast and reptile, from every dark jungle near the Equator, that there is no use trying to list them any further. Here they have been assembled, waiting for superintendents of zoological gardens from the nation's big cities. Probably there are private citizens, who have odd tastes in pets or who put on animal acts in shows, who also come here to find what they want. Mr. Buck is stocked for all requirements, whether it be a black king cobra that looks hideous and spits venom horribly, or a gorgeous blue macaw which is a joy to the eye and emits only an occasional screech. Or it may be just another tame elephant for children to ride on. The Jungle Park has quite a squad of elephants, enough to make a whole circus of the good old Barnum and Forepaugh days. It is sad to think that the thrills of the canvas and tanbark will exist no more for the children of the coming generation. The story is that the employees of the last Big Top struck for more wages than the management could pay. So the circus folded its tents like the Arab and silently stole away into oblivion, which was more than these strikers collective-bargained for.

The next best thing to the circus is this Jungle Park. In fact, so many people have made this discovery that the size of the Sunday throng requires two special traffic policemen in front of the gates. From a scientific point of view, Mr. Buck's work is notable for the fact that he has brought to this country a great many rare animals, specimens that had never been seen here before. On the back of the souvenir booklet are listed these "firsts." Besides his zoo here at Amityville he has in Singapore the largest private collection of wild animals in the world. Altogether, the Jungle Park makes an entertaining full stop to a tour of the South Shore.

CHAPTER XI

THE PARKS

JUST north of Babylon the road map shows a shred of territory set apart as the "Belmont Lake State Park." This is one of the smallest of the famous Long Island parks, but it is the capital. Here, where once stood the palatial home of August Belmont, is a new office building which is the heart and center of the whole park service. It is a handsome white edifice, standing beside a small lake. Shade trees grow to the water's edge all around that lake, and comfortable benches under their branches invite the traveler to take his ease. Across the water we can see the children—if it is vacation time—swinging madly in a playground grove, and amateur oarsmen are out on the lake taking their holiday dose of sunburn and hand blisters simultaneously. This Belmont Lake was formerly a trout pond, on which Mr. Belmont and his friends used to cast their flies, and in which the neighboring yokels used to find their own sport and sustenance, much to Mr. Belmont's wrath. Under the trees in front of the Administration Building are several large, old-fashioned guns. These came to Mr. Belmont from the squadron of Commodore Matthew Calbraith Perry, the American naval officer who went to Japan and opened up that country to the Western world. The elder Belmont married a daughter of the Commodore. And since we are here there could be no better spot to pause to consider all these Long Island Parks of which Belmont is the administration center, for in these public playgrounds, together with the parkways that link them with the great city, we have something that is not only the proud possession of Long Island, or New York state, but also of the whole country.

Already in our voyage of discovery we have come upon some of these pleasure grounds. We lingered at the very tip of the North Fork in Orient Beach State Park, stretched our legs on a bench in the shade of the cedars and looked out over the bay at Gardiner's Island. Again, on our way to Montauk Point, we went through the thick woodlands of Hither Hills, drove along the bluffs and saw on the ocean side the neat camps where motor tourists or hikers could stay. At the very end, coming up to the government reservation on which Montauk Light stands, we rejoiced in the stretch of state park there with its conveniences and comforts for the traveler. There we openly gave thanks that this stretch of glorious country, high above the sea, had not been turned over to hotels, billboards and hot-dog stands. These are only three of fifteen state parks in Nassau and Suffolk counties, of which twelve are practically complete in their development, and the others are coming on fast. How these parks came to be is a story that has been told before, but will bear retelling in brief, for it is an encouraging evidence that one does not need a political dictatorship to accomplish a great service for the public.

Long ago a State Park Commission had been established—in 1902, to be exact. This Commission met and elected a secretary. Later, after recovering from this burst of activity, it sent a report to the legislature recommending three park areas, and for this purpose the Commission was empowered to acquire five thousand acres. Then the whole group of Rip Van Winkles slumbered for two decades. Twenty years afterwards, the Commission had not obtained one acre or planted one tree. That is

THE PARKS

the familiar story of our politics.

In 1924, however, another commission was appointed with Mr. Robert Moses as its President. Mr. Moses had already, in 1918, done a magnificent job for Governor Alfred E. Smith in

BELMONT LAKE OUTLET

planning a reorganization of the state departments, and in this study Mr. Moses came upon the horrible mess in which the state parks were rotting. He went to Governor Smith with a plan for a State Council of Parks with eleven regional commissions. At first the Governor laughed at his ambitious schemes. "You want to give the State a fur overcoat, when what it needs is a suit of red-flannel underwear," he said. But Mr. Moses succeeded in convincing his chief that the idea was right, and in 1924 the New York State Council of Parks was duly ordained by the legislature, together with increased appropriations. At that time Mr. Moses took on two unsalaried jobs—which he still holds—Chairman of the State Council of Parks, and President of the Long Island State Park Commission.

When he took hold there was just one state park on Long Island, a patch of less than two hundred acres at Fire Island. This had once been a cholera quarantine station. Mr. Moses persuaded the federal officials that the lighthouse there needed only a few acres to hold it up, and that it would be well to give all the rest to the state for park purposes. The result was that the park speedily expanded from two hundred acres to eight hundred acres. Some twenty-five thousand visitors enjoy it every summer; but it is accessible only by water, and a score of Fire Island parks would not meet the needs of the hundreds of thousands of city people who drive out in their cars looking for a place to spend a Sunday beside the sea. Unfortunately, most of the hundreds of miles of beach and water front had been taken up by private owners long before, and the big problem was how to get some of that shore back into the hands of the public.

Mr. Moses made a beginning with the Hither Hills region as the first of his large parks. This was a good way off from private estates or hotels, but the year 1924 was the time when Mr. Carl Fisher was going strong with his project of a "second Miami" at Montauk. Those who owned the land were suddenly determined to hold their lots for the same soaring figures that flourished in Miami just before the bubble burst. Mr. Moses finally had to use the strong-arm weapon of "eminent domain" to get what he wanted, and it was a battle royal.

At any rate, the new Park Commission met general opposi-

THE PARKS

tion. The whole campaign is too long a story to tell here, but the August Heckscher State Park, a short distance south of East Islip, is a good example of what had to be done. The establishment of this recreation center on a former game preserve was made possible for Mr. Moses only after the most furious opposition on the part of the township and the Citizens' Committees. The fight was taken to Albany and to the courts. But at the moment when the Philistines were exulting in their victory, Mr. August Heckscher himself offered the state $262,000 to pay for the park as a gift to the people. That settled the issue, and in 1929 the park was dedicated.

So, one after another, these park areas were obtained, some by fighting, others by purchase, many by gift. These gifts were made by public-spirited individuals, such as Mr. Heckscher, and also by communities. Out of a total of about 28,000 acres in the present park and parkway system nearly 16,000 represent gifts to the Park Commission.

Sometimes, where there were no appropriations or gifts available, Mr. Moses used other means to get his park. For example, the Bethpage Park, of 1368 acres, was acquired by setting up a Park Authority, which issued bonds to cover the cost of buying the land. This seems like a daring thing to do, yet through the fees of its golf course, amounting to $140,000 a year, the Park Authority is retiring the bonds, and will soon turn the property, clear of all debt, over to the state.

The Commissioner has gone on his way victorious. The first Moses led a people into a Promised Land. This one made a Promised Land out of patches of scrub oak, beach grass and sand on one hand, while he fought off opposition with the other. But to get to these recreation and beauty spots there must be easy routes of travel, and along with the acquisition of the park areas themselves the Commissioner had to obtain rights of way for his connecting highways. These were designed not merely as highways but three-hundred-foot-wide parkways—what have been called "shoestring parks"—restricted to pleasure cars and free from crossings and stop lights.

Right-of-way problems beset the creation of these roads; but they, too, were surmounted—sometimes by a tactful detour to avoid ruining some ancestral lawn—and now there are seventy miles of incomparable parkway connecting eastern Long Island with the Bronx and Upper Manhattan. There still remains a large section of the parkway program to be completed, but that is simply a matter of time.

It is important to observe that these parkways are free from the all-too-familiar plague of advertising eyesores. There is now a state law which prohibits billboards within five hundred feet of the right of way. But, though that helps, it is not enough to prevent the disfigurement of the views from highways and bridges. Mr. Moses is driving ahead with a proposed amendment to the present law, and may the God of Battles be with him.

A very prominent feature of this parkway program is the matter of bridges. In fact, one of the Commissioner's greatest monuments is the new Triborough Bridge, so called because it connects three of the city's five boroughs. You can call it *a* bridge, but you might as well say sixteen bridges: four over the water, the supports resting on two islands in the East River, and twelve over land. Add to that fourteen miles of approaches, and you have an aggregate of the colossal piece of engineering known as the Triborough Bridge.

It is characteristic of Mr. Moses that he wasted no areas in the project. Under the bridge ends he laid out playgrounds, and on Randall's Island, which once held only institutions for

ON THE SOUTHERN STATE PARKWAY

THE PARKS

the city's insane, he laid out more recreation fields; put up the administration building for the bridge, and a city stadium. This immense "bridgeway" cost sixty million dollars, half of which came as a gift or loan from the federal treasury. But it is now a paying business because of the fees collected. It is a toll bridge, and there are more than thirty thousand cars rolling over it every day at twenty-five cents a car. The original Triborough bonds have already been retired, and a new bond issue has been sold to the public, covering what is left of the old indebtedness and the cost of the new bridge, the Bronx Whitestone, which is to be completed by the time the great rush of visitors comes to the World's Fair.

Reclaiming the site of this tremendous exposition is another one of the scalps hung up in Mr. Moses' wigwam, or if you prefer, another jewel in his crown. He, as Park Commissioner, had the say-so as to where that World's Fair was to be situated. For it should be noted here that he is also head of the park system of New York City, a very important fact because it enables him to link the city boroughs with the surrounding counties, thus disposing of local politics and personal jealousies. And, though this is not the story of the city, it should not be forgotten that Greater New York also has enjoyed the blessing of his ideas as to what public parks should be. Hitler and Mussolini never enjoyed more absolute power than he did when dictating the site of that exposition. He gave out his terms: The Fair was to take the smelly and awful area known as the Corona Dump, with its equally repulsive sister, the swampland lying to the south. Those of us who used to travel on the Fall River Line have a very distinct memory of how that dumpland looked and smelled as we passed it on the Sound. All this district was to be reclaimed to become the site of the Fair. So the old garbage area was not only to be made respectable, but actually glorified. Finally, Mr. Moses decreed that, when the big show was all over, the Fair authorities were to leave behind a new park for New York City with all the Fair buildings cleared away, and with a fine parkway around it. In this way the Commissioner planned to gain a permanent link between the Grand Central Parkway of Long Island and the Triborough Bridge.

Needless to say, the plan was accepted. The contractor set men to work in shifts so that the job would be going on twenty-four hours a day; floodlights were used at night. In nine months the dump was leveled off, including its ninety-foot "Mt. Corona." He filled in the swamp, but cut out its muck to use as topsoil, and, in short, transformed the huge ghastly eyesore (and nose sore) into what is now to be known as Flushing Meadow, site of the greatest world's fair ever seen. After that is over, this area will be the finest of Greater New York's parks.

Of the Long Island park collection all twelve that are complete can be readily identified on any road map. They extend throughout the counties of Nassau and Suffolk, from the edge of the Greater New York City area to the tips of both forks of the Island. Already some of the smaller ones are becoming crowded on a Sunday afternoon, and Mr. Moses now casts his acquisitive eye on surrounding areas. He'll get them, too. For there is no question as to the public's enjoyment and overwhelming approval of what the Park Commissioner has created for them. During the year 1937 a total of 3,500,000 people visited the national parks; but for the same period 6,300,000 came to the twelve Long Island parks, and each year the figure grows.

The assortment of recreation grounds offered to the visitor on Long Island has fortunately much variety. Orient Beach, as we have seen, is a narrow ribbon of sand with a growth of

THE PARKS

stunted cedars. Across the Bay, Montauk Point State Park is a lofty promontory reminding one of the Devonshire downs south of Exeter, in England. Behind that the Hither Hills State Park is mostly dense oak forest, flanked on one side by high bluffs overlooking the ocean. As we return along the areas on both north and south shores, it is easy to see that such natural advantages as the terrain offered have been utilized as far as possible. Sunken Meadow, for instance, on the North Shore, is a combination of lowland and beach with a high wooded bluff in the rear. The Fire Island park is a bare and wind-swept shoestring of sand that is all beach, with the Great South Bay on one side, the Atlantic on the other and a lighthouse as the "center of interest," as painters say. But all of them are provided with the things that every holiday-seeker wants, in most cases a chance for bathing, a sheltered place with tables and benches for eating, clean and modern "comfort stations," a place for children to play safely, a first-aid establishment for accidents, and protection from hoodlums and the drunk and disorderly. Probably one excellent reason for the orderly appearance and conduct of all these Long Island parks is the pervading influence of those smart-looking State Police officers who seem to be absolutely but unobtrusively on the job. Each park exploits whatever special advantage it may have, such as a lake, forest or stream. For example, Belmont has a lake with its outlet, a brook that tumbles over a dam and goes brawling off into the woods. Here there is a trail that wanders off along the stream most invitingly into a long, narrow strip of park that leads to another pond a mile or two toward the south. This Belmont Lake State Park, by the way, is already too small for the crowds of people who enjoy it.

Unfortunately Mr. Moses was born too late to save one feature for these parks of his; namely, a grove of tall pines. The Long Island trees are nothing to boast of as a rule, and most of the woodlands are covered with a growth that is small and scrubby. If there were now a grove of white pine trees, none under a hundred feet tall, what a place *that* would be to picnic in! At one time there were beautiful pine forests on the Island, but forest fires came in the wake of the Long Island Railroad, and after that somebody chopped the rest down to burn up in some smelter works, leaving behind a dismal and desolate area in the heart of the island known as the "Pine Barrens." There is some talk of transposing that into a state game preserve for hunting but it is a safe bet that Mr. Moses has his eye on that area, too. In fact there is now, north of Yaphank, one small but beautiful grove of pines—from seventy-five to one hundred years old—which may yet become the nucleus of a State park.

Out of the present collection of a dozen pleasure grounds going strong, let's visit two. The first shall be the Bethpage one, which, it will be remembered, the Park Commissioner wangled by staking his personal integrity behind an issue of bonds in the depths of the depression. This in itself is a Grade A Miracle. We shall easily find this park by looking for it just to the north of Route 24, lying between Routes 107 on the west and 110 on the east.

As we come up the drive we are amazed to see a handsome building that looks like a millionaire's country club. It is a low, rambling house in the Long Island Colonial tradition, with whitewashed brick and hand-split shingles. It spells "swank" at the first glimpse. And it gets swankier as you enter. There are the great reception rooms decorated *aux Chinoises,* also the grill, with its wainscoted walls and arching timbers overhead, and the restaurant all elegance and perfection. The locker rooms

THE PARKS

are the last word in cleanliness and perfect appointments. There are private dining rooms, if you please, which you can rent for entertaining. It all takes your breath away. The only difference between this clubhouse and that of the most opulent of Bourbons or the most royal of economic royalists anywhere in the land is that this one is on a paying basis. And anyone who behaves himself and can pay the moderate fees can enjoy all the privileges. Lunch, for example, in that handsome grill and restaurant may be bought for 65 and 75 cents and dinner for $1.25 and $1.50.

But the clubhouse is only the beginning. Bethpage is distinguished from the other of Mr. Moses' parks by having four eighteen-hole golf courses, sporty enough to suit the most fastidious. Here again the greens fee is only one dollar for weekdays, and two dollars for Sundays and holidays. It is a godsend for the golf enthusiast of the metropolitan area, for it is only forty-five minutes from the heart of New York City, and gives him the best his heart could ask for at a moderate cost.

Nor are these golf links all this park has to offer. There are tennis courts. There is a livery stable with miles of bridle paths; also a jumping course for those who are not happy unless they are risking their necks. The most striking and utterly unique feature is the polo field. Every Sunday afternoon during the season any visitor, for an admission charge of ten cents for children and twenty-five cents for adults, may watch this, one of the most thrilling games in the world of sport, and one hitherto shut off behind the hedges of private clubs. In brief, what Mr. Moses has done here at Bethpage with its 1374 acres is to give to the man of moderate means everything he could expect from membership in a country club, except initiation fees, annual dues and assessments. Bethpage is unique among public parks the world over. It is certainly what Governor Smith would have called "fur coat." This work has been criticized as "socialism"; but if this be socialism make the most of it, for Mr. Moses is a Republican.

Before leaving Bethpage we should note that out of it runs a long parkway from Massapequa on the South Shore. This is a fair sample of the kind of driveway the Commissioner plans to build someday all over the Island, connecting his recreation centers.

The second park we shall visit in this chapter is also unique the world over, but for different reasons. This is the famous Jones Beach, lying off on one of those long sand dunes that shut off the Great South Bay from the ocean. We reach our destination by a parkway which branches off from the Southern State Parkway on a line due south from Westbury. This drive leads across a causeway five miles long, over what were once salt marshes, and over three bridges to Jones Beach. This area, fortunately, had been spared from all the muck and ballyhoo of "developments" for the simple reason that nobody could get to it. So it wasn't difficult for Mr. Moses to acquire the land as a present from the two townships that owned it, Oyster Bay and Hempstead, as far back as 1926–27. What we see now, as we approach over the causeway, has all been created out of nothing but sand and marsh, as has the causeway itself.

The first object to catch the eye is a tall, graceful campanile, which is a hint of Venice. This is not, as one might suppose, a carillon tower. It is Mr. Moses' idea of how to treat a water tank. And this is typical of the whole amazing establishment as it begins to unfold before our eyes. The central part consists of two magnificent bathhouses, four thousand feet apart, connected on the ocean side by a boardwalk, and on the land

THE PARKS

side by the Ocean Parkway. The causeway on which we entered comes upon the Parkway at right angles halfway between these two colossal bathhouses. At this point stands the water

TOWER, JONES BEACH

tower, in a traffic circle. Straight in front of the tower the walk leads to the "Mall," where there are beach shops, cafeteria and café on the boardwalk.

From this center, right and left, are the wonders of this playground. As the name suggests, the main attraction of this park is its ocean bathing. There are about three miles of beach.

The East Bath House has accommodations for 10,000 bathers, besides refreshment stands, "comfort stations," and what not. The West Bath House can take care of 5400 bathers and, in addition, has a large dining room and swimming pools served with filtered salt water, which is heated in cool weather. At night there is a submarine illumination system. Between these two is the central group of buildings, on the Mall, which serves those who do not use the bathhouse facilities but go straight to the Beach. As a matter of fact, three-fourths of the people who come here do not use them. They come in bathing suits and dry off in the sun. It is one of the rules here, however, that there is no undressing or dressing in a car.

Nor is this all the story of the bathing beach. On the land side is Zack's Bay, with smooth salt water for those who don't like the surf. Here, too, is a huge grandstand, before which swimming meets are held by day and light opera is produced at night. The latter is given on a stage set out in the water, the voices assisted by amplifiers. *Pinafore,* given in such a setting, with poor little Buttercup making her entrance by boat to the gangway, must be particularly effective.

Everything about this pleasure ground is utterly different from what one usually sees in any public park. The architecture is conceived not only on a gigantic scale but in excellent taste. Fortunately Mr. Moses did not allow his architects to follow the most modern European fashions. Because these are not World's Fair buildings, but permanent structures, they can't afford to be freakish.

The whole establishment is conceived in the nautical spirit. Here and there are ship's ventilators; they are for waste paper. And those "steering wheels" are just drinking fountains having fun masquerading. Directional signs are breezy figures in cast

THE PARKS

iron; and the special sign of Jones Beach is the sea horse, which is incorporated in the mosaic designs of the flagging. There are large wire baskets for the inevitable bottles, and here and there are fireplaces in which you can have a charcoal fire for a hot lunch or supper on the beach. The Park Commissioner conceived this as a recreation park—not, like Coney Island, a place of varied amusements. To keep things shipshape there is a "courtesy squad" composed of young men who patrol the grounds, and who in silken tones and in the most Chesterfieldian manner, warn and reprove those who are transgressing the rules. They, too, are very nautical in their naval uniforms of white trousers, double-breasted blue jackets with brass buttons and jaunty white caps. These snappy functionaries rejoice in the title of "officers of the deck." It is all very salty hereabouts. Even the workmen are dressed like sailors.

The play facilities of Jones Beach are not only those of sand and salt water. Here are handball courts, deck tennis, shuffleboard, archery targets and a pitch-and-put golf course. Under yon wigwam sits a "genuine Indian Princess"—this does suggest Coney—named "Rosebud Yellow Rose." But she doesn't tell fortunes by cards and crystal ball; she teaches woodcraft to the children.

There are many free features, too, such as dancing every evening, a concert by a high-school or a W P A band every Saturday and Sunday afternoon, a class in "bodybuilding" and an exhibition of fancy diving, also every afternoon; all to be had gratis. There is a kindergarten place, and a well-equipped game area for older children. One unique advantage for mothers with infants is a special room for changing their babies' unmentionables.

For other facilities and pleasure gadgets there is a small fee.

For instance, you pay thirty-five cents for a locker and seventy-five cents for an individual dressing room. For the heated indoor salt-water pools it is somewhat more. Parking your car costs you a quarter—there is room here for fifteen thousand five hundred automobiles at one time, and some of these parking spaces face the ocean. For ten cents you can take a workout at shuffleboard, paddle tennis or archery. Some critics have argued that there should be no payments at all; but, in the first place, the Commissioner realizes that what the human being does not pay for he despises, what he does have to pay for he respects. By keeping the fees low he has made it possible for people to have a marvelous seaside holiday in surroundings such as no private club can boast—for a very small expense. In the second place, Mr. Moses is determined to make the park maintain itself. How well his ideas have worked out may be suggested by the fact that upwards of 4,000,000 people come here every year. Expenses are more than $400,000, and the intake just about meets that sum.

Before leaving Jones Beach we should notice one item that might easily be overlooked. Since a large part of the area on which all this aggregation of buildings stands is the result of hydraulic fill, the sand has nothing to hold it in a wind. On the opening day, for example, when the Governor and other notables came, a strong breeze worked havoc by blowing sand into the engines and radiators of all the official cars. Before that, this shifting of the sand was one of the gravest difficulties for the workmen on the job. A gang might come back in the morning of any day to discover that the foundations they had worked at on the day before, together with the machinery, were buried in the sand.

To hold this restless, wandering element, millions of clumps

THE PARKS

of beach grass were set out by hand—all that growth that meets the eye now—covering, now, five or six hundred acres. Then experiments were made to discover what kind of plants would stand the exposed position. It was found that some took the punishment and liked it—for example, the familiar rosa rugosa. Also, the natural dunes have been planted with bayberry, beach plum, scrub oak, etc.—designed to hold the dunes in place. Bedding flowers, like the petunia, already have been made to thrive. In a few years Jones Beach will take on the aspects of a flowering garden as well as a beach resort. One thought is bound to come to the person who visits for the first time not only Jones Beach but any one of the Long Island parks. Where are the beer cans, the pop bottles, the yellowing pages of the Sunday paper, the empty cigarette package, the lunch box? How has the great, untidy public been disciplined so that, despite the hundreds of thousands of picnickers that flock to these resorts, the grounds are as neat as a New England "parlor"? This is one of the major miracles of the whole story.

In an article for the *American Magazine* Mr. Moses discusses this very point. He explains the phenomenon in these words:

Experience has taught me that you can expect coöperation from the public in the care of parks and recreation grounds only if you give them the best. . . . Shabby playgrounds get pretty rough treatment from the average boy. They give him nothing to be proud of. . . . Mean parks make mean people.

Of course there are always the exceptions. One superintendent of a North Shore park told me that his difficulty was in keeping in position the lunch tables under the trees. Picnickers would wrench them up and put them somewhere else, out of the sun or next to their friends, and he believed that this furniture would have to be set in cement. And there are always those occasional hoodlums who simply have to be dealt with by the firm hand of the police. But happily they are very rare. The public has responded to the Park Commissioner's idea to an incredible degree. In Mr. Moses' words, "The number of people who break the rules is very small indeed. The beach looks clean even after a hundred thousand people have used it. There is no litter, no disorder, and no overcrowding."

At first it was not only the barbarians from the city slums who gave trouble. One woman of means and apparent social position drove to Jones Beach in the early days of its history and, dumping the refuse of her picnic lunch on the sand, went home rejoicing. But the officers of the Beach came upon the eyesore shortly afterwards and on one of the pieces of paper they found the lady's name and address. Then a uniformed agent of the law called at her home, laid carefully upon her hall floor a bundle containing all the refuse she had left behind and, in addition, a summons which involved the payment of a fine. That story got abroad and made a deep impression.

In short, as Mr. Moses told the newspapermen, "We promised the local people of Long Island who gave us their beach land that we would maintain certain standards, and these are being maintained." That is very modest understatement for what is being achieved at Jones Beach and, for that matter, in any of the other parks.

Like Bethpage, Jones Beach is open all the year round, though naturally it is the summer that brings the people here by the tens of thousands. It is a colorful and lively spectacle on a Sunday afternoon. Beach umbrellas flaunt their purples and oranges and greens, the sand is a dazzling white until it meets the blue green of the ocean and everywhere are the motley patches of

THE PARKS

color representing holiday costumes and bathing suits. By the way, the Jones Beach management has a rule that ladies may not let down the shoulder straps of their bathing suits. No doubt every now and then some member of the Courtesy Squad discovers a stranger unaware of this rule trying to get the perfect tan. Then he turns on the charm and with a bow and a smile says some polite formula that means, "Madam, hoist the suspenders." After all, something must be done to check the mad desire of the modern female on the beach to shed the last vestige of raiment.

To a visitor unused to the spectacle of thousands and thousands of bathers, the effect is of millions of moving arms and legs, especially legs. The "free bodybuilding class" has still much to do to improve some of the human architecture, though, of course, much is beyond repair. In addition to the ordinary run of bowlegs, knock-knees and spindle-shanks, the connoisseur can recognize Chippendale, Duncan Phyfe, grand piano, Louis Quinze and Joe Gans, with shades ranging from the strawberry of the new sunburn to mahogany, and on rare occasions even to ebony.

Probably it is too much to ask, but if in addition to the shoulder-strap rule there was one that forbad the wearing of trousers to females past thirty years of age and weighing more than one hundred and twenty-five pounds it would be an achievement for pure aesthetics. Perhaps Mr. Moses can perform this benefaction to the eye by installing mirrors in the ladies' locker rooms so adjusted as to reveal to the trousered ones how they look from aft and astern. And males who sprout an African jungle all over their chests or who have unlovely extensions and projections of their equatorial regions should be compelled to wear tops to their bathing suits or be withdrawn from circulation.

Since Mr. Moses is a miracle-worker anyhow, we will continue further suggestions for improvement, unabashed by the vision of perfection already before our eyes. There is that matter of midsummer heat. Yes, Long Island beaches, on the North Shore particularly, can be as hot as Calcutta in the dry season. The charming trained nurse at the Sunken Meadows park confessed that her chief duty lay with the treatment of sunburn and heat prostration, though once in a while a small boy would oblige by falling out of a tree and breaking his arm. The day on which I visited this park the mercury must have started to boil. A woman once asked Sydney Smith if he minded the heat. "Heat, madam," he replied, "it is so dreadful here that there is nothing left for it but to take off my flesh and sit in my bones."

There were several pink and perspiring—or should I say "glowing"?—ladies, sitting on the beach that sweltering day in overstuffed bathing suits, who looked as if they would gladly take off their flesh and sit in their bones. Perhaps it can be arranged to have air conditioning on the beaches during July and August, with artificial clouds sent up to obscure the sun, and a perpetual breeze wafted over the beach from concealed fans. No doubt these and other comforts will be attended to as soon as Mr. Moses can find time to get around to them on his agenda.

Meanwhile, where else on this planet is there a seaside park that can hold a candle, or even a paper match, to Jones Beach? And its story is not yet finished by any means. The planting is going on steadily; storm ravages have to be quickly repaired and improvements made. One of these days Jones Beach may be linked up to that other state park already mentioned, the first land that Mr. Moses took over, Fire Island. The tropical hurri-

THE PARKS

cane of September, 1938, which wrought such havoc all over Long Island, and particularly, as narrated, already at Westhampton, was deadly destructive here. The narrow strip of sand between ocean and Bay, ending in Fire Island inlet, had no protection whatever from the fury of wind and sea. The "tidal wave" swept across the whole island, fortunately taking few lives, but carrying away literally hundreds of summer homes that lay outside the park area. At the same time it gouged out new channels from the ocean into the Bay.

Up to the time of this calamity the residents were not anxious to have the park and parkway system developed further on Fire Island, because they feared that this would mean the loss of that very inaccessibility which they prized. They visioned the coming of millions in motorcars as bound to result in the end of the natural wildness of beach and sea and in the destruction of the rare vegetation, especially the groves of holly. But when the wildness of beach and sea became what it was in the hurricane, the picture looked different. The future of Fire Island itself seemed doubtful.

The wreckage of summer homes had not been cleared away when Mr. Moses came forward with a characteristically constructive plan. He said, in brief, "Drop your opposition to the plans to develop Fire Island as a link to the state's park and parkway system. The state and county authorities will then step in and save the island, not only for you but for millions of visitors in the years to come." He outlined his plan to dredge a channel on the inside of Fire Island and pump the sand upon the island to build it up and make the foundation for a new parkway to run east as far as Smith's Point. Then a bridge would be built across Fire Island Inlet, hooking up with the Jones Beach parkway and causeways. The result would be the addition of forty-five miles to the state parkway system and Fire Island itself would be protected from being washed away. For though another hurricane may not happen for another hundred years, any heavy storm can do great damage to a low sand bar which sticks up its back only a few feet above a normal high tide. Mr. Moses' plan would have meant that Fire Island would be securely moored for keeps, and no one could be more scrupulous than he to save everything of natural value, as the record of all the other parks can testify. But local officials failed to act on his suggestion because of the cost involved. One of these days they may be sorry.

The establishment of these recreation centers on Long Island in a decade was the result of a clear, original plan to start with, backed up by boundless energy, resourcefulness and courage. Those who fought tooth and nail against Mr. Moses at first have come to realize now that they did not comprehend what he meant by the word park. Now they are as proud as anyone else of what he has achieved for Long Island. And, for that matter, all Americans may feel the same sense of pride in their parks, for the nations of the Old World, whether Communist, Dictatorship or Democracy, can show nothing to match them. It was particularly fitting that one of the two Theodore Roosevelt medals for the year 1938 was awarded to Mr. Moses; for, to quote the citation, "whatever his hand has touched has achieved beauty, dignity, and a kind of utility which would have been particularly gratifying to the man in whose honor the Roosevelt medal is awarded."

CHAPTER XII

ISLAND PRODUCTS

HAVING followed the shore line of the Island, all around, north and south, we have still to contemplate all that midland part which lies between. And this we shall dispose of in one lump, without designating any routes of exploration. In fact, there is nothing much to bless the eye in this whole area that lies between the bungalows of Floral Park on the west and the boat sheds of Riverhead on the east. It is mostly a flat farming country threaded by excellent but unpicturesque highways, dotted with useful filling stations and villainous billboards. As you look from one of these great arteries of travel across the fields of potatoes or cauliflower, you see a dense fringe of scraggly pines in the background. These mark a vast, desolate wilderness that extends through the heart of Suffolk County—the "Pine Barrens." This is a jungle of scrub oak and pitch pine, stretching for twenty-five or thirty miles, and crossed here and there by state roads, to be sure, but nonetheless a wilderness. Any driver who traverses this area an hour after sundown, let us say, will see in the twilight his roadway extending straight ahead into the vanishing point on the horizon. There is not another soul on the road, not a habitation. The woods on either hand are black and soundless. You look to see if the tank has plenty of gasoline; you hope that your tire won't suffer a puncture or blowout, and reflect what an ideal spot it is to stage a holdup and murder.

They say that efforts have been made to rescue these Pine

Barrens by cultivation, but all have failed. Again and again they have been burned over, and grown up again in a worse tangle of scrub oak, catbriars and pine. Apparently here, within easy reach of New York City, is a huge tract of land which has successfully thumbed its nose for centuries at civilization.

The same Dr. Alexander Hamilton who advised the youthful Washington that the North Country Road was the best route to Boston, as mentioned in connection with Greenport, made a journey on the Island himself back in 1744. He encountered the Barrens near Riverhead and described it as "Arabia deserta." Except for the highways, it is little different after two hundred years. But there is still the possibility, as already suggested in the chapter on Parks, that Mr. Robert Moses will tackle it and transform it into a huge forest preserve; and if he sets himself to conquer the Barrens the betting will be on the side of the Park Commissioner.

The chief reason for the numerous forest fires that swept these Barrens during the last hundred years was the presence of the Long Island Railroad. This naturally had much to do with the opening up of Long Island to trade and travel, but it has had a long story of trouble. The all-rail route to Boston from New York in 1848 almost killed the Long Island Railroad because at that time it fed no town of any size east of Jamaica. Stages and ships did most of what business there was in that area, anyway. New lines were opened up to make connections with other settlements in the heart of the Island; but these, not being under one management, did not pull together until as late as 1895. In recent years the Long Island Road has suffered, like all other railroads in the country, by the highways and motor travel. Automobiles take the passengers, and the many-ton motor trucks, paying little in taxes, transport the great bulk of the

ISLAND PRODUCTS

crops of Long Island to the rest of the nation.

Yet Long Islanders say that the railroad never did carry the whole of the farm produce. Up to as late as twenty years ago a special type of farm wagon brought it to market. Late Sunday afternoons and evenings a long procession of these wagons, loaded with produce, filed through the towns, heading west. These wagons were sturdily built, the body being rather narrow between the high rear wheels. As soon as the sides rose high enough to clear the wheels, however, the wagon body widened several feet—enough to put a row of barrels along each side on this outhanging shelf. Apparently the farmers spent all Sunday morning in loading these trucks, barrel after barrel being heaped up and the whole load being covered and bound in by a white canvas tarpaulin so that the truck took on the effect of a covered wagon of earlier days. These trucks were always pulled by two well-kept horses and a continual procession of them moved along the road toward the city. They arrived at the various markets late at night or in the early dawn, ready for the morning opening. The next evening they could be seen coming home, the wagons this time empty or perhaps filled with baskets and barrels for the next load. At frequent intervals along these roads leading to and from the city were a series of inns which were little better in many cases than glorified bars with extensive sheds where the returning farmers could drive in, water their horses and then reward themselves for their long journey by getting rid of some of the money they were bringing back to the farm. If they felt a bit drowsy with their alcoholic refreshment, all they had to do was to climb into the seat and let the horses use their own good judgment about getting home.

The other type of freight a railroad depends on is manufactured goods. But a striking feature about the Long Island landscape is the absence of factory chimneys. This is a decided contrast with New Jersey, Westchester County and Connecticut, across the way. The absence of water power does not seem to be an adequate explanation, but there it is as a fact.

The Long Island Railroad may suffer also if it acts as feeder to a parental system and is therefore at the mercy of that corporation for rental of its New York station and for other expenses. But whatever the story is, the Long Island Railroad operates now at a reported annual loss of two million dollars.

The chief farm products of the Island are the cauliflower and the potato. One-third of all the cauliflower raised in the United States comes from these broad level acres in the middle section of the Island. A still more famous product is the Long Island potato. This has been called the Island's gold mine. For the last twenty years the humble spud has cashed in at an average of about eight million dollars a year. Forty-five thousand acres are devoted to it, and in addition to the actual work of cultivation there is a huge business that serves the industry, for fertilizer plants, machinery and transportation.

Nor is this all to be said about the products. Among the many distinctive items about the Island listed by the *Long Island Forum* are the following: the largest beeswax plant in the world. Just what a beeswax factory looks like is not clear to the present writer, but some day he will make a special pilgrimage to find out. The world's most powerful short wave radio telegraph transmitter is on Long Island. The shellfish industry does a business of three million dollars annually, and 300,000 bushels of clams are dug up and shipped away every year. Here is an item for California papers to copy: Eastern Long Island can brag of more days of sunshine than any other part of the country this side of the Mississippi; so say the government re-

ISLAND PRODUCTS

ports. As a result of these riches, resources and attractions, during the past ten years the population of Long Island has increased 52.6 percent. There are some who think that is quite enough.

Cauliflower and potato are the rather recent and most respectable outputs of Long Island. But thirty years ago a visitor would have told you that its chief product was mosquitoes. Dr. Alexander Hamilton reports being thoroughly bitten on his journey through the Island, especially in that "Arabia deserta." The early colonists must have suffered horribly with no screens for their doors or windows. The traveler of today who visits the North or South Shore resorts can have no idea of the scourge that used to be suffered in these parts. The present writer remembers a card party of thirty years ago, during which all the ladies were constantly slapping at their bare arms and necks with one hand while they tried to hold their cards with the other. There were screens on the windows, to be sure, but these were packed so tight with bodies of mosquitoes driven before the wind that they were actually being forced through the meshes. Some residents of Babylon, for example, until recent years used to go away for the months of July and August because even in daytime the plague of mosquitoes was so severe that the children could not go outdoors to play without being terribly bitten.

At that, some of the oldest inhabitants descended from the First Families seem to take a pride in the ferocity of these creatures and tell stories about what they used to be in ancient times. In the days of the first settlements it is said that the pioneers used to bring down the mosquitoes with crab nets and even shoot them with blunderbusses. Before that the Indians used to say that when the Great South Bay was a sea marsh mosquitoes were known to snatch papooses off the backs of their mothers and carry them off to feed their young in the swamps. And the prehistoric mosquito was said to be even larger. A fossil bone dug up on the South Shore was identified by scientists as the tusk of a mammoth, but a local sage declared it to be the proboscis of an early Long Island mosquito. Although the Museum of Natural History experts seem reluctant to verify that last hypothesis, the fact is clear that the Long Island mosquito earned a fearsome reputation, one that made even the New Jersey variety hide his diminished head.

One reason that the creature is now becoming a legend is due to a mosquito extermination commission and nearly forty years of work on the project. The lead was taken, at the turn of the century, by a group of public-spirited citizens of Long Island. Beginnings were made on the North Shore with "mosquito engineering" as far back as 1902, the first big achievement in relief from the pest coming from operations in Nassau County after some million feet of ditches were dug and the infant "wigglers" done to death with oil. Since then the work has progressed with immense strides in Queens and Suffolk Counties. Such pleasure resorts as Jones Beach would have been utterly impossible under the conditions of two decades ago.

Yet such is the natural perversity of the so-called human race that certain hunters coming to Long Island from the Big City made a raucous howl recently on the ground that the Mosquito Control was discouraging the wild ducks and therefore the work must be stopped. But no other expenditure, for whatever project, has paid such rich returns in comfort to the population of the Island, both permanent and transient, as the appropriation for mosquito extermination.

A passing mention should be made also of the famous Long

ISLAND PRODUCTS

Island fogs. It seems that the breeding place for Atlantic Ocean fogs is the South Shore, and the mating season is June and early July. Experts have claimed for the Long Island fog a greater degree of density and viscosity than fogs anywhere else on the coast. It clings with glutinous persistence, like a poor relation or a wallflower at a dance. It defies the midday sun; and even when it does depart it leaves shreds hanging on the trees like the moss on Southern live oaks.

But more interesting than cauliflower, potatoes, mosquitoes and fogs is the crop of faiths and fanatics which from the earliest days have sprung up on Long Island soil. The first of these were the Quakers. In the story of Sylvester Manor appeared Quaker exiles from New England and the heroic figure of George Fox preaching under the trees. That was only one episode in a considerable Quaker chronicle on Long Island which began earlier. In 1645 a group of Englishmen obtained from the Dutch Governor, and likewise by due purchase from the Matinecock Indians, a tract of land for a settlement. They named it Vlissingen, after the Dutch town from which these men had set forth to the New World. This is now Flushing. Here in 1680 another Englishman named John Bowne came and built a house, one that is still standing. Bowne was a Quaker, or became one soon after he arrived, and in that house he set aside a special room for Quaker meetings. Here William Penn was a guest on the occasion of his visit to Flushing, and here, eleven years earlier (1672), George Fox also was entertained on one of his preaching tours. Because so many people gathered to hear him, the usual room for meetings had to be abandoned for the open air. The congregation stood under two great oaks on the lawn while the Quaker apostle preached to them. For many years these trees were carefully cherished by the Society of Friends; but finally, when they must have been more than four hundred years old, they were felled by storm. There is a memorial stone there today to commemorate the occasion.

Before George Fox's visit John Bowne had already been in hot water with Governor Peter Stuyvesant for permitting in his house meetings of what the Governor called "an abominable sect." Since Bowne refused to budge, he was packed off in irons to Holland for trial. But as it turned out, the authorities in the Netherlands were so liberal-minded that they promptly sent him back with a tart letter to Peter Stuyvesant, saying that "the consciences of men ought to be free and unshackled so long as they continue moderate, peaceful, and inoffensive, and not hostile to the government"—a description which just fitted these Quakers.

There was also a brave woman, Lady Deborah Moody, who invited Robert Hodgson, the earliest of the Quaker missionaries on Long Island, to stay at her house. She, too, had to brave the storm of persecution from her Gravesend neighbors.

The most famous Long Island Quaker was born in the middle of the eighteenth century, Elias Hicks, of the family which has left its rustic name on Hicksville. The Society had spread far and wide on the Island by that time. Elias was a farmer's boy, and when he came to manhood he continued to till a farm, in the village of Jericho. Elias must have taken life very seriously. This is the way he notes his courtship and marriage:

In 22d year of my age, apprehending it right to change my situation from a single to a married state, and having gained an intimate acquaintance with Jemima Seaman, daughter of Jonathan and Elizabeth Seaman of Jericho, and my affection being drawn towards her in that relation, I communicated my news to her, and received from her a corresponding expression of affection. . . .

It doesn't sound very romantic, but Jemima was a good wife—she bore him eleven children—and he, except for being away so much on his preaching tours, made her a good husband.

There was nothing about his background to account for his marvelous gifts as a preacher. He had little education. Moved by the Spirit as he felt himself to be, he traveled far and wide and spoke before great audiences, not only of Quakers but of others. When this man rose to his commanding height, straight as an arrow, with burning eyes and ringing voice, the most indifferent had to listen in spite of themselves. Perhaps he had the greatest personal following in Philadelphia, where one would think this untutored farmer in his ill-fitting, drab clothes would have been ridiculed.

His *Journal* makes dry reading, but it gives a record of his astounding journeys all over the country, made, partly on horseback but chiefly on foot, simply to preach his gospel. His trips took him into Maine, into Canada, back to Ohio—through frontier country, most of it—a total of ten thousand miles. For all this he received never a penny. It was part of the fundamental belief of the Friends that it was wicked to accept money for anything so sacred as preaching the Word of God. He was satisfied, as he writes in his *Journal,* in finding "real peace in my labors."

From another doctrine of the sect, that all are equal in the sight of God, developed the Quakers' opposition to slavery. They were the earliest abolitionists, and Hicks had much to do with the passing of the state abolition act of 1827. After the year 1815 Hicks began to urge greater freedom in beliefs. His doctrines sound much like the essays of Ralph Waldo Emerson in their reliance on the "Inner Light."

In 1817 there arose at a "yearly meeting" the demand on the part of some of the Friends that an orthodox creed be adopted for the Society. This Hicks opposed with all his eloquence. The result was the great schism. Orthodox Quakers and Hicksite Quakers split apart during the years 1827–29 amid great bitterness. Most of the Long Island Friends followed Hicks. That division is now forgotten, but unwittingly Hicks dealt the Society of Friends a blow from which it has never recovered. A large number of the Hicksite sect eventually drifted into other churches, notably the Unitarian.

Parenthetically it may be added here for those interested in old American painting that Edward Hicks was the cousin of Elias. Edward was an itinerant painter, doing wagon wheels, signboards, fireboards or anything about the house, and he would sometimes try his hand even at a portrait. His chief delight in hours of relaxation was to make pictures about his hero William Penn, or allegorical scenes illustrating Isaiah's prophecy about the lion and the lamb lying down together. One dollar was big money for Edward in his lifetime. If he looks down now from where he is painting in Green Pastures, he must be vastly amused to see what thumping big prices collectors must pay now to acquire one of these quaint pictures.

Elias, the preacher, passed on to his reward in 1830, ceasing from his labors only when a sudden stroke felled him. Another sect, or cult, of a very different reputation came into being here in this same drab mid-Island area, and a generation later. It was the community settlement of "Modern Times," where the present village of Brentwood stands and not so very far from Jericho, where Elias Hicks used to have his troubles with his

ISLAND PRODUCTS

farm just when his mind wanted to be free for pious meditation.

A hundred years ago a tidal wave of Causes swept over our land. Rising chiefly in the New England conscience, it surged westward to where there weren't no ten commandments on the frontier, and south to the Mason and Dixon Line, where the only Cause that could get a hearing in those troublous years was slavery. In the strange, humorless decades of the thirties, forties and fifties, isms sprang up, flourished and died, and the crazier they were the more certain of a devoted following. Not all the inspiration came out of the New England conscience, for this was the age when Robert Owen of England and Monsieur Fourier of France were expecting to save the world by ideal socialistic communities, planted in the virgin wilderness of the New World. The most famous of these was the one at Brook Farm in Massachusetts, copied after Fourier (see Hawthorne's *Blithedale Romance*), and Robert Owen's settlement at New Harmony, Indiana.

A certain Boston inventor, named Josiah Warren, had met Robert Owen and had been completely won over to that philanthropist. Selling his factory, he joined the group at New Harmony, but after a brief stay he decided that the socialist or communist ideal checked all initiative and independence. He would find a better plan to save society. So he planted the two villages of Equity and Utopia in Ohio, and then, in 1850, came to New York to get backing for a real experiment in perfect living. He had come to believe that all government was a curse because it curbs the individual; in short, he aimed at straight anarchism. But he held to the socialist principles about wealth and profit being out-and-out robbery. "Property is theft," as Proudhon, the French Socialist, declared.

Out of the purses of the idealists (or cranks) of New York

he drew enough financial support to inaugurate his plan, and there grew up a cluster of about a hundred small buildings in the heart of Long Island which bore the title "Modern Times." Thither flocked the men and women who wanted Perfect Freedom. In the middle of it stood the "Time Store." Here the Modern-Timer would purchase what he wanted in "labor notes," or promises to pay in work. Instead of gold there was a corn standard, one hour being reckoned, measured in terms of value, by sixteen pounds of corn. And the storekeeper added to the cost and overhead of the article his own time consumed in making the sale. By and by some notes depreciated, according to the reputation of the citizen for laziness, even to the point where they weren't accepted at all.

Since the cornerstone of "Modern Times" was Perfect Freedom, it became the Mecca for every variety of crank. Whether it was diet, clothing, economics or religion—here was every man's right to do as he pleased. Women also arrived, who demanded freedom in dress. It was the age of the hoop skirt, and some of these women went abroad in short skirts revealing white cotton stockings all the way to the knee. A still greater scandal was the other group of females who insisted on wearing trousers. It should be said, however, to the credit of these apostles of freedom that none sank to the abyss of "shorts." But in 1850 a woman might as well be taken in adultery as to be seen in public wearing "pantaloons." There was one man who, for conscience' sake, went about naked, but he wasn't popular, and the Long Island mosquito made his life one perpetual martyrdom in summer.

Of course one cannot skip along the primrose path of Freedom without running into the allurements of Sex. Now Josiah Warren didn't want Sex to sneak into his economic Eden, but he couldn't keep it out with his principle of liberty for every conscience. And so Free Love cropped up. Those who lived together for a space wore a red string around the wedding finger. It was bad form to inquire into the paternity of new babies.

Opposed to this cult was the doctor-dentist of "Modern Times," Edward Newberry, who was all for breeding by eugenics rather than love. He prescribed "cross-fertilization"—blondes and brunettes, grave and gay, short and tall; that is, only opposites in type should breed. Newberry inherited his eugenics from his father, who begat eighteen children by one wife and nineteen by a second, thus doing his bit by the human race and very proud of it.

Although the founder of "Modern Times" was chiefly interested in economic freedom, the presence of free love gave the settlement its local ill fame. All the good people of Long Island sneered, snickered or thundered against the place, according to their temperaments. It was hard to keep going. "Bimeby, hard times come knockin' at de door," the panic of 1857. A few years later the shock of Civil War kicked out what was left of the financial props of "Modern Times." The apostles of Freedom melted away, and one more Noble Experiment was swept into the dust bin of forgotten causes.

The modern variants of faiths and fanatics run more to profiteers than to prophets. In 1919 a dusky clergyman, the "Reverend J. Divine" moved into Sayville, Long Island, with a group of sixteen or seventeen disciples, and set up headquarters on a quiet street. His plan of life was simple communism; that is, with himself handling the money. The faithful, known as "Angels," turned over to him all their wages, and he took care of their personal expenses. Sundays he gave free dinners, lasting in relays, all the afternoon, for any who chose to come. He advertised in the local paper as an employment agent for colored help, and did place a number of his angelic host in the kitchens of Saybrook summer residents. His following grew amazingly. By 1930 the Sayville police had a traffic problem on their hands every Sunday in front of the Divine headquarters to take care of the hundreds of negroes who flocked out of Harlem to adore their leader and get a free dinner. By this time there were one hundred and fifty angels living on the premises and new buildings had to be acquired for dormitories. There was even a house for the White Angels.

The Sayville police, all the while, cast a suspicious eye on the Reverend Divine; but his followers were decent and quiet in their behavior, and it was not easy to pin an action for fraud against their divinity. Finally, in the fall of 1931, it was decided that he was a plain nuisance and he was put under arrest. Judge Lewis J. Smith found him guilty and sentenced him to five hundred dollars' fine and a year in jail.

Four days after the sentence was pronounced Judge Smith suddenly died. To the faithful, this was, of course, the avenging act of Father Divine himself; and when the case was appealed by a negro lawyer and the decision was reversed, this, too, was another proof of supernatural power. During the five weeks that Divine stayed in jail that place of durance was all but swamped by a tidal wave of black admirers.

After regaining his freedom, the Divine One—his followers say that he *is* God—decided that Suffolk County was uncongenial. He shook the dust of Sayville from his feet and moved his heaven with its heavenly host (by this time three hundred Angels, not counting the little black Cherubs) to the more friendly atmosphere of Harlem. The rest of the history of this amazing cult belongs to the Darkest Africa of Manhattan.

ISLAND PRODUCTS

Two other Long Island settlements, with a strong foreign coloring, deserve a passing glance. One was a projected community for Slovaks at Deer Park. The leader was a certain woman who, being a Slovak herself, made herself the female Moses to lead her peasant compatriots into the Promised Land. So they scraped and saved and bought lots, and made their way to Long Island from their far country. All might have been well except that after the poor wretches found themselves dumped in a desolate area of scrub oak and pine stumps they were soon apprised of the fact that their Prophetess had neglected to obtain title to the lots she had sold, bad as they were. In short, the lady had committed a cruel, wholesale fraud on her own people, a fraud for which, despite her elaborate perjury, she was recently committed to prison.

At another dreary spot in the Pine Barrens country is Yaphank, on the edge of the tract where Camp Upton used to be in the days when we were making the world safe for democracy and shouting that the Hun was at the gate. Upton has vanished and the Hun has walked inside the gate on a free pass. Here the traveler will note "Camp Siegfried," with its entrance, beside the highway, signalized by two flagpoles. One bears the stars and stripes and the other the swastika. This is the largest GERMAN-american playground in America, covering forty-six acres, with a lake on its fringe. There are other Nazi camps at Babylon and Lindenhurst, as well as in Southbury, Connecticut, and Andover, New Jersey; but this Yaphank settlement is the most noted, or notorious, as you prefer. It was founded by one Spanknoebel, who has since fled the country on federal charges, just one jump ahead of the G-men. We are informed that only the most innocent diversions go on in Camp Siegfried. Here the boys and girls come, no doubt to learn woodcraft and how to tell birds from flowers. Perhaps they play old-fashioned games, too, like "I Spy."

Not long ago Justice Moses W. Drake, of Bay Shore, invoked the anti-Klan law against this camp, with the result that the German-American Settlement League was fined ten thousand dollars, its President, Hans Mueller, five hundred dollars and a year in jail. Five other directors were fined five hundred dollars apiece. In default of the payment of these fines Suffolk County was ready to take over Camp Siegfried. But in the summer of 1938 the sentences were all set aside on appeal. So it goes in a free country. Of course a similar camp of Americans devoted to the ideals of freedom situated, let us say, in the Bavarian Alps, would probably last about thirty seconds by the village clock, and the inhabitants thereof, if they had any further lives to live, would spend them in concentration camps.

At the time the present writer drove by, the two national flags hung morosely without a flutter. Neither seemed happy in the presence of the other. But as I contemplated the scene, a procession of little girls, two by two, forming what the English call a "crocodile," and led by two austere Fräuleins, came skipping along the road from their swim in the lake. Their tanned skins still glistened with drops of water, and they smiled merrily (behind the Fräuleins' backs). I ventured my unmistakably Aryan nose out of the window of the driver's seat, half expecting that they would break into the goose step and burst into the strains of "Horst Wessel." Instead, they behaved like typically fresh little American girls, for they cried "Ya-ay!" and waved a sassy greeting to the stranger. The kleine Mädchen don't do that in Hitlerland; such conduct is streng verboten. So, perhaps, in spite of Heils and Sieg Heils and all the rest of the rot, these youngsters who go to American schools may yet, *deo volente,* grow up to be real Americans after all.

CHAPTER XIII

SPORTS

THE level terrain of the mid-Island area, which proves so congenial to cauliflower and potatoes, attracted sport-lovers long before either cauliflower or potato was thought of. For these level lands meant playgrounds aplenty within easy reach of the Big City. But in the early days there were none of the competitive games that flourish today. Young men got their fun hunting and fishing, or wrestling and running foot races; but there was no organized game, such as baseball or football, to interest either players or spectators. Instead, the one diversion that took the place of all our present-day assortment of sports was horse racing. It was universally popular. Even in Puritan Miller Place, it will be remembered, the village elders had to pass an ordinance forbidding the pastime of racing horses in the streets.

In that same mid-seventeenth century (1664) Governor Nicolls established a race course on Hempstead Plains, though the godly among the English colonists did not look with favor on the business. But these tempting stretches of level land made horse racing inevitable, and race tracks blossomed in many places, as at New Market, Jamaica, Huntington, Massapequa, Babylon and Sheepshead Bay. Much the latest and the most famous of Long Island race tracks is the present one at Belmont Park near Jamaica.

For a taste of the excitement of the old-time race track one story will serve. Eclipse, the hero of this story, was a handsome chestnut stallion, a grandson of Diomed, winner of the first Derby. Like Messenger, whose monument we saw in Locust Valley, Eclipse had been imported into this country from England. Strictly speaking, he should be called "American Eclipse," because there was an English race horse of the same period also named Eclipse. But on this side of the Atlantic there was only one Eclipse. This horse was never beaten in a race, and he sired more winners than any other stallion of his time. Edward Troye, who painted every great race horse of his day, has left a portrait of Eclipse, painted when the steed was in his declining years but still a magnificent animal.

In 1818 Eclipse won a race against two horses then considered the best in America, but his greatest achievement was five years later, in a race advertised as "Eclipse against the World!" This was a slight case of hyperbole, for it was really a contest between North and South in the United States. The wager was twenty thousand dollars a side. The champion of the North was Eclipse of Long Island; that of the South was Sir Henry of Virginia, also a grandson of Diomed. The scene, the Union race course not far from Jamaica.

Tremendous interest was aroused over the event when it was announced. Sectional feeling rode high. Although New York state had yet to emancipate her own slaves, the newspapers blazoned "North *vs.* South, Free States *vs.* Black." Crowds took every conceivable means of transportation to the scene of the race. Twenty thousand visitors surged over the village of Jamaica and engulfed it. Many had come all the way from the South, especially from Virginia, including the eccentric John Randolph of Roanoke. Many more poured down from New York and New England, including such distinguished citizens as Rufus King and the austere Josiah Quincy, destined later to be made President of Harvard.

Fortunately the weather was fine, the last week in May, and thousands who had to sleep in barns or out under the trees did not mind the experience. The track was an oval, a straight stretch of a mile on each side with a quarter-mile turn at each end. Three heats were to be run at half-hour intervals. For the first heat Eclipse's regular jockey, Sam Purdey, did not ride, because of a quarrel with the owner. The new jockey handled the horse unskillfully and lost. The odds in the betting then soared on the Virginia horse. Then Purdey, with tears in his eyes, pleaded to be allowed to ride, and this request was granted. The second heat Eclipse won, and then the third likewise, amid the wildest excitement.

A great crowd awaited the news in Fulton Market, New York, where an enterprising hotel man, named Niblo, had arranged to hoist a flag on the top of a building as soon as the news was brought by mounted courier. After the race, a red cotton handkerchief was printed and sold as a souvenir, with pictures and text showing the rival horses with their hoofs stretched out fore and aft—the only way a horse was represented in those days—and Eclipse, of course, was shown in the lead. Even the United States mail carriers went out into the country districts bearing a red flag with the words "Eclipse Forever— Old Virginia a Little Tired."

Naturally the Southerners asked for another race with Eclipse, this time to be held in Washington, but the owner said nay. He declared that he was determined "never, on any consideration, to risk the life or reputation of the noble animal whose generous and almost incredible exertions have gained for the North so signal a victory and for himself such well-earned and never-fading renown." A bit florid, but those were the days of high-flown language, and that was the most celebrated race of the American turf.

As for Sam Purdey, who rode Eclipse in that famous event, he lies buried in St. Paul's Churchyard in New York. For many years after his death it was the custom to lay a set of racing silks on his grave at each anniversary of that race.

In all fairness to the prowess of Dixie horseflesh be it said that in 1845 another race was held between North and South. In this event Peytona of the South defeated Fashion of the North and won the purse of twenty thousand dollars. This was held at the Union race course on Long Island. Currier and Ives turned out one of their most famous racing prints of this scene.

Another sport that resounds to the clatter of hoofs is fox hunting. Nationally it is not so new an importation as one might think. Lord Fairfax followed the hounds in Virginia as far back as 1739. George Washington spent his happiest hours on the back of his favorite hunter; and Lafayette, wishing to send him a present most likely to please him, dispatched to Washington some foxhounds all the way from France. The Father of His Country in 1770 subscribed to a pack on the outskirts of Brooklyn, known as the "Brooklyn Hunt." But for all that honorable and venerable precedent, fox hunting has never taken hold in America as it has in England, despite the fact that there are now as many as one hundred and twenty-one recognized hunt clubs in this country. And our fox hunters still look to Leicestershire as the capital of their sport, following the rules of the British, written or unwritten, as closely as possible, in regard to vocabulary, dress and the etiquette of the hunt.

The vocabulary is a mystic language in itself: "Master," "whip," "M.F.H." "cubbing," "hunting post and rail," "draw-

SPORTS

ing a cover" and so on *ad infinitum*. The word "bitch" is uttered by the initiated without the quiver of an eyelash. It is only the vulgar herd who refer to the "hounds" as "dogs." Probably only those who have hunted in the Midlands of John Bull's island have really mastered the language. For instance, a "cocktail" is a horse that isn't a thoroughbred, certainly not the generally accepted meaning of the word in these United States.

The following is a sample of the fox-hunting speech as gathered from a letter, published in *Town & Country,* written by an Englishman describing an experience at a recent fox hunt in New Jersey:

The last [fox] we drew was more accommodating, and I'm sure would have given us a quick thing but for something having foiled the ground. A horseman hacking on one side of covert, perhaps. In any event after hounds checked on plow we never hit the line again. The situation, I believe, called for a Tom Smith cast. Instead, the huntsman lifted and threw off in a nearby covert.

The adventure must have been very exciting, but to us economic yokels the narrative is not quite clear.

What is harder for outsiders to comprehend is the ritual of dress. Why such a fancy getup? That topper costs twenty dollars, the scarlet coat more than a hundred and the boots a hundred and fifty. What is the sense of a silk hat on a hunt, anyway, and why call a vermilion jacket "pink"?

Perhaps a drawback to American fox hunting is the fact that it is restricted here to rich men's clubs, whereas in England farmers and villagers join regularly in the hunt. With us it still seems like an exclusive social function, and neighboring agriculturists are likely to view the proceedings with a jaundiced eye. However, the sport has been thriving on Long Island these many years. A group of gentlemen leased a farmhouse on Hempstead Plains as long ago as 1877, for the pleasures of the hunt, and imported a pack of hounds from Ireland. This was the birth of the famous Meadow Brook Club. According to one of the pioneers, the first hunt was written up in the metropolitan papers as a reckless orgy of flinty-hearted plutocrats riding roughshod over crops, amid the shrieks of farmers' wives until finally an innocent fox was torn to pieces by ravening "dogs." A modest explanation had to follow later that the only prey on that hunt was a bag of aniseed, but the first story was much better reading.

So the Meadow Brook Hunt got under way. It was soon discovered that conditions were not ideal on Long Island, for the salt air, sandy soil and strong winds make it hard for following the scent. But that did not check the enthusiasm. Once in a while something happened that was not according to the English tradition. Mr. Harry T. Peters, one of the veterans of the Meadow Brook Hunt, says in his book *Just Hunting* that one of their troubles was a deep cut of the Long Island Railroad near Syosset. This spoiled many a chase. But on one occasion when the fox ducked down into the cut and skipped nimbly along the track an exasperated huntsman dismounted, scrambled down the ravine and borrowed a handcar which he saw on the track. Then his friends were treated to the spectacle of a gentleman pumping furiously up and down on the handles of the car, his pink coattails flapping in the breeze, and the yelping pack behind. Soon Reynard was taken and slain, and the intrepid huntsman returned, pumping the handcar back to the place where he found it. That was a distinctly American touch, hunting by handcar. Certainly if the Master of the Quorn

SPORTS

Hounds had witnessed that unconventional chase he would have dropped dead of apoplexy.

Visiting English fox hunters are often pained to note lapses on the part of Americans in the field, especially in the matter of dress. "One of the fundamental traditions of fox hunting," writes the same Briton quoted above, "is adherence to the rules of dress." He notes with pain that over here we are liable to fall from grace. The American ladies have a way of wearing ornamented stock pins instead of plain, and some of the men don't know when to wear the cap instead of the topper. But if a plain yeoman may be permitted an unasked opinion, it will not be until our followers of the sport put on a comfortable tweed jacket and cap and say "Let's go, fellows," instead of "Hoicks" or "Yoicks," that the sport will really become a naturalized American citizen.

The chief fox-hunting centers of Long Island used to be Hempstead, Westbury and Cedarhurst, but the kennels are in Syosset now and the hounds are hunted east of that point. Out of the clubs originally founded for the purpose of hunting the fox other sports developed which, in popular favor, have cast the pink-coated gentlemen and their baying hounds quite in the shade. Chief of these was polo. There are now many other fox-hunting clubs in the country outside of Long Island, but the town of Westbury, Long Island, is the nation's capital for polo. The reason is that the same group of sportsmen who founded the Meadow Brook Club became interested in polo. The purposes of this organization, as set forth in its charter, were to "support and hunt a pack of foxhounds in the proper seasons and to promote other outdoor sports." Polo was the first of these "other outdoor sports." Even before the club was fairly established some of the members—Thomas Hitchcock, Sr., Oliver W. Bird, August Belmont, Dudley Winthrop, W. C. Eustis and Benjamin Nicoll—began playing polo on the area inclosed by the old race track on the Mineola Fairgrounds, only a few miles from the clubhouse. This was in 1879. Not to be outdone, the Rockaway Club took up polo also, and for some years the rivalry was fierce. The audience of rival "fans" hissed the opposing teams as if they were villains in the old-time melodrama. Rough tactics were used, too.

Once Captain Eustis of the Meadow Brook team rode up to Captain Cowdin of the Rockaway team. "I appeal to you, Johnny," he expostulated, "let us play the rest of the game decently!" Both spirit and tactics have improved since.

The sport had hardly got under way when, as early as 1886, a Cup was purchased by subscription among the players of the Westchester Polo Club of Newport, R. I., to be played for with the team of Hurlingham, the polo center of England. The official name is the International Polo Challenge Cup, and it is now owned by the United States Polo Association. The first game was played in the summer of that year in Newport, and the Englishmen won easily. In 1902 a second match was played, and again the Americans lost; but their game had shown great improvement. The English still had a better sense of team play and better ponies. In 1909 the cup was brought back to America, but our team had to import English ponies to do it. In recent years the mounts have been bred in California.

The rivalry with the Hurlingham Club still continues. Twice the Englishmen challenged and lost, in 1911 and 1913. In 1914 they won, but the Great War put an end to international polo for a while—in fact, for seven years. Then the Americans went over and succeeded in bringing the trophy back. The agreement has been made, because of the great cost involved, to hold challenge matches only once in three years. Altogether nine matches have been played against the British and one against Argentina. This record tends to make Westbury not only the national but the international capital of polo. In 1924 the Prince of Wales came to witness the match, and three years later an Indian potentate, the Maharajah of Rattam, Sir Sajjam Singh, came as a member of the challenging team, and he arrived in his East Indian regalia. Here also Gustavus Adolphus, Crown Prince of Sweden, came as a guest of the club in 1928. So this is a game not only with "class" but with color and regal splendor.

To develop the young player into the champion of future teams there are other clubs, the Meadow Lark and the Sparrow Hawk, which give the aspiring youngsters a chance to show their mettle and learn the game. There is an annual match at Westbury for players under twenty-one, the prize being the Thorn Memorial Cup, offered by Mrs. Edward C. Post in memory of her uncle William K. Thorn, who played in the first international match.

It is possible that boys of Westbury think about some other topic than polo, but nothing else appears to be half so interesting. A journalist, noting the fact that Westbury had recently rejected a plan to build a two-hundred-thousand-dollar gymnasium for its public school, remarked: "The back of a polo pony has given too many Westburyites all the gymnastics they could possibly use."

Mr. Moses' experiment in adding polo to the attractions of Bethpage State Park has already gone far toward making the sport popular among a great many who shied away from it as merely another rich man's diversion, sacred to club precincts.

DISCOVERING LONG ISLAND

In fact, it is quite possible to play polo at Bethpage at a cost not much above what many a man spends on his golf. Certainly all subsequent international matches will draw far greater crowds than Westbury has ever been called on to handle before, for we are beginning to discover that polo is a thrilling spectacle.

The International Challenge Cup, which now stands in the office of the President of the American Polo Association, is one of the quaintest specimens of design left from the eighteen-eighties. It is a huge ornate silver bowl engraved with polo scenes. From the base project six gentlemen, dressed in the athletic costumes of 1886, riding ponies which, relative to their riders, look about the size of sheep dogs. Each of these players wears a magnificent mustache and looks—in a gentlemanly way —fierce and invincible.

So far, in this casual glance at Long Island polo, we have spoken almost entirely of Meadow Brook and Westbury, but there are at least a dozen first-class fields on the Island, as, for example, the ones at Sands Point, Piping Rock, Bostwick Field and Greentree. Fifty years ago, when Mr. Hitchcock was managing the first polo team at Newport, he could count on only eight players in America, and these were as hard to get together as eight prima donnas. Nowadays there are probably as many as eight hundred players, and there are more than fifty recognized teams who compete in annual tournaments. In this extraordinary development the Long Island clubs have taken the lead.

The Meadow Brook Club was a pioneer in fox hunting and polo, as we have seen; but fifty years ago another game was suggested to the directors, a curious form of amusement which was said to be popular in Scotland. It consisted of clouting a small white ball over a field into a succession of holes in the ground. This game had nothing to do with horses; players had to foot it all the way, and perhaps it was largely for this reason that those Centaurs of the Meadow Brook organization could not see anything in it. So that club passed up the opportunity of fathering the game of golf in this country.

Long before—just a hundred years, in fact—while the British were occupying New York, a man advertised in the *Royal Gazette* as follows: "To the Golf Players. The season for this pleasant and healthy Exercise now advancing, Gentlemen may be furnished with excellent CLUBS and the veritable Caledonian BALLS by enquiring at the Printer's." Evidently the officers of the Scotch regiments found some place in or near the city for their sport. Historians say that there was also a regular golf course in Charleston, South Carolina, in the year 1786, and ten years later Savannah boasted one. But these did not last. A hundred years later some people began playing in Yonkers, known among themselves as "the apple-tree gang." That sacred apple tree of 1888 is still enshrined on Palisade Avenue in Yonkers. Another attempt was made to stir up interest in the game at Tuxedo, but without success. For the real birth of the game in America we must go to the Shinnecock Hills of Long Island. In fact, the men who backed that first course there did not know of anyone else in the country who was interested in the game.

The treeless sea dunes and moors of a large section of the Shinnecock region suggested the landscape of Scotland, where the game flourished. The initiative in this enterprise seems to have come from a Scot named Duncan Cryder, and it was he who selected the Shinnecock Hills. In 1889 Messrs. Cryder, William K. Vanderbilt, Jr. and E. S. Mead (of the publishing house of Dodd, Mead & Company) went to Europe to find someone to lay out the links. In Biarritz they discovered a young professional, Willie Dunn, then in the midst of building a course. Dunn swung on a ball, to show how the game went, and drove it all the way to the next green. The gentlemen from America were deeply impressed. It looked so easy. At once they engaged Dunn to lay out the Shinnecock course, and there in 1891 he constructed twelve holes. This was the first incorporated golf course in America. The following summer a clubhouse was completed, and American golf got under way. The labor on these links was furnished by the Indians of the reservation, and it was found that the ground was covered with the ancient burial mounds of their red ancestors. Some of these served as bunkers.

The first members of this club were a distinguished group. One of them, the architect Stanford White, a former Tile Club member, designed the clubhouse. Another was Elihu Root. In a very short time all Southampton was enthusiastic about the new game, and soon the directors were faced with the problem of a waiting list. To the original twelve-hole course (thus restricted for economy's sake) was added soon a nine-hole course for the ladies.

At the outset these pioneers took their sport very seriously. They had the feeling that one must dress for the game as scrupulously as for fox hunting. Since Willie Dunn went about the links attired in the bright red jacket he wore when playing in Scotland, the members of the Shinnecock Club all blazed forth in scarlet coats with monogrammed brass buttons; also they wore white collars, and knickers with heavy golf stockings or white flannels. For an American summer sun those jackets and woolen stockings were very uncomfortable, but the Shinnecock players endured them bravely, happy in the thought that they were correctly attired. The following year Willie Dunn, while setting out another course in New Jersey, was chased by a bull. He just had time to cast off his red coat and vault a fence. After that, although young ladies in high pompadours still went out to the links in their scarlet jackets, the fashion speedily went out for the men. Even Willie Dunn did not invest in another blaze of red after the bull finished with the first one. And as the game spread like a prairie fire all over the country, players arrayed themselves for comfort, regardless of what the well-dressed golfer wore at St. Andrews.

So, in brief, runs the story of the birth of golf in America. What it has become in the forty-five years or so since then needs no telling. On Long Island alone there are nearly a hundred courses today. Golf has given the American business and professional man something to live for; it keeps him miserable over his hooks, slices, foozles and what not. But until he passes on to his reward he hopes against hope that his score will improve. It is noteworthy, too, that this game which began among a few very rich men accoutered in scarlet and monogrammed buttons has long since entered the phase of public golf courses in our parks, where very unpretentious citizens are enabled to try their luck at keeping their heads down and their eyes on the ball.

Among the pioneers of the Shinnecock Club was mentioned the name of Mr. William K. Vanderbilt, Jr. It was not long after he had done his part in founding the first organization in America devoted to the game of golf that he became interested in a strange new contraption, the horseless carriage. In order to encourage development in this country of the new vehicle, which the French had named "automobile," Mr. Vanderbilt inaugurated a series of international races to be held on the long, level highways of the Island. In order to attract the best that the world had to offer among makes of cars and racing drivers, he offered a cup and a prize of twenty thousand dollars. Although these "Vanderbilt Cup" races did not last many years, they were such a sensation in their time that they deserve to be rescued from oblivion.

Earlier European races had been run with the usual road cars, over existing highways. For the first Vanderbilt race of 1904 special racing cars were constructed, but they still used an ordinary dirt highway, except for a film of oil that was laid to keep the dust down. The route was a round of thirty miles to be run ten times, following, a good part of the way, the old Jericho turnpike. At the worst of the turns some dirt had been heaped up to bank the road, though cars were supposed to make a right-angle turn as best they could.

On the straightaway, at the starting point, a grandstand was put up, and here was a score board on which the fans could watch the relative positions of the racers. But the stand held only a minute fraction of the audience. Multitudes lined the course and packed the curves and turns.

The first trophy race had been a novelty, but as a spectacle of danger and thrill it caught the popular fancy. When the third event was held, October, 1906, crowds of undreamed-of proportions poured in a resistless flood to the scene. They came by any and every mode of conveyance, most of them by rail to Mineola and from there tramping three miles to the course. Society people came in their own cars by the dawn's early light in order to obtain points of vantage near the starting point. In those days anyone who owned a car was readily distinguished from the common herd by his costume—duster, goggles, gauntlets, rubber jackets and puttees.

SPORTS

But whether the mob came on foot or by bicycle or by old-fashioned buggy, most of them pressed to get a place near a famous "hairpin turn" at one end of the course, and this was most desirable because it was the spot of greatest peril to the racers. If anyone was going to be killed, this was the most likely spot. So, long before the starting gun banged, ten thousand people and five hundred automobiles were jammed at this point. A barrier had been erected there, but the crowd tore it down.

The worst feature of their behavior was that here and elsewhere they not only pressed close to the track but, when they thought no car was coming, would amble out on the road and take a look. The local constabulary were helpless in the face of the mob, for it was afterwards estimated that there must have been three hundred thousand of them. To the racers themselves this spectacle of an unruly horde of spectators overflowing the course was the greatest terror they had to face. In European races the crowd was always handled in style by the gendarmes and the army. In fact, the veteran racer who won the prize that day confessed afterwards that when he saw the mass of people milling around and over the road he almost quit before starting.

There were seventeen contenders that day and they boomed away from the starting point at intervals of one minute. By the time the last man was off, the first was halfway round the first lap. That made it difficult for an onlooker to get any idea how the race was going, and after the first lap or two the spectators found the spectacle rather dull. As each car went roaring past they surged all over the road. A bugler high up on the grandstand would spy a car coming and give a warning blast. "Car's coming!" the cry would go up. Other officials would wave red flags frantically and the people would scuttle off the road.

If a racer had to stop to replenish gasoline or change tires, the car would be surrounded instantly by a group of the curious. Other racers would shoot past, grazing their coattails. At last one of these imbeciles ambled out in the middle of the road just in time to be struck by a car going at full speed. He was instantly killed and his mangled body flung into the group of spectators. The chief attraction had been the fact that this automobile race was considered the most perilous form of sport yet invented, "compared with which," one journalist wrote, "Ben Hur's chariot race was a mere kindergarten diversion." No one expected that the one fatal casualty of the day would be a spectator.

It was a miracle that the drivers did come through unscathed that day. In addition to the antics of the crowd, the hairpin turn and the right angle at Krug's Corner, the road had many soft spots, which sometimes sent a car hurtling into space with all four wheels in the air. One unspeakable human rat tossed out a broken bottle on the track. Louis Wagner, the French contender, struck this object and blew a tire with a terrific bang. That accident might have cost his life, and it nearly cost him the victory he eventually won.

This race made the third consecutive time that the French had won the Vanderbilt trophy. The band played the Marseillaise politely but without enthusiasm, and the crowd surged away in all directions to reach home as best they could. The American hope had been pinned on a young man with just the name to win, "Daredevil Tracy." But his tires went all to pieces and he never had a chance. Once he skidded at a turn and knocked down a drunk and a small boy. The drunk, of course, was not hurt, but the boy's leg was broken. Coming as near as that to what might have been a double killing brought no inspiration to our Daredevil Tracy to put on any extra speed for the rest of the race.

Because of the death of the spectator, already noted, and the near escape from death of many another, Mr. Vanderbilt decided to call off any more international races on the Jericho turnpike. But he did achieve his purpose, that of stimulating American manufacturers to build better cars.

Mr. Walter Pritchard Eaton reported this third and last international race for the *American Magazine*. He called his story "Mile a Minute Madness"; but, as a matter of fact, some of the cars went as high as eighty or even a hundred miles an hour in their spurts. In summing up the lessons of the race Mr. Eaton said:

"Another thing the race has shown, so the builders themselves admit, is that the limit of speed for gasoline cars has been reached. They can go no faster and stay on the ground or hold together. . . . It looks as if the automobile had reached its speed limit. We have to turn elsewhere for our next speed thrill."

That was expert opinion in 1906.

All the reporters of that race agreed that, although people flocked to see the event by the hundred thousand, the race was very disappointing as a spectacle. As one man remarked when the affair was over, "Brrr! Bang! Whizz—! and a bad smell, and then some more of the same. That's all I saw of the Cup Race. I hope Mr. Vanderbilt got a better run for his money than I did!"

Although he felt it necessary to abandon these international races, Mr. Vanderbilt still kept up his enthusiastic interest in the advancement of motoring. In that last year of the Cup Race, 1906, he headed a corporation known as the "Long Island Motor Parkway, Inc." This company undertook the construction of a special roadway for automobiles, to be maintained by tolls, running from Lake Ronkonkoma in the middle of the Island to the Horace Harding Boulevard in the metropolitan area. In its day this motor highway was considered one of the wonders of the world, but it never was a financial success. As the great public roads and parkways developed during the last thirty years it became outmoded and was recently closed. Mr. Vanderbilt conveyed portions of it to the counties of Nassau and Suffolk, to the Long Island State Park Commission and to Greater New York. The part that is included in the metropolitan area is now used as a bicycle path. But this motor parkway was a splendid beginning made by a public-spirited private citizen toward the great transformation which the motorcar has brought about in our state and national highways.

If the village of Westbury is the polo capital, its neighbor to the west, Forest Hills, is the capital of lawn tennis. But the latter community cannot lay claim to the honor of originating the game in this country as Southampton can boast of golf in its Shinnecock Hills. Those, by the way, are real hillocks if not hills, but you can sweep the entire scene with your telescope without detecting the slightest eminence to justify the name "Forest Hills." For that matter, there has probably been no "forest" here, either, since the red man went his way. It is one of those names real-estate people invent when they want to sell off land which is as flat and bare as the kitchen table. In truth, like its neighbor, Kew Gardens, it echoes the name of a suburb of London.

To go back to origins, the famous West Side Tennis Club grounds and buildings here at Forest Hills are a comparatively recent affair. The game was introduced into this country in

SPORTS

1874, when players sported Dundreary whiskers and full beards. Staten Island and Nahant, Massachusetts, still fight over the distinction of having marked out the first tennis court in the United States. Anyway, the first championship was played for in the year 1881.

The West Side Club was formed by some New Yorkers in 1892, with courts at 89th Street and Central Park West. The growing metropolis kept pushing them uptown to 117th Street and Amsterdam Avenue, until they were forced out of their last refuge at 238th Street and Broadway. Land on Manhattan being now too costly, it was necessary to move elsewhere. Why not Long Island? For a while debate waxed fierce and long over the relative charms of Kew Gardens and Forest Hills, but finally the latter won. Ten acres were bought there for the club, and the necessary buildings put up. These new grounds were selected for the setting of the 1914 Davis Cup contest.

So rapidly grew the popular interest in the game that in 1923 the club built the present concrete stadium, which seats nearly 14,000 spectators. Together with the marquee, the seating capacity can be increased by about 500. Within the ten-acre lot belonging to the club are nearly sixty courts, twenty of them of grass. By contract with the United States Lawn Tennis Association the national championships are held here for a period of years. Here also, in alternate years, are staged the contests for the Wightman (women's) Cup, between Britain and the United States, if we possess the cup.

Those are reasons aplenty for calling Forest Hills our national capital for tennis, as Wimbledon is for the British Isles. In a sense, too, it can claim to be a world center for the game, because in addition to the many important contests staged on its courts, the West Side Club has a membership of more than eight hundred, and is the largest organization in the world devoted exclusively to tennis.

Like golf, this game was originally the sport of a few gentlemen of leisure, who put on tight knee breeches and a little round cap, twirled their long mustaches and popped a ball about on a none too even lawn. Their ladies, in bustles, tight skirts and garden hats, used to play, too. They made futile passes at the ball and hoped that they weren't getting too red in the face. This was the tennis of Du Maurier's pictures in *Punch*. To hoi polloi the game in those days was the very synonym of sissiness, just the thing for Little Lord Fauntleroys to play with their Dearests.

In the half century since it was transplanted to America a tremendous change has taken place in the character of the game all over the world. Needless to say, the fierce, slashing style of play today takes every ounce of stamina that the most masculine of he-men can summon to his racket. Perhaps the most striking change in the story of the game is its great popularity. It is the most democratic of these single-player contests. It is far cheaper in time and money to play than golf. The result is that the ball boy of yesterday may be the champion of today.

Out of that very circumstance, however, has grown the present-day problem of amateurism. Under the old conditions, in England, a player, being a gentleman of leisure, paid his own expenses as a matter of course. But a young man, here, who has a living to make can hardly be expected to give up all his time to playing the tournaments or pay the expenses involved. Even forty or fifty years ago players without money were helped financially. At present, the situation seems to be falling into confusion and it has resulted in some of our best players going, one after another, into the professional ranks. Here is a problem

SPORTS

for the International Lawn Tennis Federation to solve.

On the walls of the stadium are tablets bearing the names of the great players of the past, many of whom have fought out their contests on these courts. And there have been battles royal here. If any single match were to be selected for mention, probably most tennis enthusiasts—at least of the older generation—would agree that the choice should fall on the singles between Norman E. Brookes of Australia and Maurice E. McLoughlin of California. This memorable duel of rackets took place in August, 1914, the first year in which the club had opened play on its new grounds.

In this Davis Cup series the Australians won three matches to the Americans' two, and thus carried off the cup. But there was comfort in the magnificent performances of McLoughlin, who defeated the two stars of the Australian team, Brookes and Wilding, with both men playing at the top of their games. It was the first of these matches, the one with Brookes, that was the memorable one. "A titanic battle ensued," wrote the editor of *American Lawn Tennis,* "from which the Californian emerged victorious after one of the finest and closest matches in the history of the game. The first set will go thundering down the ages as the greatest exhibition ever seen." Anyone who witnessed it will contend that after a quarter of a century it is still the grandest exhibition of tennis ever seen. That first set lasted about an hour and three-quarters; and when it was over, the audience was fully as limp with exhaustion as the players.

It was one hundred per cent tennis all the way. One miraculous shot followed another as the spectators gasped and applauded. The games seesawed back and forth, alternating with the service. On the eighteenth game Brookes forged ahead to forty-love on McLoughlin's serve. If he could win any one of the next three points the set and the match would be probably won for Australia. For Brookes' service looked unbeatable. At this critical point McLoughlin flung himself on the ball with all his strength and shot it over the net like a bullet. He then brought the game to deuce. Then he suddenly changed his pace and rushed to the net with a chop-volley. This point was followed by a clean service-ace. The score was now nine-all.

So that duel went on until the thirty-first game, when the American broke through his opponent's service to lead at sixteen to fifteen. The next game on McLoughlin's service was hotly contested every inch of the way, but finally the latter shot it out on fast drives and won, seventeen to fifteen. That set won the match; for although Brookes fought hard during the next two sets, youth was on the side of his opponent. The American took the next two sets at six to three.

That extraordinary score of seventeen to fifteen was not duplicated again in a Davis Cup series until 1923, when it was repeated in a doubles match. But there was no comparison between the two for a combination of endurance and skill. "That Brookes-McLoughlin set," wrote Mr. S. W. Mayhew in his *Quest of the Davis Cup,* "still stands as the most memorable of all sets in the contests for the trophy."

McLoughlin later defeated Wilding of New Zealand. That was the last match that great sportsman from the Antipodes was destined to play. He dropped his racket for a rifle, and in May, 1915, was killed in battle in northern France. Strange to say, a fortnight after the Davis Cup series, McLoughlin lost the championship of the United States to Richard Norris Williams, 2nd, who had just been defeated by both Brookes and Wilding. It was the first indication of a strange sequel, unique in tennis history. After that incomparable performance on the Forest

SPORTS

Hills courts in the Davis Cup matches, McLoughlin's game went to pieces, and his brilliant career as a champion came to a sudden and inexplicable end.

The same level fields that attracted horse racing, polo and tennis to Long Island were also ideal for airports. Although aviation is ninety-nine per cent business to one per cent sport it would never do to omit mention of it, because of the fame of the flights made from these Long Island plains. Glenn Curtiss began experimenting with his planes on the Island as far back as 1909. After the Great War two of the Service aviation fields were preserved, Mitchel Field for the army and Floyd Bennett for the navy. In addition, there are two commercial airports, Curtiss and Roosevelt.

These were the starting places for the spectacular flights that filled the newspapers and thrilled their readers in the last dozen years. There was Lindbergh's solo performance, in 1927, to the Le Bourget airport in France. This was followed by Chamberlin and Levine's nonstop flight to Eisleben, Saxony. In the same month of June, Byrd took off across the Atlantic but, blinded by a fog over Le Bourget airport, went back to the Channel for safe landing and crashed on the beach. Three years later Post and Gatty jumped off from Roosevelt Field and, by a series of hops from England to Germany, to Russia, to Siberia and to Alaska, made their way back to Floyd Bennett Field in 7 days, 18 hours and 49½ minutes. Of very recent fame (1938) was the flight of Howard Hughes, who also circled the globe from Long Island to Long Island but by a different route. And there was that Douglas Corrigan, who, according to his story, took off for California and found himself in Ireland.

But of all these stories the most famous still is that feat of

Lindbergh's. As an obscure young mail pilot he entered the competition for the Raymond Orteig prize of $25,000 for the first to make a nonstop flight from New York to Paris. Lindbergh's rivals were Commander Byrd, who had been the first to reach the North Pole by airplane, and Chamberlin, then the most noted air pilot in America. But both these men were held back by accidents or legal difficulties. Lindbergh was a dark horse, and his plane, *The Spirit of St. Louis,* was an odd-looking contraption of a design that did not impress anyone favorably.

Finally Byrd and Chamberlin mended their planes, recovered from injuries, settled their difficulties and were ready to go. But the weather was bad, and the crowds, after waiting to see these men make their start, returned home. On the morning of May 20, 1927, Lindbergh stepped into his plane and started off, despite the fact that the clouds hung low and the rain was still falling. His plane was so loaded with gasoline that it had trouble in leaving the ground, nor did the muddy condition of the runway help. Then, reaching a spot of hard ground, the plane took the air, but it narrowly missed hitting a tractor and some telegraph wires as it climbed. Finally, she was safely in the air and off.

Lindbergh followed the coast to Newfoundland, flew low over St. John's to check his bearings and then headed out over the Atlantic Ocean. A storm covered his wings and fusilage heavily with sleet, which weighed the plane down, but he made Ireland safely, flying low so that his plane could be identified. Then across the Channel and up the course of the Seine, he soon arrived, guided by flares and rockets, at the airport of Paris—Le Bourget Field. He had made the flight of 3610 miles in 33½ hours, a record that still holds.

The rest of the Lindbergh story is too familiar to need re-

SPORTS

telling. The tumultuous welcome home, the idiotic frenzy of publicity that beat upon his head, the dreadful tragedy that entered his home, the subsequent flight to England and then to Germany and France to escape the perpetual assault by photographers and reporters. Indeed, it may well be said that this young man's life might have been infinitely happier if he had never made himself a nation's idol. And the whole story stands as a bitter commentary on the vulgarity of a certain section of the American press, which denied this young man any right to privacy for either himself or his children.

The foregoing catalogue of sports—and it is by no means complete—has dealt with activities that, like the cauliflower and potato, flourished in the flat lands of mid-Island. For the last item on the list we shall return to that coast line which has been called "New York's seashore." For this sport is fishing, and game fishing at that. For some reason fishing for the market seems to have fallen on evil days along the North Atlantic coast. The fishing that has made Long Island dear to the heart of the angler is carried on simply for sport. So, while aviation may scarcely be allowed inclusion as an amateur activity, because most of the fliers at least have been out for the cash prizes, here is something carried on entirely for fun.

The famous fishing centers are Greenport, Montauk, Freeport and the Rockaways; but there is no cove or inlet on the long coast line that is not ruffled by the fishermen's oars, and whipped by their lines. During the season the Long Island Railroad runs special excursion trains for fishermen from New York to Montauk.

There are all sorts of methods, as there are all sorts of fish. One type of enthusiast stands on the beach and flings his hook out into the surf. You will find him under the bluff at Montauk Light, or along the beaches at Rockaway. The surf angler thinks that this method is the most sporting way to take a game fish. Others take a boat well offshore to various fishing grounds that are the deep secret of the local wiseacre whose boat and services have been hired for the day.

A man who has parked his homemade trailer in Hither Hills State reservation will probably go out in a small boat by himself and take his chances on bringing home something for supper. Others take to the fishing grounds in elegant and dazzling motor cruisers. But whether it is a "pumpkinseed" or a yacht doesn't seem to make much difference with the booty brought back to port when the sun goes down. An innovation is the provision of the Freeport Boatsmen's Association that every boat in the organization must go out with a pair of carrier pigeons. In case of accident, or even a walloping big catch, a bird is released with the news, and a boat from shore is out in half an hour to bring help. Some boats even have a two-way radio-telephone system, but that does seem a bit of too much. One of the blessings of a day's fishing, anyway, is to get away from the telephone.

But whether it is surf angling or boat angling, the waters offer the fisherman a wide variety of game, and these are fish that put up a fight; striped bass, channel bass or red drum, bluefish and weakfish merely start off the list with the favorites. Weakfish, it may be added for the novice, is not so named for lack of muscle but for his tender mouth. He is likely to wrench off, leaving some of his jaw on the hook.

These fish have an accommodating way of running at different seasons. Flounders come in March; when they disappear weakfish and sea bass arrive, staying through the summer and until about the middle of October. To make the summer program still more lively, the bluefish, mackerel and tuna appear in early July and stay on through September.

The last-named fish deserves special mention. He is called the "deep sea torpedo," and is the special pet of a large group of anglers. Yet up to only a few years ago nobody knew anything about him. Once in a while a tuna was caught, but for some reason, despite his size, he failed to excite interest. The discovery of the tuna is credited to certain gentry of a by-gone era known as bootleggers. They used to go offshore in their boats and make profitable contacts with rumrunners. While waiting, they used to amuse themselves by fishing. Soon they found that they were dealing with a ferocious creature that raced off with all their tackle. When finally they built up a stout enough line and hook, they brought in the tuna. In doing so they discovered that, huge as it was, every ounce of a tuna fish was full of fight. When repeal put an end to their illicit activities it occurred to them that something might be done with the tuna to bring in revenue. Result: a brand-new and highly profitable aspect of Long Island fishing. Whole fleets of boats and their skippers do nothing but take the city fellers out to the tuna hunt.

They say you should wait until just after a storm—which means you must have a good seagoing stomach—and then you troll. What you tie on the hook for an allurement may be a bunch of feathers, a pork rind or your necktie—you never can tell what will take the tuna's fancy—but once he is hooked, the man at the other end of the line has his hands completely occupied. The tuna is not only immensely strong but full of guile. He grows to great size. The largest one taken off Long Island so far, caught by Mr. Francis Low, weighed seven hundred and five pounds. To the Scriptural inquiry, "Canst thou draw out Leviathan with an hook?" the tuna fisherman answers, "Sure!"

He has a picture ready to prove it, too. Everyone who comes in with a tuna seems to make for the nearest cameraman and has himself photographed with his tuna and his own self-satisfied smirk. It may indeed be darkly suspected that local photographers of Freeport and Montauk keep large stuffed specimens ready for fishermen to pose against. There are too many of these monstrous catches. Anyway, such a picture must make a big impression back home in Davenport or Keokuk.

So, all in all, in its fishing Long Island has its chief sport, attracting every class of angler from the farmer's boy, running away for a little while from the bugs on his father's potato plants, to the Big Shot from the metropolis, who also is running away for a holiday from similar pests on his industrial plants. If Long Island is a great playground for the sportsman of every stripe and variety, doubtless the largest, most democratic army of devotees is the one armed with the rod and reel.

In all this flat area so famous among sportsmen there are suburban and summer communities growing so rapidly that they threaten one of these days to form an unbroken chain of dwellings from Glen Cove to Freeport. If one of these towns is to be selected as the "sweet Auburn, loveliest village of the plain," let it be Hempstead. To be sure, it is hardly a village any longer, for it has a population, by census, of nearly 13,000—by booster advertising, of 20,000. It has all the pleasant appurtenances of a residential town without being too citified, and its location makes it the green heart of all this area of racing, polo, fox-hunting, golf and aviation. To the east lies the Meadow Brook Hunt Club. To the north are the Mitchel and Roosevelt

SPORTS

flying fields, the Mineola Fairgrounds, and the International Polo Field. Farther north we find more polo fields, country clubs and what not, all the way to the Sound. South of Hempstead, just outside the boundaries of the town are the Hempstead Lake State Park and the Southern State Parkway, making a direct route to Jones Beach. This Hempstead Lake is another one of those famous Long Island bird sanctuaries. It is a rendezvous for wild duck. Here flock the black duck, the American teal, the European widgeon and the European teal. The last two are rare species in America. In fact, no one seems to know how they happened to abandon their home scenes to disport themselves in the waters of Hempstead Lake after their nesting time near the Arctic Circle. Finally, it is only a hop, skip and jump to the wharves of Freeport, where the boats are waiting to take the angler out after the game fish.

Hempstead is worth a garland of praise on its own account, too. It is distinctly a home town, without the blight of factories, tenements, freight yards and dumps that has ruined so many a community of equal size in New England. As some visitor remarked, "The entire city has the appearance of a park." If we took the entire original Hempstead township in, too, as a part of our "Sweet Auburn," we should include all those other delightful home and summer communities from Great Neck, Port Washington, Manhasset, Glen Cove, Roslyn all the way south to the clustered villages on the Atlantic shore, for the township boundaries used to run clear across the Island. That was in the day when the village of Hempstead had two churches and a dozen houses.

Right on the edge of the present town is Garden City. That is worth pausing briefly to consider, for it has a unique history. Unlike all the other towns in this area, it has no pre-

Revolutionary past. It was deliberately founded seventy years ago by a rich philanthropist who had his own idea of what Utopia should be. In 1869 A. T. Stewart, the merchant of New York, decided to spend a part of his fortune in founding a city which should be a Garden of Eden without the serpent. To keep the reptile out, he drew up a formidable set of rules and regulations for the settlers. These were written into the deeds, and every property-holder disregarding them could be prosecuted by the others. Despite various battles in the courts, these restrictions still hold. But, strange to say, the ungrateful human critters made it plain that they did not wish to be dragooned into the Kingdom of Heaven, and for the first few years the voice that breathed o'er that particular Eden was heavy with disappointment. Another noble experiment bogged down, in spite of the most beautiful specifications.

In 1876, after the well-meaning gentleman's death, his widow erected in Garden City a fine Gothic cathedral, with a Bishop's Palace and a boys' church school, all as a memorial to her husband. At the same time, some of the stiff regulations for the citizenry of the town were quietly dropped, and soon the new settlement began to thrive. Now Hempstead is quite proud of her great-granddaughter.

Of course, to be only seventy years old is mere infancy for any community on Long Island. The township of Hempstead goes back to the early seventeenth century, when all the rest of the Island to the west belonged to the Dutch. For many decades its most famous landmark was a hostelry known as the "Sammis Tavern," after the name of the family that owned and operated it. This was dispensing ale and strong waters here in the village to thirsty travelers as far back as 1680. A hundred and ten years later President Washington was an honored guest. He wrote in his diary that "ye inn was a hospitable place and full of good cheer." A Sammis waited on him then. In 1861 the farmer boys came shuffling in, half-exultant and half scared, to sign up as volunteers in response to the call of Father Abraham. The innkeeper then was a Sammis. In the next generation officers and men in khaki came in for refreshment before they embarked for Cuba, and another Sammis was the proprietor.

Unfortunately there were no public-spirited citizens to save this, the oldest tavern in the country. For a space of two hundred and twenty-three years the business was conducted in the same building by the same family. Seven generations were born in that inn. But an accursed modern-improver had to come along and knock it down. Some patriotic citizen, however, put up a tablet on the present building to say that "General George Washington was entertained in 1790 at the Sammis Tavern located on this site." The memorial bears a bas-relief portrait of the President; but we have many of these, and it would have been more interesting to have kept a picture of the old tavern itself. For it had much to do with historical events before and after that visit. It saw Dutch officers and befeathered Indians come and go, and for seven long years during the Revolutionary War British officers in scarlet made merry in the taproom.

Now the Hempsteaders were outspoken Loyalists when that war began. So also was the rector of St. George's Church. But they did not enjoy the army occupation overmuch, for despite the citizens' huzzas for King George, the British helped themselves to what they wanted with a ruthless hand. They came down like the wolf on the fold, paying naught for their plunder in silver or gold. Cattle, grain, lumber, hogs and chickens—all were impressed into His Majesty's service without a by-your-leave.

Nor were the invaders scrupulous about the two places of worship. They took over the Presbyterian sanctuary as a combination granary and stable, first ripping out the pews and the flooring. They pulled up, also, the headstones from the graveyard to use as hearthstones for their campfires. Long years afterwards, in 1840 to be precise, one Stephen Gildersleeve of Hempstead made a formal written statement to the effect that it was a matter of common knowledge in his childhood that the redcoats were sometimes scared away from their posts by the ghosts of the Presbyterians whose graves they had desecrated. Yes, sir! All the old folks of that generation knew this to be a fact. So let's hope that these ill-mannered "lobsterbacks" were sufficiently terrified to make them think twice about playing the vandal in churches or churchyards thereafter.

These soldiers seemed to take special pleasure in making fun of the Presbyterians, for when they tried to hold meetings on the Lord's Day the regimental band would follow to their place of service, which was a barn, and as soon as the minister began his sermon the band would begin to play.

As for St. George's, in spite of its being Church of England, in spite of its rector's loud denunciation of the rebels, in spite of the fact that its patron saint was no less than the patron saint of England, the British officers made this sacred edifice an army storehouse, too. Once the soldiers amused themselves by shooting at the gilded cock that served as the weather vane. Some of the parishioners quietly removed it by night and hid it in the cellar, together with the font and the silver chalice that Queen Anne had given.

The present building dates from as late as 1822, but it still carries aloft the same weather cock, its holes neatly plugged, and in the church are still to be seen the silver chalice and the old font. All in all, the Tory Hempsteadians discovered that their Policy of Appeasement did not work out so successfully as they had hoped.

Naturally the patriots of Long Island had no love for the Tory village. When finally the British troops left to embark for England, the victorious rebels came trooping into Hempstead to express their sentiments. The rector of St. George's had to make a quick jump, not only out of town but off the Island, for he was particularly unpopular. The next incumbent was an Englishman, too, but he had been long enough in the colonies to become an ardent American. The first thing he did was to paste a new set of prayers for the President and Congress over the page where the petition is made for the King, the royal family and Parliament. That prayer book is one of the cherished relics of the present church.

There was so much feeling in the town between the patriots and the loyalists that in 1784 the former broke off from the others by forming the new township of North Hempstead, leaving South Hempstead to the Tories. The latter name was applied to the old village of Hempstead. Later it quietly dropped the "South" and became plain Hempstead again, and its citizens became as good Americans as any to be found in the northern township.

Before taking leave of Hempstead we should doff our hat for a moment beside the grave of Henry Eckford, who is buried here. He was a Scot who came to America via Quebec and set himself up as a shipbuilder in New York. In the War of 1812 he built ships in record time for the navy on Lake Ontario. Afterwards he became the naval architect for the Brooklyn Navy Yard, and it was there that he produced the seventy-four-gun ship of the line, the *Ohio,* whose figurehead we observed at Canoe Place. This was said to be the finest ship of her class at that time. President Jackson wanted him to plan a reorganization of the American navy, but he was thwarted by the politicians. Other countries, however, were glad enough to get his services, and at the time of his death he was in Constantinople. His remains were brought to Hempstead that they might rest near his neighbors' and friends.' It is worth remembering that he was in the front rank of those great ship designers of the first half of the nineteenth century, that period when American clippers were the finest in the world.

CHAPTER XIV

OLD BROOKLYN

1. The First Hundred Years

EARLY in this voyage of exploration it was discovered that all the western end of our Island had been bitten off by the Big City. In fact, the marks of its teeth already extend as far east as Hempstead and Garden City. Heaven knows when all the rest of Nassau County will be devoured. And after that what can preserve Suffolk from the same suburban fate? So far in these pages all this closely built area to the west has been ignored as being merely the bedroom of New York and not really Long Island at all.

But ere we leave this vast, citified territory with its miles upon miles of tenements, gas tanks, garages, amusement parks, apartment houses and bungalows, we should for the sake of old times say a few words about the metropolis of this region, Brooklyn—that old Brooklyn so beloved by the citizens of long ago. Today, alas, nobody has a kind or even a respectful word for the place. The gag writers for radio and movies harp on its name as if it were the world's greatest municipal joke. "He's from Brookalyn," is in itself supposed to be the signal for rude laughter. In baseball the "Dodgers" seem to dodge successfully any place in the league except a lowly one. And so it goes among the comedians, amateur and professional. But this attitude of scorn and ridicule is uncalled-for and most reprehensible. After all, it is only the crude idea of humor cherished by Manhattanites of the baser sort.

DISCOVERING LONG ISLAND

It was not ever thus, and does not deserve to be now. Never was a community so maligned. The city—or rather, borough, for it was joined with Manhattan forty years ago—has a great deal to be proud of. Its Prospect Park, Institute of Arts and Sciences, Museum of Art, charities, hospitals, libraries, foundations for education, are all well worth a good thumping boast apiece. And there are charming streets and corners left over from the old-time Brooklyn, which strangers seldom see. For example, the people who live in those unpretentious brownstone houses on Brooklyn Heights enjoy a view across the East River and harbor of the great city itself which is unrivaled by any vista in all Manhattan. For that matter, it would be hard to match that scene anywhere else among the habitations of men. Dawn or sunset, noon or night, summer or winter, it is always fascinating, always different, always beautiful. To the east rise the magnificent piers and span of Brooklyn Bridge. Directly ahead stands that colossal pyramid of Manhattan office buildings, their straight lines broken by delicate wreaths of steam during the day. By night the great mass is all atwinkle like a Christmas tree with its thousands of lighted windows. To the left, at the entrance to the harbor, stands Miss Liberty with upraised arm and torch looking down upon the great ocean liners as they come and go. At night, radiant with floodlights, she looks like some heavenly apparition, a sort of welcoming angel at the gate of the New World.

Unfortunately, only a few people are in the secret of that stupendous scene. To strangers, Brooklyn seems like a succession of dreary streets, up which trolleycars clang and groan between miles of monotonous brick buildings shadowed by noisy elevated railroads. The dwellings and shops along the chief arteries of travel seem inhabited by queer, swarthy immigrants

OLD BROOKLYN

from out-of-the-way corners of the planet such as Beluchistan, Belgrade and Beersheba. For the three bridges built to the east of Brooklyn Bridge have served as conduits to drain off into Brooklyn the overflow from the East Side of Manhattan. What were once pleasant suburbs, like Williamsburgh, became largely submerged, and the flood spread through many sections of Brooklyn.

But this does not by any means spell the whole story of modern Brooklyn, which still holds to its historic position as the city of homes and churches, of parks, museums, schools and libraries. Strangers who travel by trolley or elevated never see the heart of real Brooklyn, those quiet streets away from the thoroughfares where the old houses are, and where the traditions of a hundred years ago still hold up their heads proudly. Let us turn back the pages of its history even further than a century in order to look first at the little Dutch village of the seventeen hundreds.

It is pleasant to discover that the original settlers bought their land honestly from the Indians; this initial purchase took place in the year 1636. It was only six years after that date that a regular ferry service was established with the thriving town of New Amsterdam across the neck of the Sound, which came to be known as the East River. Like other towns in the New Netherlands colony, the name harked back to an original Breuckelin—a municipality in the province of Utrecht, Holland—a name signifying "marshy land."

Toward the end of the century the sons of these first settlers saw the Duke of York take over the entire colony, and thereafter they had to learn to be good Britishers. Then, later, when rebellion broke out against a British Ministry, the great-grandsons of these Breuckelin citizens had to learn to be Americans. It was a hard lesson, too, for the town was in the hands of the enemy for more than seven years, and to be a rebel sympathizer was not healthy.

Here, on August 27, 1776, in an area long since covered by city blocks, Washington's army fought the Battle of Long Island. In this engagement the inexperienced officers and men of the rebel force were pitted against a trained army of ten thousand British and Hessian soldiers; naturally the Americans suffered a severe defeat. This compelled Washington to retreat to New York and then up the Hudson.

Although this meant that he had to abandon the Long Island area to the enemy, he needed to keep informed of British troop and fleet movements and the character and extent of their fortifications in and about this New York area. As every schoolboy knows, Nathan Hale gave his life in this service. But what few readers of history know is that, all through the war, Washington was kept informed by some remarkably brave and skillful intelligence agents working on Long Island. So carefully did these men conceal their identity that practically no one knew who they were, besides Washington himself and the closest members of their own families, even after the war was over.

Mr. Morton Pennypacker, the historian and antiquarian of Suffolk County, whom the reader met in the East Hampton Library, recently unearthed a large amount of material which reveals the service that these spies performed, and for the first time identified who they were. Several of these agents besides Nathan Hale were caught and executed, but they went to their death revealing nothing to the enemy. Others operated with success to the end of the war. We have already had a glimpse of their activities in connection with the story of André at Oyster Bay. The village of Setauket on the North Shore, which has been visited in these pages, was an American spy center, and from here one of the ablest of these men, Abraham Woodhull, conducted his operations throughout the war. Once his father was tortured by Colonel Simcoe's Rangers to make him confess what the British suspected must be going on, but the old gentleman endured the suffering without a word. John Jay and Robert Townsend related the story to James Fenimore Cooper, who made it the basis of the tenth chapter of his novel, *The Spy*.

Woodhull and his friends used a code book in which, for example, the figure 10 stood for New York, and 20 for Setauket. In addition, he had a liquid stain which, when washed over a letter, revealed writing done in invisible ink. James Jay, the brother of John, claimed to have invented this, which he called "white ink." After a few minutes this would fade out and the writing could not be brought back again. Such messages, of course, were written between the lines of ordinary letters. All of Woodhull's dispatches were helpful to Washington, and one of them was received just in time to save a French fleet from capture.

Another code used by these men was a clothesline on which news could be hung out in terms of a family wash, according to a system known to the courier riding by. Half a dozen handkerchiefs, for example, carried a definite message; a combination of one petticoat with so many handkerchiefs would mean something else, and so on. Whether the clothesline ran east or west, north or south, also had a significance. Here was where the patriotic women and girls did their bit, and although it may have struck Sir William Erskine or Colonel Simcoe that almost every day seemed to be washday on Long Island they never suspected what those clotheslines were for.

Sally Townsend's brother Robert, of Oyster Bay, also was

active in this intelligence service and, as has already been narrated, had much to do with the detection of André's plot involving Benedict Arnold. Robert's cousin Ann had married Major General Green of the British army. With Colonel Simcoe and Major André living in his own home and flirting with his sisters, and Cousin Ann the consort of a British general, Robert Townsend found his family relationships decidedly complicated during the war. Throughout the war he operated in New York City. He was named in the American dispatches always as "Samuel Culper, Jr." or by number as 723; while his friend, Abraham Woodhull, was "Samuel Culper," number 722. Tallmadge, working on the Westchester shore, was officially "John Bolton."

There was another slant to this hazardous work that sometimes had a comic side. The British officer in command at various points tried to induce citizens of Long Island to form companies in the service of His Majesty. To make the offer more attractive it was given out that such volunteers would not be called on for fighting but to help the army of occupation keep order and to bring in supplies. Washington actually encouraged some of the patriots to enlist in this service because, in British uniform, they were able to accomplish more for the American cause than in any other way, chiefly in matters of intelligence.

The British officers found these Americans very unsatisfactory. They never amounted to much on any of the jobs assigned to them, whether it was bringing in forage or cutting up cordwood. The captain of one of these Loyalist companies was that same Daniel Youngs who delivered Sally Townsend's note to her brother Robert in the André affair. Youngs, wearing the British uniform, performed important service during the war by

BROOKLYN BRIDGE

letting Washington's agents pass through the Island without interruption.

The other important links in the intelligence chain between Woodhull at Setauket and General Washington were Caleb Brewster, to whom Woodhull gave the messages, and Austin Roe, who took them from Brewster and every week went over the Fulton ferry to meet a secret courier in New York. This ferry was the only possible avenue of information, because the Sound was tightly watched by British men-of-war.

Somewhere, on either the New York or the Brooklyn side where that old ferry used to run, there should be a historical marker to keep alive the memory of the intelligence service that passed back and forth at this point during the Revolutionary War. The men who conducted that work knew that if once the slightest suspicion fell on them they would be sent to the hangman without mercy.

One other memory of the Revolutionary War associated with Brooklyn is that of the prison ship *Jersey*. Any form of imprisonment in the eighteenth century was brutal, but for sheer horror the old hulk that incarcerated the wretched captives from the rebel forces during the Revolution is still hard to surpass. It is the "Black Hole of Calcutta" in American history. Today, in Fort Greene Park in Brooklyn there rises a tall shaft to the memory of the men who died on that ship. But for a long time their bones lay in neglect.

In 1803, when Tammany Hall was not the synonym for political corruption that it has been for seventy years, the club presented a memorial to Congress asking for a decent tomb for the victims. The hasty burials during the war left, after a score of years, some of the bones actually exposed, and there was not even a wooden marker in their honor. But Congress was not interested in dead heroes who could not vote. Finally, in 1808, Tammany itself assumed the duty and erected a small vault, with a temporary shed over it, standing near the Navy Yard in Brooklyn at the end of Front Street. The club held a public funeral and reverently laid in this vault the bones they were able to collect from the original burial ground on Gowanus Creek. When, after many years, the present monument was erected, the sandstone slab which Tammany Hall had set up was transferred to the new vault beneath the shaft, where it remains today.

The *Jersey* had been dismasted in 1776 as unseaworthy and placed in Wallabout Bay, four years later, as the chief prison ship for the New York area. The name of the Bay does not appear on road maps but it is that indentation used by the Navy Yard in Brooklyn, lying on the hither side of the Williamsburgh Bridge. Near the head of this bay flowed Gowanus Creek.

Into this hulk were jammed the American prisoners, sometimes well over a thousand at a time, but as they died by scores they made room for newcomers. Because the ship reeked with germs of pestilence, no one from shore dared to go aboard to try to better the condition of the captives. Every morning the cry went up on board, "Rebels, turn out your dead!" The corpses would then be dragged out in their blankets, if they possessed them, tossed into boats and their fellow captives, under armed guard, had to row ashore and bury their shipmates. Eleven thousand and five hundred prisoners died here in Wallabout Bay.

The following narrative was written by a Thomas Andros, one of the few who succeeded in surviving imprisonment aboard the *Jersey:*

OLD BROOKLYN

On the commencement of the first evening, we were driven down to darkness, between decks, secured by iron gratings and an armed soldiery. And now, a scene of horror, which baffles description, presented itself. On every side, wretched, despairing shapes of men could be seen. Around the well-room an armed guard were forcing up the prisoners to the winches, to clear the ship of water, and prevent her sinking, and little else could be heard but a roar of mutual execration, reproaches and insults. During this operation there was a small, dim light, admitted below, but it served to make darkness more visible and horror more terrific. When I first became an inmate of this abode of suffering, despair, and death, there were about four hundred prisoners on board, but in a short time they amounted to twelve hundred; and in proportion to our numbers the mortality increased. All the most deadly diseases were pressed into the service of the "king of terrors," but his prime ministers were dysentery, small pox, and yellow fever. There were two hospital ships near to the Old Jersey, but these were soon so crowded with the sick, that they would receive no more. The consequence was, that the diseased and the healthy were mingled together in the main ship. In a short time, we had two hundred or more sick and dying, lodged in the fore part of the lower gun deck, where all the prisoners were confined at night. Utter derangement was a common symptom of yellow fever, and to increase the horror of the darkness that shrouded us (for we were allowed no lights betwixt decks) the voice of warning would be heard, "Take heed to yourselves; there is a madman stalking through the ship with a knife in his hand."

When the war was over and the redcoats took ship for England, in November, 1783, they left this grisly souvenir behind, still lying at anchor, and as no one else wanted it the *Jersey* gradually rotted herself out of existence.

DISCOVERING LONG ISLAND

Only one character will be introduced from this early period of Brooklyn history, and to meet him we must go back to the days when the village of Breuckelin was a typical Dutch community trying to live peaceably with its neighbors of the English colony to the east. But every now and then some band of ruffians would come over by night and raid the town. One of these armed hoodlums or holdup men was a certain John Scott. Governor Peter Stuyvesant found out that Scott had an evil reputation even among his compatriots, and made ready for him. The next time Scott tried his gangster tactics he was arrested and clapped into jail. That happened in 1654. This was Breuckelin's early experience with this person. But Scott was not weary of ill doing. After being run out of Connecticut he seems to have started as a blacksmith and cattle-raiser in the region of Southampton, Long Island. But he had dreams of big deals in real estate. Later he laid his plans to gain personal dominion over a vast area. He set out, in fact, to be nothing less than the Lord of Long Island.

This man must have been as smooth and slippery as an oyster, for all his life he succeeded in making people believe him and always to their sorrow. Giles Sylvester, of Shelter Island, for example, lent him some money, which Scott never returned. Sylvester's opinion of Scott was expressed in these words, "If the gallows hath him not, he will rot whilst he liveth." As his deals grew bigger he added to his name the military title of "Captain," and hinted at his aristocratic family in England.

In 1660 he returned to London in order to join the throng of needy royalists who clamored for patronage after the Restoration. While in England he sold twenty thousand acres on Long Island to a friend, land to which he had no title. This was the incident referred to in the story of Mt. Sinai in an early chapter.

Then he took the jewels of his friend's wife and brought their son to Long Island. There he pawned the jewels, and, as we have seen, sold the youth into slavery. This accomplished, he went gaily on his way. Now he called himself "Colonel Scott," a gentleman, he said, who was very influential in the court of Charles the Second. He bluffed, lied, cheated—one of his victims being Richard (Bull) Smith of Smithtown—but somehow he made himself one of three commissioners to treat with the Dutch. He had himself referred to as "The President of Long Island." At the head of a troop of cavalry he galloped into Breuckelin, crying that the place belonged to England, by God. "Bring out your Governor Stuyvesant," he shouted, "and I will run him through with this sword!" To show how brave he was, Scott knocked down a small boy who had neglected to take off his hat. That was Scott's way of getting revenge for the time he had been locked up in a Breuckelin jail a few years before.

Since he had all the air and manner of a Big Shot, for a while he carried all before him. He showed the Dutch commissioners a large parchment document giving him by royal grant the whole of Long Island. There was only one slight omission; namely, the seal and signature of the King, but all the other flourishes were there and the bluff impressed the Dutchmen.

Meanwhile he continued to sell land that did not belong to him, and the law was never quick enough to catch up with him. Soon, he believed, he would have it all arranged to become Lord of Long Island and then he could snap his fingers at pettifogging lawyers and sheriffs. But something slipped up. Charles the Second, when the raid on New Amsterdam had been accomplished, gave Long Island not to "Colonel" John Scott but to Brother James, the Duke of York. So the grandiose plan built up on such an elaborate pyramid of fraud and lies suddenly tumbled to the ground. There was a growing hue and cry against Scott for "villainous and felonious practices." Gone was the glittering prospect of a Governor's Palace erected on Brooklyn Heights in which the Lord of Long Island could hold his court. Indeed, it became increasingly evident that he would have to get out of the province or the bailiffs would have him. So he slipped away on a vessel bound for the Barbados, posing as a Quaker suffering for conscience' sake. Thereafter Brooklyn knew John Scott no more.

But ere he fled he had succeeded in wangling a bit of revenge on the Duke of York. Having some pretentions to map making, he was permitted to make suggestions as to the boundaries of the new colony of New Jersey, granted to Berkeley and Carteret. He arranged it so that the eastern boundary followed the Hudson River, thus depriving the province of New York of the western shore of its great river and harbor. That is the reason why the businessman of today who commutes from Jersey City to New York goes from one state to another, and why New York City cannot swallow, as additional boroughs, all its trans-Hudson population. The first English governor, Nicolls, was furious when he learned what had been unwittingly done in London, and put his finger on the responsible man. He already knew something of the fellow's record. "Scott," he said, "was born to work mischief."

So "Colonel" John Scott, "The President of Long Island," was known no more in these scenes except for the lingering odor of his frauds, more and more of which kept coming to light. But though at this point he leaves the story of old Long Island and Brooklyn, his career of villainy had scarcely begun. He never deviated into decency even by accident. In the end he succeeded in committing a triple treason, by selling out, in turn, his own country, Holland and France, by spy activities, according as it suited his purse. In due time he was exposed by Samuel Pepys, the man of *Diary* fame, and Scott had to flee to Norway for his life. But at last King William the Third granted him a pardon and he came back to England to die in the atmosphere of respectability. Brooklyn has known some choice rogues, especially those crooks who ruled the City Hall and exploited the immigrant vote to their own profit, but, compared with John Scott, even the politicians of the old Brooklyn machine were mere amateurs.

II. The Nineteenth Century

When the second war with Great Britain fell upon Long Island it found Brooklyn still a small country town; but as New York forged ahead in the succeeding decades to its dominating position as the most important seaport and the largest city in the country, its suburb across the East River began to wax great likewise. As the consort of New York, Brooklyn was bound to be affected by all the forces and events that made the history of the metropolis. Politics, panics, immigration, war, invention—in all these Brooklyn had her share of the effects. Ere long it became the largest suburb in the world and the third largest city in the nation.

In its history there have been many eminent figures, notably philanthropists and divines. In fact, Brooklyn used to take pride in being known as the City of Churches.

Probably the noblest character in the Brooklyn of the nineteenth century was both clergyman and philanthropist, Dr. Richard Salter Storrs, pastor of the Church of the Pilgrims. He was noted not only as a pulpit orator but also as a citizen who was at the head of every movement for the public good during his long life. He never quite enjoyed the national reputation of his contemporary, Henry Ward Beecher, but he was not far behind, and in personality he was of finer quality. At any rate, since Brooklyn has been the City of Churches, we shall turn to look upon two gentlemen of the pulpit. One is utterly forgotten. As a matter of fact, he never lived in Brooklyn; he briefly touched it with his presence on a few occasions and went his way. The other is still the most celebrated of the long muster roll of Brooklyn clergymen and one of the most famous in the history of the country. For more than forty-five years he has stood in bronze facing Borough Hall. Both men are interesting, but for utterly different reasons.

The first was the Reverend Eleazer Williams, an Episcopal missionary to the Indians. On a Sunday morning in February, 1853, he assisted the Reverend Francis Vinton in the communion service at Grace Church, Brooklyn Heights. By a strange circumstance it happened that the Duke of Württemberg, then traveling incognito in the United States, was a member of the congregation. Now German Dukes do not attend episcopal services in an American church unless for some special reason. The next day the Duke's aide called at the Rectory to inquire who the clergyman was that had assisted in the service. He said that as soon as Mr. Williams entered the chancel the Duke whispered in great excitement, "Who is that man? It is so. If there is anything in a family resemblance he *is* a Bourbon. He is a Bourbon, no doubt. He is the image of Charles the Tenth."

This astonishing observation did not surprise Mr. Vinton, as might be expected. In the year 1844 he had met Williams in

Newport at the home of Mrs. O. H. Perry, where the missionary had come to ask financial help for his work with the Indians. On the table in the drawing room lay a handsome set of books, a history of the French Revolution, a recent gift from a French admiral whom Mrs. Perry had entertained. While waiting, the two clergymen turned the pages of this work to look at the pictures.

Suddenly [wrote Vinton afterwards] I saw Williams sitting upright and stiff in his chair, his eyes fixed and wide open, his hands clenched on the table, his whole frame shaken and trembling as if a paralysis had seized him. I thought it had. I exclaimed, "What's the matter?" I rose quickly to rouse him for no answer came. It was a minute before he could speak. But with great effort he raised his hand and pointing to one of the woodcut portraits at the bottom of the page, said with great difficulty of utterance, "That image has haunted me day and night as long as I can remember. 'Tis the horrid vision of my dream. What is it? Who is it?"

There was no name on the page, but Vinton looked up the picture by its number in the Contents and read, "Portrait of Simon, to whose care the Dauphin had been committed in the prison of the Temple." Vinton shut the book while his companion still gazed "as if fascinated while overwhelmed with unutterable horror."

Then for the first time he talked to Vinton about a strange experience he had had. On a visit to America in 1841, the Prince de Joinville, son of Louis Philippe, had apparently sought out the Indian missionary in the West, at Green Bay, Wisconsin; and, after asking to see certain scars as marks of identification, exclaimed, "Mon Dieu, you have rights you know not of!" He then offered Williams a formal abdication to sign, saying that for his signature King Louis Philippe would grant him a princely compensation. Williams said that, after considering the matter for some hours, he had declined with thanks. It was the first intimation he had ever received that he was not the son of the man whom he had always regarded as his father, the half-breed Williams. But he had no memories of his childhood before he was thirteen or fourteen.

Early in the same year in which Eleazer Williams officiated in Grace Church, Brooklyn, another clergyman, named Hanson, had written an article for *Putnam's Magazine,* on the same theme; namely, that this missionary to the Indians was no less than the lost Dauphin, son of Louis the Sixteenth and Marie Antoinette. Hanson and Vinton got in touch with each other. In the summer of that same year, 1853, they persuaded an aged half-breed Indian chief of the Oneida tribe, on his way back from Washington, to stop in New York. There, in the presence of these two clergymen and on oath, the old sachem told this story. He said that in 1795 Eleazer Williams, when a boy of ten or twelve, had been brought to Ticonderoga by two Frenchmen and consigned to the care of the man Thomas Williams, who became his foster father. He said, further, that the boy seemed "fou," or not in possession of his faculties, and was weak and sickly. The few words the boy spoke at that time were in French. Later, while bathing in Lake George, said the chief, Eleazer struck his head on a rock and was nearly drowned. Afterwards that blow on the head seemed to restore the lad's normal mental powers except for his memory, which was still a blank up to the day of his accident. As it happened, Eleazer Williams himself was staying in New York at the time the Indian chief was giving this testimony, attending to the printing of his translation of the Prayer Book into the Iroquois language, and he came in to see his old friend, with whom he conversed for a while in the Indian tongue.

Later, Hanson learned that the Duchesse d'Angoulême, the Dauphin's sister, once declared that when her brother should be discovered, if he were really yet alive, he could be identified

ELEAZER WILLIAMS
(*After the daguerreotype by Brady*)

by a scar on the back, on his shoulder, in the form of a crescent. This had been made by the surgeon at the time that the Dauphin was inoculated for smallpox, in order to make a positive identification mark, in addition to the inoculation incision. Hanson and Vinton agreed, therefore, to try to verify this mark the next time that Williams came to New York. On his subsequent visit to Brooklyn, where he officiated again for his friend at Grace Church, he readily consented to permit Hanson and Vinton to look for the scar. There they discovered both the marks, the scar of the inoculation and near it, on the shoulder, a crescent, three-quarters of an inch in length, a mark that Williams did not know he bore.

So, briefly, ran the evidence in this strange story. Several doctors examined Williams and testified that he showed no evidence whatever of Indian blood. This conclusion is borne out by such portraits of him as are extant, notably a daguerreotype of him by Brady, taken in 1853. More than thirty years afterwards the historian Benson J. Lossing reviewed the evidence at length in an article written for the *Independent*. In this he inferred his own belief that Eleazer Williams was actually the lost Dauphin, thus corroborating the story current in Royalist circles that a dead child had been substituted for the Dauphin, who, though wrecked in mind and body, still lived, and that he had been spirited away to America.

Williams died in 1858. To the last he always seemed more disturbed than pleased over this story of his royal birth and claim to the crown of France. Certainly he made no effort to capitalize on the facts. He was slow-witted—a Bourbon characteristic—and quite content to spend his life trying to serve his earliest friends, the Indians. As a young man he had fought for his country in the War of 1812 and had been badly wounded in the Battle of Plattsburg. He made no capital of that fact, either. One biographer says of him that "his character and life were exemplary." He seemed to be happiest when preaching to his Indian congregations, and translating hymns and prayers into their language.

On the other hand, another biographer, in the *Dictionary of American Biography,* says pish, tush and nonsense to the whole story, concluding with the statement that this missionary was

OLD BROOKLYN

"repudiated by the Indians he served" and "was known in Green Bay for his deceit, indolence and hypocrisy." So there you are, as often happens in historical riddles. But if the last estimate is true, then not only the missionary himself but his two clergymen friends, Hanson and Vinton, and the aged Indian chief were a pack of liars in a conspiracy to defraud the public, and that is hard to believe. Indeed, there are students of history today who incline to the opinion that when the congregation looked upon an elderly, bald-headed clergyman officiating in the morning service with his friend, the Rector of Grace Church in Brooklyn, they were looking on no less a personage than Louis the Seventeenth, the uncrowned King of France.

The second clerical figure, the man more closely associated with Brooklyn than anyone else of his generation, was the Reverend Henry Ward Beecher. But, of course, being a Congregationalist, he did not wear the priestly garb of the Established Church. In fact, he used to dress in a breezy way that did not suggest the pulpit at all. People said of him that he looked more like a farmer. His preaching, too, was breezily unconventional and he had his pulpit cut away to give him more room to march up and down. While he preached he liked to make the congregation laugh, and this was one reason why his church, the Plymouth, used to be crowded every Sunday. Henry was a younger brother of that sternly moral Catherine Beecher to whom the reader was introduced in East Hampton, and of that Harriet Beecher Stowe who wrote a story about slavery that was a best-seller everywhere—except south of the Mason and Dixon line.

Henry also was all for abolition. Once, in 1848, he put on a startling act in the Broadway Tabernacle in New York. The meeting was called to raise a ransom for two runaway negro girls. With another clergyman, Beecher called for contributions from the congregation in order to buy their freedom. "A slave auction in the pulpit!" It was a sensation. Henry was a good showman. He knew how to handle audiences, too. In 1863, when the cause of the Union looked pretty hopeless, Beecher was sent to England to speak, in order to create a more favorable attitude there toward the North. At that time it looked as if Great Britain would recognize the Confederacy any day and perhaps break the blockade as well. In Liverpool he was met by a great audience bent on howling him down, but he stood before them, fearless though alone, until he had said his say. He repeated that stormy experience in other cities, but he made the Englishmen listen to him by the extraordinary magnetism of his personality. Indeed, he is credited with having accomplished a great deal toward creating British sympathy for the cause of the Union. By the time the war was over he was the most celebrated preacher in America. Above all, he was the pride of Brooklyn, its foremost citizen.

Then came annus domini 1872. Someone in that year printed a limerick which has since become famous:

> The Reverend Henry Ward Beecher
> Called a hen a most elegant creature.
> The hen, pleased with that,
> Laid two eggs in his hat,
> And thus did the hen reward Beecher.

Usually credited to Oliver Wendell Holmes, the verse appears to have been composed by Alphonso Ross, managing editor of the Boston *Daily Advertiser*. In 1872 newspapermen began giving a great deal of space to Henry Ward Beecher, little of which was devoted to his sermons. The reason goes back to some queer people whose lives became tangled up with Beecher's.

Chief of these were Theodore Tilton, a young journalist on the staff of the *Independent;* Victori Claflin Woodhull, editor of a radical weekly and an apostle of "The Untrammelled Life"; Tilton's wife, a Sunday School teacher in Plymouth Church; and the Suffrage leaders, Susan B. Anthony and Elizabeth Stanton Cady. Out of these characters grew the famous Beecher-Tilton trial, which dragged on for six months, and which ended in a virtual acquittal for Beecher. During that time his church and most of the metropolitan papers stood by him loyally. But the suit had cost him a fortune, and he went back to the lecture platform to pay his debts. At first, because of the publicity attendant on the trial, he met with coldness and hostility, but his extraordinary personality won over his audiences to him. This was true even when he appeared in Richmond, Virginia, where he had against him the added handicap of his reputation as an Abolitionist; and again in England, where he had been lampooned as a "pulpit Barnum." On his death in 1887 he was still the pastor of Plymouth Church, Brooklyn, and a few years later his admirers erected the statue in bronze which faces Borough Hall today.

Henry Ward Beecher and Richard Salter Storrs were not the only Brooklyn preachers of the latter half of the nineteenth century who were nationally famous. There were at least three others, T. DeWitt Talmage, Charles Cuthbert Hall, and Theodore L. Cuyler, whose names were household words all over the country. S. Parkes Cadman, who recently died, carried on the same high tradition of civic and religious service into the twentieth century. It is a curious fact that so large a proportion of the outstanding Protestant clergymen of the nation were to be found in Brooklyn rather than in Manhattan.

No doubt these men would seem very old fashioned today. They knew nothing about modern booster methods or high pressure salesmanship in the church. The older men would certainly have been shocked at the present fashion of praying into the microphone. But when they stood in their pulpits on a Sunday morning they did not face a sparse scattering of elderly ladies. In a Broadway phrase these preachers "packed 'em in." Many of the worshipers in their congregations came regularly over the ferries from New York, summer and winter. It was men like these, not the buildings they preached in, that made Brooklyn the "City of Churches."

Mention might be made of various events in nineteenth-century Brooklyn history which once loomed large in the newspapers of their day and have since been forgotten. The Brooklyn of Civil War days saw the building of the famous *Monitor* near the Navy Yard, and the tremendous Sanitary Commission Fair to raise money for the wounded soldiers. In the decade following the war occurred the greatest fire disaster in the city's history, the burning of the Brooklyn Theater, December 5, 1876. Kate Claxton was then playing *The Two Orphans*. During the performance the scenery caught fire from the footlights. A panic followed, and next morning two hundred and seventy bodies were discovered in the ruins.

But if only a single story is to be related the obvious one is that of the Brooklyn Bridge, the first and still the most beautiful of all those spiderweb structures that span the East River. The idea goes back to 1811, when Thomas Pope, a bridgebuilder of New York, came forward with a plan to construct a "flying lever" arch from Fulton Street, New York, to Fulton Street,

Brooklyn. Pope made a model of his bridge and published a book explaining his plan in detail, illustrating the way the bridge would look with a handsome steel engraving. But he was unable to get financial support; most people thought that the idea was crazy.

Two more generations passed, content in the belief that crossing between New York and Brooklyn would always be by water. But the Civil War was scarcely over before the bridge idea was revived. The science of engineering had made great strides since the day of Pope. This time the proposal received a popular backing, because of the bitter winter of 1866–67, during which the East River was so choked with ice that the Brooklynites spent more time on the trip between their breakfast tables and their desks than if they had made the journey from New York to Albany. Again, in March, 1871, citizens made the crossing over the ice on foot, as they had done twenty years earlier.

Of course there were always the croakers who still declared that a bridge never could be built, and the aesthetes who tore their hair over the prospect of what they called "a shocking deformity." This from a generation that doted on mansard roofs, with frills, and cast-iron dogs! But by this time the cold-water brigade could not stop the project. In 1867 the plan was organized, and John A. Roebling was appointed the engineer. He had recently built the suspension at Niagara. Roebling plunged into the work with all his characteristic energy. But in 1869, while he was locating the site of the Brooklyn tower, a ferryboat lunged against the platform on which he was standing and drove a timber upon his foot, crushing it. A fortnight later he was dead of lockjaw. So before the work was actually begun, its chief engineer was killed.

At this juncture his son, Washington A. Roebling, picked up

the task from his father's hands. Two years later a fire started in the caisson of the Brooklyn tower. Roebling stayed too long in order to make sure that every sand hog had been rescued, and he came down with "caisson disease" or "the bends." From that time on he was confined to his sickroom. But from his bed the indomitable man continued to direct the work for eleven years to its triumphant completion.

It was a herculean undertaking. Every week it became more complicated. The government insisted that the span must be five feet higher above the water level than in the original plan. The politicians of both cities interfered, in the hope of swag, causing needless and costly delays. And so it went.

When at last a cable had been swung from tower to tower, E. F. Farrington, the master mechanic, knowing that the men might be reluctant to work on that cable so high over the water, rigged a "boatswain's chair"—a small piece of board suspended on an overhead ring connected with a "traveler" rope. Then he let himself go, waving his hat cheerily, and made the dizzy journey across the East River to the applause of shouting citizenry, gathered on the housetops on both sides of the river, and the tooting of the steamer whistles below.

Finally, after thirteen years of labor, and an expenditure of some sixteen millions, the bridge was declared finished; 1595 feet in length, it was the greatest bridge in existence. And it was the "Brooklyn" Bridge, because that city had contributed two-thirds of the cost. A grand opening was staged on May 24, 1883. There was oratory by Congressman Hewitt of New York, and by Dr. Storrs, the clergyman of Brooklyn. President Arthur, in frock coat and top hat, flanked by Cabinet officers, army and navy bigwigs, ambassadors and other such impressive personages—all in full dress and luxuriant whiskers—conducted a formal opening of the bridge. On the river below, naval vessels —pitiable wooden relics of the Civil War—boomed away in salute with their ancient smoothbores. That night Brooklyn celebrated with the biggest show of fireworks ever seen. Washington Roebling, the chief hero of the whole story, could witness only what he could see from the window of his room, but after the ceremony the President and his staff paid him a special call to congratulate him.

It is an old superstition that no bridge will endure "unless there is a man buried beneath." Of the 600 workers, 20 were killed outright; 110 suffered from the caisson disease, of whom three died almost immediately—how many more succumbed eventually is not known. These figures do not include the first fatality, the death of the elder Roebling.

A few days after the opening, other fatalities followed. It was Decoration Day; since the cars were not yet running, a huge holiday crowd came with a rush to cross the bridge on foot. There was no dividing line between the throngs who were moving in opposite directions. In addition, the thoroughfare was blocked by numerous peddlers who were trying to sell to the crowd. Soon there was a melee of excited men, women and children, pushing in opposite directions. The jam became so great that a panic broke loose. Under the pressure of human bodies, the guardrails broke and victims were hurled to the car tracks below. Others were trampled underfoot. Before order was restored twelve had been killed and many more injured. That was the worst day the great bridge has ever seen.

For another incident of a brighter sort we should turn to the brief but spectacular career of Steve Brodie. He was a young

Irishman living on the Bowery, and he yearned to become famous. "I gotta get publicity," he told his friend Isaac Myers of the curio shop.

"Vy don't you jump from the Brooklyn Britch?" suggested Myers.

"Mebbe I will," Brodie replied.

Now a certain Mr. Odlum of Brooklyn had already tried that feat the previous year (1885). But he had struck on his side, and passed on into another world instantaneously. No one had tried it since. But now rumors began to circulate on the East Side of a hundred-dollar bet that Steve wouldn't dare to do it; the bet was a fake, but it aroused interest. Just when he would make the leap, however, was kept a secret. Suddenly, on July 23, 1886, Brodie's friends announced that the great jump had been made in their presence. They declared that Brodie had climbed the rail of the bridge, dropped into the water and had been picked up by a barge that happened to be passing. The story threw the whole East Side into wild excitement.

At the same time, there were skeptics, even on the Bowery, who held that Mr. Brodie had caused a dummy to be dropped from the bridge, that he himself had dived from some place of concealment under a dock, swum under water and come up in midstream ready to be taken aboard the barge. To this day nobody knows whether Steve Brodie ever made the leap, and probably the doubters are now heavily in the majority. Certainly he never performed any similar feats of daring before or after.

Two years later he essayed to swim the Niagara Rapids in a rubber suit; but as he had selected a winter day, he found the water too cold and insisted on being hauled out immediately. This was rather ignominious, but he said that he would have done the Rapids O. K. except for the water being so cold. He was always deaf to numerous suggestions that he repeat his alleged leap from Brooklyn Bridge in the presence of more witnesses. "I done it oncet, didn't I?" he would answer in an aggrieved tone.

But he made great profit from the story. He set up a saloon at 114 Bowery, which became a famous resort for prize fighters and a mecca for the slumming parties and "rubber-neck" wagons. Money poured in daily and nightly in a golden torrent. Not content with the profits from his saloon he turned to the stage, still capitalizing on his alleged exploit. In the early nineties he starred in a play called *On the Bowery,* in which he nightly leaped from Brooklyn Bridge to save the heroine, who had just been hurled into the East River by the silk-hatted villain. That was a tremendous success with the melodrama public. As a specialty between acts he sang "My Poil Is a Bowery Goil," and as an encore—he was always encored—"The Bowery, the Bowery, I'll never go there any more!"—a song that gray-haired men can still remember.

In his saloon, among many other ornaments, was a large oil painting depicting the Brooklyn Bridge and himself poised in midair. Near it hung the affidavit of the barge captain that he had picked Brodie out of the river. Who could ask for more convincing evidence?

At his bar he used to condescend to drink with his customers, provided that they paid five cents for his glass of beer. For him this was a small whisky glass, and he drank chiefly foam. But, at that, he was incessantly sipping beer. Ere long diabetes was upon him, and in 1901, before he was forty, he made another leap into a cold river; this time it was the Styx.

In his day Steve Brodie was a popular hero, almost in the

same class with John L. Sullivan, and even now the slang phrase still persists: "To do a Brodie," meaning to make a big jump. Long after his death a man was still hired to pose in front of the Brodie saloon to impersonate the hero, in order to oblige the gullible sightseers. Yet the whole fantastic legend is probably nothing more than a brazenly unscrupulous answer to the cry, "I gotta get publicity."

So the Brooklyn Bridge came into existence and began to collect its legends. It was hailed by *Harper's Weekly,* which issued a special Bridge edition for the week of the opening, as "one of the mechanical wonders of the world." A poet contributed a verse called "The Nuptials," in which "Manhattan takes fair Brooklyn for his bride." A fussy critic wrote at great length in the same issue about the unfortunate "masses." He said that some of the details were "shabby and flimsy . . . while the design of the iron stations at either end is grossly illiterate and discreditable to the great work." Still, he could not help admiring the great span. "This aerial bow," he wrote, "as it hangs between the busy cities . . . is perfect as an organization of nature."

All that was more than half a century ago. Day after day the bridge now carries far more traffic than it was ever designed to bear, yet does so with perfect safety. At the time of the opening day in 1883 the sky line of New York showed church spires as the highest points, and a six-story building was considered tall. On the surface of the East River there were still many square-rigged sailing ships. Needless to say, the whole scene has been transformed beyond recognition. Beneath the bed of the East River run those great tubes through which tens of thousands now rush at express speed every day from one city to another. But the Brooklyn Bridge still serves, and serves well; it is even now the most famous object associated with the name Brooklyn. Whether or not certain details are "flimsy" or "illiterate," as that captious critic wrote, this structure has been the delight of painters and etchers throughout the entire half century of its existence. Among all the mighty bridges of the world it is still unique for its combination of stupendous size and grace.

CHAPTER XV

"THE WORLD OF TOMORROW"

"MAGNIFICENT! Colossal! Stupendous!" At this point the distinguished visitor's vocabulary gave out. He was Captain Anthony Eden on a brief visit to the United States, and before returning to England he had been taken out to Flushing Meadow to see the buildings of the New York World's Fair. It was on a bleak December day, three months before the opening of the exposition, but even then those reverberating adjectives were fully justified.

The point may be raised that most people will come to the great spectacle first and visit the rest of Long Island afterwards, but the position of the Fair at the very end of this voyage of discovery was deliberately chosen in order that it should make a climax to the whole story, ending in a shower of superlatives and fireworks. For there never was anything on the scale of this exposition attempted on this earth, and whichever way we look we must turn to the pages of the trusty thesaurus to find appropriate words for this unprecedented undertaking. No restrained language will serve. We shall have to unpack and dust off all those booming adjectives that the publicity men of the old-time circus used in their ballyhoo and on their flaming posters, and which in a later, softer-spoken era have been allowed to gather cobwebs.

In the first place, what is this Greatest Show on Earth all about? Specifically, it celebrates the one hundred and fiftieth anniversary of the inauguration of the first President of the

"THE WORLD OF TOMORROW"

United States, George Washington, a ceremony that took place on the balcony of the old Federal Hall in New York City, then the acting capital of the young republic. On November 6, 1935, the newly appointed directors of the Fair met for the first time to plan the great project. Already, in our discussion of the Long Island parks, mention has been made of how Flushing Meadow was selected for this purpose; but it will bear repeating here that the area on which the World's Fair now stands was, only a few years ago, a city dump. At the heart of it stood a mound of smoking ashes known at "Mt. Corona," which was a monument to twenty-five years of dumping refuse at this spot. Surrounding this heap of ashes, tin cans and other non desiderata of a metropolis, was a tidal marsh, through which the Flushing River struggled with difficulty toward the Bay, carrying its own cargo of sewage. There was nothing that the Fair could utilize, no trees, no grass, no lakes—nothing but garbage, ashes, sewage, rats, mosquitoes and smells. That was Flushing Meadow before June, 1936.

In three months after the first meeting the Board of Design had a plan ready, and as soon as this was approved the gigantic task of transforming this dismal area was begun. This plan had to be thought out so as to provide, especially in the matter of planting, not only for the layout of the Fair but also for the municipal park which is to flourish here after the Fair has ceased to be.

No time was lost in beginning work, and as soon as the tractors and scoops began turning over the mud, the World's Fair became live news. Mr. Grover A. Whalen, President of the Fair, has shown a genius for publicity. Never for a day, while the work was in progress, have his countrymen been allowed to forget that The Greatest Show on Earth was developing on the outskirts of New York. And his advertising devices were not of the usual kind. When motorists bought their 1938 license plates from the state, they were surprised to see, on every one, "New York World's Fair 1939" stamped into the metal. The same legend was repeated on the issue of the following year. So, wherever a driver of New York state took his car, he willy-nilly advertised the Fair.

But it was not enough to keep his fellow citizens reminded; Mr. Whalen planned a way of "telling the world" by the most spectacular method possible, a round-the-world flight. In a huge "Wright Cyclone, twin-motored, Lockheed, cabin monoplane" Mr. Howard Hughes and four companions soared up from Floyd Bennett Field on Sunday morning, July 10, 1938, and came roaring back to the same flying field, safe and sound, after circling the globe in a record-breaking swoop of 3 days, 19 hours, 14.1 minutes. Of course the name of the plane was "New York World's Fair 1939." This flight more than cut in two the record made by the late Wiley Post. Probably the greatest danger experienced on the entire journey was the welcoming crowd of some twenty thousand enthusiasts who fairly engulfed the plane when it landed home again.

Another unusual bit of publicity came from the sinking of the "Time Capsule." This was a metal cylinder which was lowered to a depth of fifty feet in the swampy ground beneath the site of the Westinghouse Electric and Manufacturing Company building at the Fair. This Capsule was filled with objects illustrating the civilization of the present day, with the idea that the container should not be opened until the year 6939. These evidences of our culture, as selected for posterity, consisted of a can-opener, a lady's hat of the current style, a Bible, a toothbrush, a safety pin, a pipe, some children's books, a camera,

"THE WORLD OF TOMORROW"

cigarettes, fountain pen, etc. Chewing gum seems to have been overlooked. Then there was a bundle of fabric materials, like cotton, wool, rayon, etc. There was a pictorial record, too, consisting of a news reel, showing twenty characteristic scenes: President Roosevelt speaking at Gettysburg, Howard Hughes returning from his flight around the world, Jesse Owens winning the hundred-meter dash at the 1936 Olympics, a Harvard-Yale football game, a Big League baseball game, the Navy in review, the war in China, May Day in Moscow, and so forth. This was made up by the RKO Pathé Pictures, Inc. In addition to the news film there was a quantity of micro-film representing the equivalent of a hundred books, from a mail-order catalogue to a detailed treatise on the life of our day—a total of 10,000,000 words.

A magnifier was included for reading the microfilm. All these evidences of modern civilization were stowed in the Capsule and the oxygen was replaced by nitrogen in order to prevent rust. To make sure that posterity will not forget to look for it at the proper time five thousand years hence, copies of the *Book of the Record of the Time Capsule* were sent off to selected libraries all over the world.

The preparation of this volume is a story in itself. It was designed by the expert, Mr. Frederick W. Goudy, in order that its appearance might be worthy of the antiquity which it is destined to attain. Printed on permanent, 100-pound paper, with special inks, it is bound in royal blue buckram, stamped with genuine gold and the signatures are sewn by hand with linen thread.

The book contains a message, asking that it be preserved and translated into new languages as they appear; a description of the capsule contents and the exact latitude and longitude of the

DISCOVERING LONG ISLAND

deposit to the third decimal point in seconds. In addition, instructions are included for making and using instruments to locate the Time Capsule by the methods of electromagnetic prospecting.

Also, in order to save our speech from extinction and make it intelligible, the book includes an ingenious "Key to the English Language" devised by Dr. John P. Harrington of the Smithsonian Institution, containing a diagram of the perversities of English grammar and a mouth map showing how each of the 33 sounds of English is pronounced. If this key doesn't do the job, there are multilingual texts, after the fashion of the Rosetta Stone, and a dictionary of colloquial English.

We can only hope that whatever survivor of the genus *homo sapiens,* or maybe *pithecanthropus erectus,* who happens to be wandering around among the ruins on Flushing Meadow five thousand years hence, will be sufficiently interested to dig up the Capsule and try to make sense out of its contents.

Finally, there was the happy thought of extending an invitation to the King and Queen of England to attend the Fair on their projected visit of friendship to America, an invitation which was graciously accepted. All in all, no other exposition of this kind has ever enjoyed anything like the extraordinary amount of favorable publicity during the months in which the process of building went on.

Perhaps the directors would instantly raise the objection that there never was an "exposition of this kind"; that this show is unique, sui generis, not just another one of those World's Fairs. There is some ground for this proud boast. Reader, do statistics leave you cold? Very well, here is a cooling mouthful for a hot day:

Area of the Fair grounds, 1216½ acres. April 30 is the date of

"THE WORLD OF TOMORROW"

opening, and the Fair season will run through the end of October. An attendance of more than 60,000,000 is expected, with a daily average of 250,000. The total cost of the project is estimated at $156,000,000. There will be parking space for 35,000 cars at any one time. Transportation facilities will be capable of handling as many as 165,000 persons an hour. The charge for admission for adults is seventy-five cents and there will be no free passes. Out of the profits of the enterprise, the first $2,000,000 will be turned over to the City of New York to use in the development of the site of the Fair as a permanent park after the exposition is over. Additional profits are to be divided equally between the City and the State of New York for educational and charitable purposes. The exposition in Chicago in 1933 proved so successful that it was carried over another year, and it is a good bet that this Fair will break that record. There we are for some round figures, and certainly these are rotund, especially that one about 60,000,000 paid admissions.

What, in general, can be said about this magnificent, colossal, stupendous, and so forth, exhibition, one that is literally the Greatest Show on Earth? First of all, this Fair has a Theme,—"Building the World of Tomorrow." Hence the visitor need not be surprised to see on every hand architecture such as he has never imagined before: wide, windowless buildings; cylinders, cones, spikes, chunks, hunks, prows of ships; a Gargantuan cash register which keeps tally of the number of admissions; a monster powder puff—all weirdly unexpected forms. On these surprising shapes are still more astonishing colors. Here is a vast area of buildings divided into color zones, gold, red, blue; and sometimes the boldest colors combine on the same wall. Elsewhere, although the surfaces themselves are plain, vividly painted murals on a Brobdignagian scale stretch across the front.

DISCOVERING LONG ISLAND

The men who designed and painted these murals are the best exponents of their art in America, and here on these walls they let themselves go with a splash and a bang. Sculptors, too, have had their fling, not only in the groups and the fountains, but also on the façades of the buildings, creating huge figures, sometimes in gay color. Traveler, do not look for any pretty-pretty, Venus and Adonis sort of thing. For example, the figures representing the characters of American folk lore, such as Paul Bunyan, Strap Buckner and Johnny Appleseed, are not reminiscent of Praxiteles or even of Hart, Schaffner and Marx. They suggest, rather, the comic strips of a Sunday paper; but, to be sure, they are supposed to be comedy characters.

Among the 60,000,000 visitors who are expected to surge through these avenues there is bound to be a violent difference of opinion as to whether these architectural, mural and sculptural fantasies are artistic or—to coin a word—just bizarre-tistic. That is to be expected. The directors made no attempt to create the architecture, painting, sculpture, or landscape design of the future. But there was the idea of giving an exhibition of the worthwhile ideas and forces at work now, out of which some things may develop in decades to come. No restrictions were laid on architects, sculptors or painters, and the men were selected with the idea of representing a wide gamut of taste and manner. Perhaps if there was one principle on which they all agreed it was to avoid the commonplace. Surely they have done that. On the other hand, in the section devoted to the exhibits of the States, traditional architectural forms were used, each related to the current style of the period of colonization.

The main axis of the Fair runs from the Federal Government Building at the east to the Chrysler Motors Building at the extreme west; that is, it crosses the Fair grounds at their widest

"THE WORLD OF TOMORROW"

point. Very appropriately, since the Constitution began to operate at the time of Washington's inauguration, the main thoroughfare on this axis is called Constitution Mall. The line of the avenue is so drawn that if it were extended it would pass through the middle of the base of the Statue of Liberty in New York Harbor. Lined with shade trees—ten thousand have been planted on the grounds—with broad walks and a series of fountains, this Mall will give the finest vista of the Fair. The most striking features of the Mall are the famous Trylon and Perisphere, the needle and ball which have become, long since, the symbol and trade mark of the Fair. From this center, the other streets radiate like the spokes of a wheel to the three zones of color, yellow to the west, crimson to the north, and blue to the east.

In these different zones are grouped the industries, sometimes many in a single building, elsewhere in individual exhibition buildings erected by single companies such as the Ford, DuPont, General Motors, National Cash Register, Borden, U. S. Steel and many more.

To the north of the Fair grounds is Flushing Bay, newly dredged and furnished with a marine basin for visitors who come by boat. Between the water and Roosevelt Avenue is the chief parking area for automobiles. To the south are two lakes, Fountain—formerly called Meadow—and Willow, both dredged out of the muck of the old swamp. Along the eastern shore of Fountain Lake, for the length of a mile, stands the amusement section. At the head of the lake is an amphitheater of brick—one of the permanent structures—facing the stage which lies on the surface of the water, where elaborate dramatic spectacles are to be enacted.

So much for a general idea of the ground plan of the Fair.

Much careful thought has been expended on the comfort of the visitor who will be going to and fro through this area. To help him get about, there is a fleet of buses, swiftly moving vehicles that stop only at specified points and bowl round the outside limits. There are also tractor trains and wheel chairs—these two for a generation that has forgotten the use of its legs. Perhaps citizens of the World of Tomorrow will not be able to walk at all. Better yet, under the trees have been placed many benches, where the sight-seer may rest. No world's fair ever before had half enough of these simple comforts. Yet on some holiday the crowd may be so great that even these multitudinous benches will look like those few loaves and fishes of which the Disciples remarked, "What are these among so many?"

One exceedingly important consideration is the health of the visitor. If some 60,000,000 human beings are due to stream through these Fair grounds during the summer of 1939, a large number of cases needing first-aid treatment must be reckoned with. It did not seem wise to set up a complete hospital for the six-month period. Instead the directors adopted a system similar to the "Triage" plan in use by the French army during the World War. For this purpose six first-aid stations are set up, with complete equipment, at strategic spots in the grounds. Each has a waiting room, doctor's office, nurse's office, a male and a female ward with from four to ten beds each, and a surgical room. One of these stations has been in use since November, 1937, and another was opened in September, 1938, to handle the accident cases in the construction work. The whole plan for medical and first-aid treatment is not to provide hospitalization but to keep the seriously ill patients only so long as they need to be put in condition for transportation to the city hospitals. For this purpose the Fair maintains a fleet of the most modern

"THE WORLD OF TOMORROW"

ambulances to take the sufferers to the hospitals in Queens, Manhattan and the Bronx. Special equipment is provided for cases of drowning and intoxication.

In all this prodigious organization it is possible to select only a few features for special mention. To return to Constitution Mall, at the western end is the Federal Building facing a parade ground, flanked by the buildings of the nations, more than sixty in all. Of the major countries of the world only two are not represented here, China, which has enough to occupy its energies merely to survive; and Germany, which feels rather stuffy about the United States anyway.

Between the buildings representing the various nations stretches a parade ground planned to be wide enough to accommodate 50,000 marching men. The western end of this area is formed by the great, oval Lagoon of Nations. This was once the very center of the muck and water of the old Flushing Meadow swamp. It was something of a problem to make a foundation that would hold the fountain that occupies the middle of the Lagoon; this was solved finally by laying a wire mesh over the oozy mud and on top of that a cotton burlap, over which great quantities of gravel were dumped before a dependable bottom was formed.

The most striking object to be seen between this Lagoon and the Perisphere is the towering statue of Washington, sixty-five feet high, standing to the left of the Mall. The Father of His Country is here represented in civilian dress, as he appeared on the day he arrived in New York to take the oath of office. He stands with his gaze fixed on the great Perisphere, as if he were wondering what the World of Tomorrow would bring forth for the nation he did so much to create in the World of Yesterday. Sixty-five feet is a dimension that makes this the largest portrait statue in the world, if we except the rock monuments of Egypt; and perhaps that is about right to suggest his proper stature in our history. Behind him stand four allegorical figures, representing the Freedoms of Press, Religion, Assembly and Speech.

So much of the sculpture is conceived on this gigantic scale. For example, not far away from this group is the sundial by Paul Manship, with a "gnomon" fifty feet long. The index of this dial is supported by the Tree of Life, under which are the three Fates, busy with the thread of man's existence, after the Greek myth.

But it would be an endless task even to begin to enumerate the fountains, sculpture groups, murals, and all the other ornamental details in a scene as vast as this. Instead we must concentrate on the heart of the Fair, the Mall, and the Theme Center, the Trylon and Perisphere. The Mall stretches out in a straight line for almost a mile, its course interrupted by five lagoons and five waterfalls, all asparkle with fountain jets. The parade ground at the eastern end is balanced at the western extremity by the Transportation Area, the scene of the railroad and motor exhibits. Along its entire length the Mall is lined with shade trees between fifty and seventy feet in height. Along a part of the route there is a double row of red maples on each side. Bordering the fountains and pools lie brilliantly colored beds of flowers. For example, the Netherlands contributed a million bulbs, mostly tulips.

Trees, fountains, waterfalls and flower beds, however, are an old story. The unique feature of Constitution Mall is the pair of structures which constitute the Theme Center of the Fair, the Trylon and Perisphere, together with the curving ramp of the Helicline. This is certainly something original. Indeed, before this combination of needle and ball was adopted, 1035

"THE WORLD OF TOMORROW"

sketches had been scrutinized and discarded. The very words Trylon, Perisphere and Helicline are also new, having been invented for the purpose. What the solemn lexicographers think

TRYLON AND PERISPHERE

about these additions to the language is not on record, but it won't make any difference.

The Trylon is so called because it stands high like a pylon but has three sides. It is so slender and sharp as to suggest a surgeon's lancet. Its juxtaposition to the great ball of the Perisphere makes it hard to realize that this narrow spike is 145 feet higher than the Washington Monument. But there is no elevator to the top of this spire. The Trylon serves chiefly as the entrance and exit for the Perisphere. The visitor enters through the door at the ground level, steps on one of the two escalators and is transported up fifty feet to the entrance of the Perisphere. After he has seen the show in the interior, he emerges at an exit—Barnum would have called it the "Egress"—which opens on the ramp or Helicline, down which, by an easy grade, the sightseers walk back to the ground level. The name "Helicline" comes from two Greek words meaning "spiral" and "slope."

Tall as it is, there were no special, difficult problems in the construction of the Trylon. But with the Perisphere the engineers had new and complicated knots to unravel. Never before had anyone tried to build a huge hollow ball that should serve as a theater. As a bit of home work in spherical trigonometry and calculus, it was full of headaches. The chief engineer for the Perisphere confessed that the problem of stresses and strains involved in the building of this colossal ball was the most difficult he had ever attempted. Nor was it merely a matter of building a hollow ball eighteen stories high that should stand firm on a foundation of ooze and muck. The interior also presented difficulties for which there was no precedent. This had to be a theater, twice as large in area as the Radio City Music Hall in New York and an entirely new kind of theater at that. For here the audience must revolve slowly around the interior, and the entertainment is to go on below, above and all around. All this meant problems in acoustics, lighting, moving-picture effects on a concave surface, together with sound effects. In addition there was the installation of a moving gallery that should swing smoothly and noiselessly around the entire circumference

"THE WORLD OF TOMORROW"

of the sphere.

The "theme" of the pictorial display inside is the same as that of the entire Fair, the World of Tomorrow. As the visitor steps off the escalator and into the interior of the Perisphere, he takes his stand on a moving platform. From this he looks out on what appears to be limitless space of sky. Below lies "Democracity,"—another coinage and one not too easy to pronounce—which represents what a community could be if it were built not in the helter-skelter fashion of our cities but as a result of regional and municipal planning. This is the ideal city which the world of tomorrow is expected to create. As he gazes, the visitor is conscious of being moved gently through space. Lifting his eyes from the scene below, he sees the sky above him changing. Night turns to dawn, then to sunrise, daylight, sunset, and to night once more—the whole cycle of twenty-four hours taking place in six minutes. During the "night" stars and planets may be recognized in their proper places as in a planetarium. As day comes, delicate clouds float across the blue. The climax is reached when an advancing host seems to march across the sky to the sound of music, indicating that free democracy triumphs in that world of tomorrow. The effect is tremendous.

By day this Trylon and Perisphere will be the only white objects on the Mall in the midst of a rich pattern of colors. The Perisphere by day, thanks to a clever arrangement of fountains at its base, will look like a huge white bubble, supported lightly on jets of water. At night the white surface will receive a play of lights which will make it seem opalescent and transparent, filled with moving clouds of colored mist.

What in brief are the distinguishing features of this World's Fair? This, by the way, is the second international exposition staged by Father Knickerbocker. The earlier one was held in 1853, the "Crystal Palace," occupying the area of Bryant Park at Forty-second Street and Sixth Avenue. It was considered wonderful in its day and amazingly big, for it spread over practically all of a city block. This Crystal Palace also was supposed to be a vision of tomorrow. A reporter for the New York *Illustrated News* declared that the exposition "solicits our gaze for a sweet sunprint of the glowing future—science and art in an amicable wrestle for the smile of beauty. . . . In the poetry of notable events the Crystal Palace may be termed the *Iliad* of the nineteenth century." (This was newspaper style in the fifties.) The whole of that exposition could have been put into the Perisphere of the present Fair. The first, outstanding feature, therefore, is size. Everything here is on an immense scale.

The second feature is the note of modernity. Except for a few historic echoes, like the replica of Independence Hall, the buildings try for unusual effects. If, to hardshell conservatives, some of these seem lunatic, it should be remembered that a psychologist recently prophesied that, at our present mounting rate of insanity, two hundred years hence there won't be a single right-minded American left.

There are some of us with gray in our hair who remember with unfading enthusiasm the White City of the World's Columbian Exposition of 1893, especially that stunning Court of Honor with its Peristyle shining snow-white against the blue of the sky and the deeper tone of Lake Michigan. All that architecture was of the Renaissance—the World of Day before Yesterday. It was all stately, dignified and beautiful. Leonardo and Cellini and Michelangelo would have liked it. But this new architectural manner is amusing and stimulating anyway. Some interesting developments are sure to come out of it.

"THE WORLD OF TOMORROW"

Despite the extreme character of some of these modernistic buildings at the present Fair, the Board of Design exacted uniformity on four points. None of the exhibition buildings should have an upper floor. There should be no windows; only interior lighting. The inside area must be divisible into units of twenty feet square or multiples thereof. Finally, all aisles in the exhibits must be twenty feet wide. Also the structural plans call for stucco on light steel frames. Outside of these requirements the imaginations of the designers were allowed free rein.

Closely related to this modern approach to line and form is the color scheme. "This exhibition city presents color cocktails at every turn, and will send the visitor away with a new set of color impressions. Here an atmosphere of gaiety, of holiday spirit and of contrast to the drab modern city has been established by the use of carefully modulated colors. From the White Theme Center, avenues stretch away like the spokes of a wheel, and down each vista are seen the gradually deepening tones of a primary color. Unlike the snow-white Chicago Fair of 1893 and the multi-colored Century of Progress Exposition of 1933, The New York Fair depends for its effect upon definite color progressions, leading to strong accents at the focal points. This scheme binds together over a hundred buildings of contrasting architectural form and relieves the monotony of acres of unbroken walls. Against it the many mural paintings give points of added interest and, by their bright colors, sharpen the general color effect." In brief, the visitor gets an eyeful.

But chief of all these distinctive characteristics of the Fair, at least as far as the present observer may be trusted to judge, is the lighting. This is the achievement that is likely to make the deepest impression on the visitor's mind. The Fair will be at its best by night, and that best is something never matched before.

Already the play of colored lights on the Perisphere has been noted but that is only one detail in the lighting plans for the Constitution Mall. To anyone standing at either end the great esplanade will look like a setting in jewels. It will appear like a huge lavaliere laid down the length of a mile, and set with emeralds, rubies, turquoises and the great opal of the Perisphere. The 600 trees that line the avenue will be lighted from beneath by the new capillary mercury tube. From this the coloring matter of the leaves will fluoresce and become a shimmering, luminous green.

The center of the light displayed on the Mall is the Lagoon of Nations. This pool is nearly 800 feet long and 400 wide, into which three of New York City's blocks could be set. Under the water in the middle of the oval is a platform nearly 400 feet long, on which are mounted 1400 water nozzles, 400 gas nozzles, containers for fireworks, lighting boxes and rotating color drums. All this paraphernalia is concealed by having the parts exposed above water shaped liked the blossoms of water lilies.

Other "flowers" are outlets for sound projectors. The idea is that in this Lagoon display an entirely new form of artistic composition is presented—light, water, flame, music and fireworks, blended into one great but formally arranged pattern. The operation of this prodigious symphony of light, sound and color is handled in a room on the roof of one of the government buildings, where three men operating a control board, something like an organ console, directed by a chief operator, conduct the play of the various element. The show in the Lagoon begins shortly after dark every evening and lasts half an hour.

A second evening exhibition of light is held at the head of Fountain Lake. This is to entertain the crowd that tends at that time toward the amusement area. Here, also, the entertainment

"THE WORLD OF TOMORROW"

lasts thirty minutes. This show, however, is on a greater scale, as befits the size of the lake and its far-reaching shores. For this display there are five floating barges which can be shifted from one place to another for varying the pattern of the display. Some of these have huge water pumps and are provided with lighting equipment, much the same as that set up on the Lagoon of Nations. Others carry searchlights masked to throw light up on white smoke, which is produced by still other barges. Five more take care of five captive balloons, which form the crown of the picture, and these floating platforms hardly more than begin the catalogue of equipment. As for the character of this spectacle, Mr. Grover Whalen has summed it up briefly by saying that it will be a combination of Niagara and Vesuvius—water, smoke, lights, color, fireworks, sound. It will be a grand riot of all these elements. In fact, when Mr. Whalen was looking for a single word to describe it, all he could think of was "chaos."

As for the fireworks, none but the best pyrotechnician in the world would suffice for what the Fair proposed to do. After a while this expert was discovered—Mr. John Craig, the same who as a young man was responsible for the brilliant displays given in the Chicago exposition of 1893, as well as the famous fire-work spectacles given at Manhattan Beach during the 1890's and early 1900's. There was at the same time, outside the Fair grounds, a special fireworks entertainment given every night in the city. This was called "The Siege of Sebastopol." Mr. Craig designed that too. Now, forty-five years later, he was discovered living in retirement on Staten Island, where he was occupied in raising potatoes. Characteristically, Mr. Craig fertilized his garden with damaged gunpowder.

Called to the new Fair, Mr. Craig is working out in pyrotechnic terms the designs created by Professor James Labatut of

Princeton, which call for the most elaborate and carefully designed pyrotechnics. For example, on the evening of the Fourth of July, Fountain Lake may see a reproduction of the battle between the *Monitor* and the *Merrimac,* with the frigate *Congress* ablaze in the background.

So much for a few hints as to the sort of thing the visitor can see. Each individual must make his own discoveries here in the Fair grounds as well as elsewhere on this journey. He will learn that when he is tired he can sit under shade trees or sun umbrellas in the patio of the Ford Building listening to music, while cars filled with sightseers run gaily round the ramp of the exhibit. Or he will gaze in wonder at that gigantic model, nearly as long as a city block, showing a colored, lighted, architectural, high relief picture of New York's metropolitan area comprising more than four thousand electrically wired buildings and a third-rail subway system. This diorama is taller than a three-story building. It is exhibited by the Consolidated Edison Company. Or he may look at that other diorama, the Horizons and Highways model, produced by General Motors, showing another scene extending for nearly a quarter of a mile and covering 30,000 square feet of flooring. Here the visitor sits in a comfortable chair and makes his sightseeing tour on an escalator-conveyor system equipped with a sound device that describes the important features to be noted. The scene will include a metropolis of a million inhabitants, two sister cities of three hundred thousand each and a vast crountryside of farm land and suburb threaded by superhighways. One sees it as if one were a disembodied spirit riding on a cloud. Then there are fascinating nooks in the Old World villages, over in the amusement section. There are ten thousand other absorbing things to see which lie waiting to be discovered. An exposition on a scale

"THE WORLD OF TOMORROW"

as huge as this will have to be visited not once but many times, or as long as the seventy-five centses hold out, before one can have any adequate conception of what there is here.

Incidentally, the Fair is the first to be ready on time for the opening. The Chicago Columbian Exposition was a whole year late, and even then was not entirely in shape when the crowds began to arrive. The directors of the New York Fair set as a dead line a day an entire month before the April 30 on which the President was scheduled to make the formal opening. That extra period of thirty days was set aside for the installation of exhibits and for training the personnel so that from the hour of opening everything should proceed smoothly and the huge crowds should be handled without friction.

At the very beginning of the enterprise Mr. Whalen told the press that the Theme of the Fair, or its purpose, rather, is "the creation of a better and fuller life—the advancement of human welfare. . . . All the goods and ideas thus far developed will be displayed in a connected sequence, so that, seeing what is available to them, visitors to the Fair will be inspired to work with their fellow citizens for a more worthy future." He said also that it was going to be "glamorous, fascinating and dynamic." It is certainly all of that and more. Indeed, as we try to express in some compact phrase the total effect of this World of Tomorrow, back we come to the same adjectives with which this chapter began: Magnificent! Colossal! Stupendous!

INDEX

Amagansett, 168 f.
America, the, 48 f.
Amityville, 220 f.
Andre, Major John, 19 ff., 61, 88, 300 f.
Arbuthnot, Vice-admiral, 87, 150 f., 163
Arnold, Benedict, 21 f.
Aviation, 285 ff.

Babylon, 214 f.
Battle of Long Island, 7
Beecher, Catherine, 156 ff.
Beecher, Henry Ward, 156, 316 ff.
Beecher, Lyman, 154 ff.
Bethpage Park, 234 ff.
Bispham, David, 147, 176
Block, Adrian, 6
Blue Point oysters, 210 f.
Bowne, John, 253 f.
Brewster Homestead, 46 f.
Brodie, Steve, 321 ff.
Brookhaven, 208 f.
Brooklyn, 297 ff.
Brooklyn Bridge, 318 ff.
Bronx-Whitestone Bridge, 3
Bryant, William Cullen, 12 f., 76, 173
Buek, Gustave H., 134 f.
Buell, Samuel, 137, 150 f., 154

Camp Siegfried, 261 f.
Canoe Place, 191 f.
Caroline Church, Setauket, 45
Casa Basso, 205 ff.
Chase, William M., 148, 189 f.
Clinton Academy, 126 f., 130, 151
Cooper, James Fenimore, 110 f., 115 ff., 128, 301
Corbin, Austin, 179 f.
Currier and Ives, 49, 266
Cutchogue, 59 f.

Dana, Charles A., 13
Dayton, Ebenezer, 142 f.
Deurcant, Mary Willemsen, 141
Dominy House, East Hampton, 125 f.
Duck Industry, 194 ff.
Duck Shop, 220 f.
Dyer, Mary, 106

East Hampton, 6, 12, 81 f., 86, 90 f., 119 ff., 167 f., 186
East Marion, 75 f.
East Setauket, 46
Eckford, Henry, 295 f.
Eclipse, 263 ff.
Execution Rock, 10

"Father Divine," 259 f.
Fenn, Harry, 76 f., 91, 101, 108, 131, 145
Fireplace, 90, 163
Fisher, Carl G., 180 f., 228
Fishing, 287 f.
Flushing, 4, 253
Flushing Meadow, 3
Flying Eagle, the, 43
Ford, James, 209
Forest Hills, 4, 280 ff.
Fox, George, 23, 107, 253 f.
Fox-hunting, 266 ff.
"Frank Buck's Jungle Park," 222 ff.
Frank Melville Memorial Park, 44
Fuller, Margaret, 13

Garden City, 291 f.
Gardiner's Bay, 65, 77
Gardiner, David (Senator), 80, 82 f., 92, 96
Gardiner, John, 83 f., 141
Gardiner, Julia, 91 ff., 108, 148
Gardiner, Lion, 6, 79 ff., 98, 140 f.

INDEX

Gardiner's Island, 69, 75 ff., 163
Gilmer, Ann Elizabeth, 93 f.
Godwin, Parke, 13
Golden Parrot, the, 107
Golf, 273 ff.
"Goody Garlich," 81 f., 91, 142
Greenport, 64 ff., 99 ff., 114
Guild Hall, East Hampton, 122

Hale, Nathan, 21, 30, 300
Hardy, Commodore Thomas, 30, 61, 64, 88 f.
Hart, Joshua, 38 f.
Heckscher Art Collection, Huntington, 30 f.
Hempstead, 290 ff.
Hercules figurehead, 192 f.
Hicks, Edward, 256
Hicks, Elias, 33, 36, 254 ff.
Hither Hills, 169 f., 228, 233, 288
"Home Sweet Home" house, 131 ff.
Hook Mill, East Hampton, 124
Hopper, Edward, 117 ff.
Horsford, Eben N., 104 f., 111 f.
Huntington, 29 ff.
Hurricane, the, 115, 144, 183, 196 ff., 214, 245

Indian names, 9 f., 59
Indians, 7
Islip, 212

Jamaica, 4
James, Thomas, 137, 141
Jersey, the, 303 ff.
Job Wright house, 23 f.
John Drew Memorial Theater, 129 f.
John Hulbert flag, 194
John Milton, the, 138, 175
Jones Beach, 236 ff.

Kew Gardens, 4
Kidd, Captain William, 79, 83 ff., 109, 128, 141

Lathrop, George Parsons, 77, 90 f.
Lazy Point, 165
Leaves of Grass, 34
Lexington, the, 50 ff.

Library, East Hampton, 122, 127 f., 148
Life and Adventures of Joshua Penny, the, 62 f.
Lindbergh, Charles A., 286 f.
Locust Valley, 14, 17, 28, 46
Lossing, Benson, J., 7
Louie V. Place, the, 211 f.

McAdam, John L., 212 f.
Mahan, Rear Admiral Alfred T., 195
Matinecock Meeting House, 15 f., 46
Meadow Brook Club, 268 ff.
Menhaden, 100 ff., 164 f.
Messenger, 17
Millard House, Miller Place, 57 f.
Miller Place, 51, 54 ff., 58
Miranda, General, 109 ff.
"Modern Times," 258 ff.
Montauk, 163 ff., 180 f., 201, 228
Montauk Point, 166, 169, 177 ff.
Montauk village, 170 f., 201
Moran, Thomas, 130, 147, 161
Morley, Christopher, 4, 14
Moses, Robert, 98, 181, 227 ff., 248
Mosquito control, 252 f.
Mount, William S., 42, 128
Mount Misery, 53
Mulford house, East Hampton, 129, 133, 146

Names on Long Island, 9
Nicoll, Gloriana Margaretta, 212 f.
Nissequogue River, 39 f.
Northport, 36, 40 f.

Old Field Point, 42 f.
Old Horse Gray and the Parish of Grumbleton, 117 f.
Onderdonk mill, 11, 128
Orient, 76
Orient Beach State Park, 77
Orient Point, 75 f.
Oyster Bay, 61 ff.

Park City, the, 22
Parks, 225 ff.
Payne, John Howard, 121, 131 ff., 146, 151 ff.

INDEX

Penny, Joshua, 61 ff.
Pennypacker, Morton, 78, 127, 133, 300
"Pharaoh, King David," 176 f.
Picturesque America, 99, 101, 108, 114, 131, 145, 169, 173
Polo, 269 ff.
Port Jefferson, 27, 47 ff., 53
Porter, Commodore David, 216 f.
Princeton, the, 92 ff., 139
Promised Land, 164

Queensborough Bridge, 3
Quogue, 194

Raynham Hall, 18
Roebling, John A., 319 f.
Roebling, Washington A., 319 ff.
Roosevelt, Theodore, 18, 24 ff.
Roslyn, 11 f.
"Rowdy Hall," East Hampton, 123

Sag Harbor, 108 f., 155, 160 f.
Sagtikos Manor, 214 f.
Saint George's Church, Hempstead, 293 ff.
Saint Luke's Church, East Hampton, 122, 135 f., 160
Sammis Tavern, 292 f.
Sands, John, 28
Scott, John, 53, 306 ff.
Setauket, 44 ff., 300 f.
Shelter Island, 69, 77, 99 ff.
Shinnecock Hills, 148, 188 ff., 273 ff.
Shinnecock Reservation, 7, 189 ff.
Smith, Richard, 37, 307
Smith, Colonel William, 37
Smithtown, 36 ff.
Sigourney, Lydia, 172 f.
Simcoe, Colonel John G., 10, 61, 301 f.
Southampton, 6, 184 ff.
Southold, 6
Sports, 263 ff.
Spy system in the Revolution, 300 ff.

Sterling, Earl of, 79 f.
Stockton Captain Robert F., 92 ff.
Stony Brook, 40 ff.
Sylvester, Grissel, 105 f.
Sylvester Manor, 102 ff.
Sylvester, Nathaniel, 105 ff.

Tallmadge, Benjamin, 21 f.
Tennis, 280 ff.
Tile Club, Introduction, 131, 145 ff., 158 f., 162, 170, 176 ff., 189
Townsend Manor, 72 f.
Townsend, Robert, 20 f., 301 f.
Townsend, Samuel, 18 f.
Townsend, Sarah, 19 ff., 302
Triborough Bridge, 3, 230 f.
Tryon Hall, 217 f.
Tyler, Alexander, 139
Tyler, John, 92 ff., 108, 148

Vanderbilt, William K., jr., 275 f.
Vanderbilt Cup races, 275 ff.

Wallace, John, 137, 159 ff.
Warren, Josiah, 257 ff.
Washington, George, 1 f., 7, 11 ff., 20 f., 28, 37, 65 ff., 72, 128, 215, 266, 300, 302 f.
Water Mill, 183 ff.
Webster, Daniel, 37 ff.
Westhampton Beach, 196 ff.
"Whaleboat men," 58
"Whalers' Church," Sag Harbor, 115
Whitefield, George, 72 f., 107
Whitman, Walt, 31 ff., 101, 173 f.
Williams, Eleazer, 310 ff.
Wilson's Sail Loft, 48 f.
World's Fair, 3, 326 ff.
Wyandanch, 141, 176

Yaphank, 261 f.
Youngs, Daniel, 21, 201, 302

349

974.72

Coram Public Library
Coram, New York